AF555952

Transformation of Education

Transformation of Education

Dr. G. Visvanathan
Professor, Department of Education,
Annamalai University, TN
and
Dr. S. K. Panneer Selvam
Assistant Professor, Department of Education
Bharathidasan University, T.N

RANDOM PUBLICATIONS
NEW DELHI (INDIA)

Transformation of Education

ISBN 978-93-5111-529-8

Published in 2015 in India by

RANDOM PUBLICATIONS

4376-A/4B, Gali Murari Lal, Ansari Road
New Delhi-110 002
Phone : +9111-43580356, 011-43142548, 011-23289044
e-mail : sales@randompublications.com
info@randompublications.com
randomexports@gmail.com

Reprinted 2025

Type Setting by : Shah Computer Graphics, Delhi-110094
Printed at : Replika Press Pvt. Ltd.

Contents

4

5

6

7

8

9

24

25

26

27

28

42

1

Value Based Distance Education-
A Challenge

Introduction

After independence, India had made tremendous progress in the field of education, though mostly quantitative in nature. Earlier, education was available only to the elites in society, and a large majority of poor and marginalized people remained illiterate. Political considerations have an important role in the expansion of higher education, especially at the state level. The state government experienced tremendous pressure from the public to establish more and more colleges and universities. In a democratic society, even the strong governments find it very difficult to resist such pressures and are compelled to succumb to the same. These considerations have led to fast expansion of higher education in our country, which in turn, has adverse impact upon its quality. Therefore, in order to insure access and education of a reasonably good quality, we must think of some alternative system capable of supplementing the role of conventional system, and distance education is one of such alternatives. One of the most significant developments in the field of education during the last two decades has been the acceptance, spread and growth of distance education through open learning systems in most parts of the world.

Definition of distance education

How distance education is best defined or differentiated from other educational approaches has been the subject of much debate. From the perspective of many educational technologists, distance education is "inexorably linked to the technology" and seems to be viewed as different from other forms of education, a factor which may contribute to course development and acceptance problems.

ICN (2003) defines distance education as: A formal learning activity which occurs when students and instructor are separated by geographic distance or by time, often supported by communications technology such as television, videotape, computers or mail. Moore Kearsley defines distance education as (1996): Distance education is planned learning that normally occurs in a different place from teaching and as a result requires special techniques of course design, special instructional techniques, special methods of communication by electronic and other technology, as well as special organizational and administrative arrangements.

A broadening of the definition of distance education is urged by Barker, Frisbie and Patrick (1989) who acknowledge correspondence study as the historical foundation of distance education but suggest that there are really two forms of distance education. One is the traditional correspondence- based distance education which is independent study oriented and the second is telecommunications-based distance education which offers the teaching and learning experience simultaneously (1989, p. 23).

The terms 'distance education' and' open learning' have been used in different contexts with somewhat different meanings. Distance Education has been defined as an educational process in which a significant proportion of the teaching is conducted by someone removed in space and/or time from the learner. Distance Education programmes have often used a combination of educational media, old and new, varying from print to broadcasts to audio and video recordings, and included opportunities for face to face study as well as learning from recorded material. Distance education is now internationally recognised and accepted as an alternative channel for providing broader access to education in a cost-effective manner; wider and diversified curricula and a means for continuing life-long education. Increasingly new categories of clients are seeking better education; the young who for one reason or the other are not able to join a college or university; adults who want to acquire a diploma or degree; professionals who want to keep pace with technological change; persons required to discharge responsibilities for which their formal education does not equip them; those who do not want to get uprooted from their environment and do not want a disruption from their responsibilities at home and/or in their offices; and those who look for education at their door step. Many of these categories may not fit in with the normal admission criteria and find that their aspirations may not be fulfilled through the conventional system of education. This is also a time of convergence between the worldwide need to extend and develop educational opportunities and the development of new communication technologies viz. sophisticated printing methods, audio based technology, video technologies; computer based technologies; and satellite communication, making it possible for learners to get access to the world's knowledge from the remotest and most inaccessible areas.

Education is the vehicle of knowledge, self-preservation and success. Education not only gives us a platform to succeed, but also the knowledge of social conduct, strength, character and self respect. The greatest gift education gives us is the knowledge of unconditional love and a set of values. These values include the simple difference between right and wrong, a belief in God, the importance of hard work and self respect. Education is a continuous learning experience, learning from people, learning from success and failures, learning from leaders and followers and then growing up to be the person we are meant to be.

The elements of a value-based education can be found not only in the subject matter, but in the learning styles which are employed, the scheduling of the classroom, extracurricular activities, and parental involvement. The value-based education is therefore organized so as to secure the fullest possible development of body, mind and heart; and a fruitful channelization of the life-energy in pursuits that contribute to the growth of both internal and external personality. It offers a sufficient training of the mental faculties in the fields of various humanities and sciences. It ultimately provides the requisite help, through a powerful spiritual atmosphere, for the soul to come forward and gradually begin to govern a balanced, peaceful and spiritually awakened life. Therefore, value based-education is instrumental to unfold and nurture the ideals of life. Education that does not help promote human virtues will not do any good to the society; it will rather mislead the entirety of humanity.

According to Gandhi: "The real difficulty is that people have no idea of what education truly its. We assess the value of education in the same manner as we assess the value of land or of shares in the stock-exchange market. We want to provide only such education as would enable the student to earn more. We hardly give any thought to the improvement of the character of the educated. The girls, we say, do not have to earn; so why should they be educated? As long as such ideas persist there is no hope of our ever knowing the true value of education".

Professional Ethics and Value Education

The rapid developments in science and technology and the challenges of globalization are posing additional challenges to the education system in the country. This is also the time when parental care to the children is on the wane. The adverse effects of the media on the mental development and moral values of the younger generation are being felt increasingly in all spheres of life. Gross consumerism has distorted the outlook of persons into one of equating possessions with richness. Exploitation of natural resources is proceeding without reference to sustainability. The hiatus between the rich and the poor is getting wider. While the education system needs to keep pace with the scientific and technological developments in terms of building the skills and knowledge, it also needs to address the more fundamental issues of the social and moral consequences of such unregulated activities. In this context, there is now a growing demand to lay greater emphasis on education to inculcate, nurture and develop values, particularly among the youth of the country.

Implementation of value based education in distance education:

Talking about VBE (value based education) is quite an easy job, but implementing it in distance education a daunting task, which needs the strongest determination. Actually, unless we can create a very healthy and pleasant educational environment, VBE cannot be implemented at academic institutions. First of all we should all fully agree that without VBE we cannot have a safe society, a developed country and a harmonious family environment. Therefore, we need to find out some practical ways to apply VBE, e.g. starting with junior classes, developing a strong commitment of all academic institutions, encouraging parents for their persistent support, producing more trained and dedicated teachers, establishing supportive administrative teams and the like. A well organized library equipped with relevant reference books and audio-visual cassettes of course helps as an additional and supportive means and resource to inculcate the value based education in the children.

Recommendations

1. The need of the hour is to inculcate human values in the University students who are learning through distance mode, like quest for peace, adherence to truth and right conduct, non-violence, compassion, tolerance, love for all living beings, respect for the Motherland and the glory of its culture and traditions, in order to promote societal concern and responsible citizenship; so that such an effort is in the interest of the students, society and the nation.

2. It is entirely feasible to inculcate 'values' in the students at the distance learning level, and there are several institutions in the country where such value-based education is imparted with impressive results. However, it requires sustained efforts to practice, absorb, and assimilate values.

3. It is desirable that human values should permeate and form part of the teaching in all disciplines and subjects.
4. Syllabus for a compulsory paper of appropriate credits at the undergraduate level of all disciplines, to stress human values and the duties laid down in the constitution [Art. 51 – A], and the same may be suitably supported by the methodology and examination/evaluation criteria facilitating a learner-centric approach.
5. Alternately, the compulsory paper on "Environmental Science", recently introduced by UGC, may be suitably elaborated to bring forth environmental concerns in the backdrop of human values. However, introducing an optional paper on this subject, with the possibility of giving some incentives for taking such papers may not be a wise step.
6. Recognizing the special role of teachers in this effort, it would be desirable to impart them the necessary skills and insights into value education by devising suitable orientation courses and extending support to institutions for imparting such training.
7. Human Values should be the guiding parameters for governance processes at higher education institutions. The University system may take note of this. Also, our government considers taking suitable measures for disseminating this information in the higher education system.
8. Due recognition should be given to the expanding socially relevant role of open education and to explore the methods of communicating and internalizing 'Human Values' among the students. Special attention should also be given to develop appropriate study material for this on a priority basis through proper supportive measures.
9. The evaluation criteria of institutions should be so spelt out as to give due weight to the inculcation of human values, and that the 'Healthy Practices' identified during the Assessment exercises be widely disseminated by NAAC for the benefit of other institutions.

10. It is important to realize that we live in a fast changing world, dictated by the developments in technology. Quick access to information has made knowledge creation fast, and the multiplier effect has made it even explosive. It is increasingly difficult to anticipate changes and respond to them with creative purpose. Designing courses with relevance to the future and developing the necessary manpower to deliver them is a challenging task. All this calls for a team of professionals in different areas to come together to develop proactive strategies for distance education to meet the future demands. A Strategy Planning Body and an Institution to design and develop futuristic courses for transferring them to the Universities and Colleges may be created.

11. There have been significant changes recently in the policies on financing of Universities in India affecting the pattern of financing and expenditure in the Universities. Given the increasing importance of distance education in higher education, it is important that the State continues to take major responsibility of financing the Universities. All other sources of income, including fees should be viewed only as peripheral. It is to be noted that reliance on students' fees has its own limitation.

12. Universities have to attempt seriously to improve the pattern of allocation of resources between various activities and items of expenditure. Core academic activities should obviously receive top priority.

Conclusion

There is a famous saying - better late than never. So we must start now. Educators worldwide are now quite worried; therefore they have started various packages and discussions at their level. Names could be any - Holistic Approach to Education, Global Education, Democratic Education and Home Schooling System (USA), Alternative Education etc. They are all working for VBE directly indirectly, formally or informally. So we must awake and work now.

In fact the bright future of our nation depends on the children as there is a saying –"If you plan for one year, plant rice. If you plan for ten years, plant trees. If you plan for 100 years, educate children". Our ancestors gave us the highest message of value based education. Consequently, the time has again come to revive and restore our ancient knowledge based on VBE in this modern age without being biased, extremist, prejudiced and orthodox. It is only ancient knowledge which will change the attitudes of our children making them complete human beings; in return they will change the entire human society.

Reference

1. Lederach, J. P., 1995. Preparing for peace: conflict transformation across cultures. New York: Syracuse University Press.
2. National Institute of Education and UNICEF Colombo, undated (c). 'Peace education activities from Sri Lanka.'
3. Asif Ahmed, "Importance of Distance Education in India" Coldeway, D.O., Devlin, L.E. & Holmberg, B. (1989) Distance education as a discipline.
4. Evans, T. & King, B. (1991) Beyond the text: contemporary writing on distance education. Geelong: Deakin University Press
5. Holmberg, B. (1990) On European distance-education research.

2

Preparation of Self Instructional Material for Distance Education

Distance education is institutional concept of education centered round self-directed learning by means of correspondence courses with an integrated element of communication technology and facilitated with tutorial sessions, seminars etc. to meet the need for enlargement of teaching force, improved professional standards and modernization of teaching methods, distance learning system provides alternative ways of gaining established qualifications. The content of such courses cannot depart from the normal; the difference of learning experience arises from the presentation of the self-learning course materials and from the situation of students and, therefore, different pedagogic skills are required. The term self-learning material is used for the specific items used in a lesson and delivered through various media formats such as video, audio, print and so on. This paper discusses the preparation of self-learning material for distance education.

Distance education has been accepted as an effective and viable alternative to formal education system all over the world. The term distance education is used to cover various forms of study at all levels, where the students are not in direct contact with their teachers. With the progress of new sophisticated technologies, multi-media instruction is being carried out in all distance education institutions. This includes print Self-Instructional Materials, Audio and Video (broadcast and cassettes modes), telephone, computer and video disks, Tele-Conferencing, etc. However, printed material is the major medium of instruction in the most of the distance education programs.

Development of self instructional material is a challenging task and is quite different from the material meant for formal education. According to Rowntree, “the self-instructional materials must carry out all the functions a teacher would carry out in the conventional situation. . . guiding, motivating, intriguing, expounding, explaining, provoking, reminding, asking questions, discussing alternative answers, appraising each learners progress, giving appropriate remedial or enrichment help . . . and so on”.

Importance of Printed Material

Of all teaching media, printed material is an important and significant. The stimulus to learning which it offers depends primarily on the teaching skills which it incorporates, and on the sense of progressive mastery of the subject which the student derives from it. Further, the printed material can provide the nucleus round which an integrated sequence of broadcast programmes, of directed activities, of discussion groups and face to face teaching can, as resources allow, be built up for all these reasons, the package of printed material dispatched to the students at regular intervals is an indispensable component of distance learning systems.

Textbook Vs Self-Instructional Materials

It is very important to understand the major difference between a textbook (normally used by a learner in a conventional system of education) and a SIM (study material supplied to a learner in an open and distance learning system of education). Lockwood, (1997) made a comparative study of a traditional textbook and self-instructional materials. In his study he listed the following differences:

Textbooks	Self-Instructional Materials
Assumes Interest	Arouses interest
Written for teacher use	Written for learner use
No indication of study time	Gives estimation of study time
Designed for wide market	Designed for a particular learners
Rarely state aims and objectives	Always gives aims and objectives
Structured for specialists	Structured according to needs of learners
Little or no self-assessment	Major emphasis on self-assessment
Occasionally offers summaries	Always offers summaries
Dense content	Content unpacked
Readers views seldom sought	Learner evaluation always conducted
No study skills advice	Provides study skills advice
Can be read passively	Requires active response
Aims at scholarly presentation	Aims at successful teaching

Characteristics of self-instructional material

Self-explanatory: The content is self-explanatory and prepared for self-learning. The learner is able to read through the material systematically and get a clear grasp of whatever has been presented.

Self-contained: The written text is self-contained so that a learner does not immediately need additional sources. All information required by the learner is included. This does not mean that additional reading will not be required. What is essential is that the material received is complete in itself and the learner later can build on it with additional material if required.

Self-directed: Self study materials are written in such a way that the student receives guidance, hints and suggestions at each stage of learning. Clear objectives, simple explanations, sequential development, apt illustrations, and appropriate learning activities are utilized. The material performs the role of a teacher.

Self-motivating: The study materials are highly motivational for the learners. Some ways in which this is done is to draw attention to known facts, relate this knowledge to familiar situations and make the entire learning relevant to the learner's real life context.

Self-evaluating: In order to optimize learning, the learners should know whether they are proceeding on the right track. Self-evaluation in the form of self check questions, exercises, etc. will assist in making this possible. The course writer provides an evaluation system by providing an appropriate number of self-check exercises, activities to check the progress of the learner.

Learning through self-instructional materials is catching on throughout the world in the developed as well as the developing countries. These are now available both in computer managed as well as traditional print forms. Some instructors find such material useful even though they are available for teaching in the classroom.

Conclusion

Any mode that fits the conditions of the country may be adopted /adapted. Emphasis should be on establishment of an internal faculty feasible use of media and above all, on a group of eminent writers for developing instructional material. Although there are aids to writing self-learning materials and training can be given enhance skills, authorship remains a highly personal trait. In theory it would appear the person best suited to write the package would be one with the subject matter at his fingertips as he would not need to research the topic experience. However, suggests that except in exceptional circumstances the subject matter expert is the last man to write it. Experts fail in three ways:

1. Where they have great depth of knowledge and enthusiasm for one particular area of subject, they give this detailed coverage to the detriment of the rest of the package.
2. Because they are expert in the subject matter they find it difficult to foresee the difficulties that it presents to the learner are to prone to overestimate his basic knowledge.
3. They have no experience in visualization and produce scripts that are virtually impossible to illustrate.

The writers must be deductive critical, creative thinkers who also need to have good visual creativity and be capable of sympathy with the students. Efforts should, therefore, be spent in searching out those with flair who know how to research a subject with a capacity for logical analysis. It is also essential that his academic content of the course and the ways in which they will be taught must be thought of as a single operation by a simple group of people. To aid comprehension of teaching points, the text should be sensibly illustrated. If the illustration is not visualized by the writer(s) at the same time it will not be possible to tie up the illustration with the text exactly. Finally the textual material needs editing. The editing process should include:

1. Technical review, to ensure that the content is technically correct.
2. An educational technology review, to ensure that as far as possible without developmental testing the sequence and structure is likely to enable the students to learn.
3. Elimination of ambiguities, repetitions and errors of grammar and spelling and checking that cross-references are correct.
4. Making adjustment on the balance and coherence of course coverage.
5. If several authors are involved coordinating their efforts to a single style.

References

1. Lockwood F (1997), Developing *Self Instructional Material for Open, Distance and Flexible Learning,* Pre ICDE Conference Workshop Report, Pennslyvania State University.
2. Rowntree Derek (1994), *Preparing Material for open, distance and flexible learning: An Action Guide for Teachers and Trainers,* Kogan Page, London.

3

Influence of Modern Technologies on Enhancing Learning Chemistry Through Distance Mode

Introduction

Change is the key element for the twenty first century that poses many challenges and enormous pressure on our daily life, work and society. Political, economical, social and technological environments are changing significantly and rapidly. Information and Communication Technologies (ICT) transform all aspects of education and distance education (DE), which is a rapidly growing segment. The advent of the internet as a means of information access and distribution and the explosive growth of the World Wide Web (Web) have transformed distance teaching from a broadcast mode to an interactive one. To succeed in teaching at a distance, the entire faculties and related people must get involved in the development of courses and curriculum.

The most important component of chemistry learning is the abstract component. A strong abstract component is one of the most challenging elements to deliver effectively at a distance mode (kenepobl et all. 2005). The effective designing and delivery of abstract components for distance chemistry learners, therefore, becomes essential to support and sustain learner's interest in chemistry. The use of modern technologies to overcome the challenges of learning chemistry through distance mode. This article discusses the use of various options of Modern Technologies for influencing the enhancement of learning chemistry through distance mode.

Current Practices of Chemistry Learning

Current practices of instruction exhibit certain characteristic features in chemistry learning:

1. Lecture – and laboratory – oriented subjects are often presented with few, if any, linkages established between them
2. Students are passive in lecture courses.
3. Students often do rote exercises in the laboratory that are unrelated to either the conduct of modern chemistry or to the subject matter of the lecture component.
4. The administration of the lecture – laboratory experience is often fraught with difficulties that stem from a lack of resources, time constraints, and personnel that have inappropriate training.
5. The student is passive with respect to his/her entire educational experience;
6. Collaborative work is not valued;
7. Teachers are assumed to be omniscient;
8. The course content is stable;
9. The course is homogeneous.
10. The subject is presented as homogeneous with little idea of its relationship to the real world or to other disciplines; and laboratory – oriented experiences, whether they be manipulative data analyses or cognitive, are often nonexistent.

Finally, the structure of chemistry instruction has changed little since the early part of the century from which time we have direct knowledge of what was happening in the formal instructional processes for chemists.

Modern Technologies

Modern Technologies enhances the level of learning through distance mode is highly appreciable then and there. The quality of lesson material, curriculum transaction, follow-up works, and evaluation process are highly enhanced. Even in today's scenario a lot of skill development courses also pursued through distance mode. Internet, Web-based instruction, Virtual laboratories, Teleconferencing are some of the very popular technology systems which are widely used by the students.

Internet

The internet as a medium of learning is explored to the maximum for the creative use and positive impact of such knowledge on the learning process. Topics from recent advances in the subject are allocated to them. Through internet search, the students acquire the latest know how on the assigned topics and compile the projects in the form of a brochure.

Web

Based instruction (WBI) is defined broadly as any form of innovative approach for delivering instruction to a remote audience in which the Web is included as a tool. Presently, several Web sites have been developed to provide learners with access to instructional resources from a distance. However, Hill (1996) noted that, most course-based or learning sites simply post course materials. In such instances, use of the Web falls far short of the potential this medium affords. According to Casey (1998), currently used Web models of learning can be identified as one of the followings:

1. The Web as Source of Information: This is the simplest use of the Web. It is used as a convenient place to store supporting information for traditionally offered courses.
2. The Web as Electronic Book: Many institutions have moved to use of the Web to present information in a more structured way for teaching process. Students use the screen to read materials, activate multimedia a demonstrations, and take self-correcting quizzes or other activities. The course material is mostly factual information, which is to learn from the Web page and any accompanying media. There is no interaction between teacher and the students through the Web.
3. The Web as Teacher: Some Web – based courses include some form or personal communication between students and other students via the use of email and perhaps char rooms.
4. The Web as a Communication Medium between Teacher and Students: In this model, students learn from the teacher but "through" the Web and not "from" the Web. Thus, the Web acts as the communication medium for the necessary interaction. A model such as these aims to mirror a face – to – face learning environment, within students will be able to establish some of human relationship with the teacher.

Virtual laboratories

Virtual laboratories detail the preparation, essential equipment, and method relevant to the practical and students then actively perform experiments themselves with simulated responses. Virtual laboratory presents a range of equipment on-screen and may offer a very high degree of interactivity. Training through audiovisual aids can play an important role in medical education.

Teleconferencing

It is a new mixed model approach for DE combining satellite teleconferencing with hands-on activity session. It was developed to adjust for many of the disadvantages associated with DE and traditional in person training. The mixed model used live teleconference speakers. Video clips, interactive call-in sessions and local sessions.

Conclusion

The field of education all over the world is swept by a paradigm shift that is the result of a new awakening in the teaching – learning process. The onus is now on the learner and the teacher is now looked upon as a facilitator. Understanding that the traditional chalk and talk method can no longer enthuse the students, the college continuously strives to innovate methods that will sustain their interest and make the learning process more productive and interesting. Innovative teaching can take many forms. Educators must learn to change with the times and the methods offered for instructing students. These changes will ultimately benefit the students and the education system.

Refernces

1. Barron, D.D. (1990). The Use of Distance Education in United States library and Information Science: History and Current Perspectives. *Education for Information*. 8, 325- 339.
2. Bothma, Theo J.D. and Snyman Retha (MMM). (2000). Web-supported teaching in the Department of Information Science at the University of Pretoria: a case study. In 66th IFLA Council and General Conference, Jerusalem, Israel, 13 – 18 Aug, 2000.
3. Brine, Alan and Feather, John. (2002). Supporting skills development – LTSN-ICS. In 68th IFLA Council and General Conference Bangkok, Thailand, 18 – 24 Aug, 2002.
4. Casey, D. (1998). Learning “From” or “Through” the Web: Models of Web Based Education.
5. Dibbon, David. (2000). Innovative Teaching Working Group: A Proposal. Education 4361. December 10.

6. Gilbert, L. & Moore, D.R. (1998). Building Interactivity into Web Courses: Tools for Social and Instructional Interaction. *Educational Technology*, May-June, 29- 35.

7. Hall, Katherine (2000). Distance Education: an insider's view. *AALL Spectrum*, May.

8. Hill, J.R. (1996). Distance Learning Environments via the World Wide Web. In Khan, B.H. (ed.) Web-Based Instruction. New Jersey: Educational Technology Publications.

4

Factors Affecting Quality in Distance Education

Distance education, or distance learning, is a field of education that focuses on the pedagogy, technology, and instructional systems design that aim to deliver education to students who are not physically “on site”. Quality in distance education has been studied mostly from a top-down approach, from administration and faculty to students. This paper provides decision makers with 32 trends that affect distance learning and thus enable them to plan accordingly. The trends are organized into categories as they pertain to students and enrollment, faculty members, academics, technology, the economy, and distance learning. All the trends were identified during an extensive review of current literature in the field. In response to these trends, distance learning may rise to meet student needs and overcome funding challenges that traditional institutions cannot. Distance education administrators must resolve concerns with faculty and university administrators to ensure adequate support, as well as to develop the needed course management systems and teaching strategies. Technological advances and increased fluency will continue to open opportunities for distance education.

Although higher education institutions are changing to favor distance education, the complexities of major transformations will require patience.

Introduction

Distance education, or distance learning, is a field of education that focuses on the pedagogy, technology, and instructional systems design that aim to deliver education to students who are not physically "on site". Quality in distance education has been studied mostly from a top-down approach, from administration and faculty to students. This paper provides decision makers with 32 trends that affect distance learning and thus enable them to plan accordingly. The trends are organized into categories as they pertain to students and enrollment, faculty members, academics, technology, the economy, and distance learning. All the trends were identified during an extensive review of current literature in the field.

Quality principles

1. Accreditation and Assuring Quality in Distance Learning
2. Benchmarking Quality in Online Degree Programs: Status and Prospects
3. Distance Education: Guidelines for Good Practice
4. E-Learning at the Crossroads: What Price Quality?
5. Guidelines for Creating Web-based Student Services for Online Learning
6. Implementing the Seven Principles: Technology as Lever
7. Identification of Key Issues in the Development of Sustainable e-Learning and Virtual Campus Initiatives
8. Maintaining the Delicate Balance: Distance Learning, Higher Education Accreditation, and the Politics of Self-Regulation
9. NACOL National Standards of Quality for Online Courses

10. NACOL National Standards for Quality Online Teaching
11. Principles of Effectiveness for Serving Adult Learners
12. Program in Course Redesign (PCR)

Thirty Two Trends Affecting Distance Education

1. The current higher education infrastructure cannot accommodate the growing college-aged population and enrollments, making more distance education programs necessary.
2. Students are shopping for courses that meet their schedules and circumstances.
3. Higher-education learner profiles, including online, information-age, and adult learners, are changing.
4. The percentage of adult, female, and minority learners is increasing.
5. Retention rates concern administrators and faculty members.
6. Traditional faculty roles are shifting or "unbundling."
7. The need for faculty development, support, and training is growing.
8. Faculty tenure is being challenged, allowing for more non-traditional faculty roles in distance education.
9. Some faculty members are resisting technological course delivery.
10. Faculty members who participate in distance education courses develop better attitudes toward distance education and technology.
11. Instructors of distance courses can feel isolated.
12. Faculty members demand reduced workload and increased compensation for distance courses.
13. Knowledge and information are growing exponentially.

14. The institutional landscape of higher education is changing: traditional campuses are declining, for-profit institutions are growing and public and private institutions are merging.
15. There is a shift in organizational structure toward decentralization.
16. Instruction is becoming more learner-centered, non-linear, and self-directed.
17. There is a growing emphasis on academic accountability.
18. Academic emphasis is shifting from course-completion to competency.
19. Education is becoming more seamless between high school, college, and further studies.
20. Higher education outsourcing and partnerships are increasing.
21. Some advocate standardizing content in learning objects.
22. Technological devices are becoming more versatile and ubiquitous
23. There is a huge growth in Internet usage.
24. Technological fluency is becoming a graduation requirement.
25. With the economy in recession, there are fewer resources for higher education and higher education, initiatives, such as distance education.
26. Funding challenges are the top IT concern for many.
27. Lifelong learning is becoming a competitive necessity.
28. More courses, degrees, and universities are becoming available through distance-education programs.
29. The Internet is becoming dominant among other distance-education media.
30. The distinction between distance and local education is disappearing.

31. The need for effective course-management systems and Web services is growing.

32. There is an increasing need for learning and teaching strategies that exploit the capabilities of technology.

Factors affecting the cost-efficiency of distance learning systems

1. The number of learners enrolled.
2. The size of the curriculum
3. The number of years over which courses are offered without change
4. Containment of course development costs
5. Sharing course development costs
6. Technology choice
7. Labour market practices
8. Structural practices

Factors restricting the distance education

The funds

1. For institutions: continuing costs of installing, maintaining, using, and upgrading technology to support distance services
2. For students: computer, associated software and charges to the Internet service provider

The system of evaluation

1. Distance education has difficulty in controlling cheating because of the lack of teacher control.
2. With the development of technology, the system of evaluation will be improved.

Conclusion

In response to these trends, distance learning may rise to meet student needs and overcome funding challenges that traditional institutions cannot. Distance education administrators must resolve concerns with faculty and university administrators to ensure adequate support, as well as to develop the needed course management systems and teaching strategies. Technological advances and increased fluency will continue to open opportunities for distance education. Although higher education institutions are changing to favor distance education, the complexities of major transformations will require patience.

References

1. Anderson, T. (2001, November/December) The hidden curriculum in distance education: An updated view. Change. 33(6): 28-35.
2. Bates, T. (2000) Distance education in dual mode higher education institutions: Challenges and changes. Online: http://bates.cstudies.ubc.ca/papers/challengesandchanges.html
3. Dubois, J. R. (1996) Going the distance: A national distance learning initiative. Adult Learning. 8(1): 19-21.
4. Kariya, S. (2003) Online education expands and evolves. IEEE Spectrum. 40(5): 49-51.

5

Factors Affecting Quality in Distance Education

Introduction

The factors presented in this article were identified during an integrative literature review, conducted to summarize the current state and future directions of distance education. Books, journal articles, reports, and web sites were selected based on their currency (most references were published within the last 3 years) and relevance to distance education, information technology, and impact on the larger, higher education community. Themes emerged as the analysis progressed regarding students and enrollment, faculty members, academics, technology, the economy, and distance learning. The citations were then ordered in sub categories and specific factors as follows.

Student/Enrollment Factors

1. The current higher education infrastructure cannot accommodate the growing college-aged population and

enrollments, making more distance education programs necessary.

2. Students are shopping for courses that meet their schedules and circumstances.
3. Higher-education learner profiles, including online, information-age, and adult learners, are changing.
4. The percentage of adult, female, and minority learners is increasing.
5. Retention rates concern administrators and faculty members.

Faculty Factors

1. Traditional faculty roles are shifting or "unbundling."
2. The need for faculty development, support, and training is growing.
3. Faculty tenure is being challenged, allowing for more non-traditional faculty roles in distance education.
4. Some faculty members are resisting technological course delivery.
5. Faculty members who participate in distance education courses develop better attitudes toward distance education and technology.
6. Instructors of distance courses can feel isolated.
7. Faculty members demand reduced workload and increased compensation for distance courses.

Academic Factors

1. Knowledge and information are growing exponentially.
2. The institutional landscape of higher education is changing: traditional campuses are declining, for-profit institutions are growing and public and private institutions are merging.

3. There is a shift in organizational structure toward decentralization.
4. Instruction is becoming more learner-centered, non-linear, and self-directed.
5. There is a growing emphasis on academic accountability.
6. Academic emphasis is shifting from course-completion to competency.
7. Education is becoming more seamless between high school, college, and further studies.
8. Higher education outsourcing and partnerships are increasing.
9. Some advocate standardizing content in learning objects.

Technology Factors

1. Technological devices are becoming more versatile and ubiquitous.
2. There is a huge growth in Internet usage.
3. Technological fluency is becoming a graduation requirement.

Economic Factors

1. With the economy in recession, there are fewer resources for higher education and higher education, initiatives, such as distance education.

2. Funding challenges are the top IT concern for many.
3. Lifelong learning is becoming a competitive necessity.

Distance Learning Factors

1. More courses, degrees, and universities are becoming available through distance-education programs.
2. The Internet is becoming dominant among other distance-education media.

3. The distinction between distance and local education is disappearing.
4. The need for effective course-management systems and Web services is growing.
5. There is an increasing need for learning and teaching strategies that exploit the capabilities of technology.

Among the above factors, in this article the distance education factor is presented in detail.

Distance Learning Factors

(i) More courses, degrees, and universities are becoming available through distance-education programs

The literature is replete with evidence of the growing demand for distance education. The annual market for distance learning is currently $4.5 billion, and it is "expected to grow to $11 billion by 2005" (Kariya, 2003). As Oblinger and Kidwell (2000) have noted, the International Data Corporation (IDC) expects a 33% growth rate in distance education over the next several years. Some analysts predict that demand for distributed education will grow from "five percent of all higher education institutions in 1998 to 15 percent by 2002". Others have asserted that up one-half of traditional campus programs will soon be available (alternatively or exclusively) online (Finkelstein et al.2000).

Organizations from within and outside higher education are adapting to accommodate the growth in distance learning. For example, "human resource professionals and hiring managers are becoming more accepting of online degree credentials". Further, more and more university systems are "spinning off" new "virtual" or "online" universities-for example, Penn State's World Campus, Arizona Regents University, California Virtual Campus, and many others.

Some reasons for this remarkable growth include efforts to expand access to more students, alleviate capacity constraints, capitalize on emerging market opportunities, and serve as a catalyst for institutional transformation (Oblinger & Kidwell, 2000). Another factor influencing growth may be competition with other institutions. "Universities offering distance education are often perceived as modern and technologically competent, thus creating a competitive advantage". Distance students include both the traditional continuing-education students (i.e., adult learners) and growing numbers of younger, on-campus students (Anderson, 2001). One estimate is that as "many as half the students in online courses are from the traditional 18- to 25-year-old student cohort who normally take campus-based courses" (Roach, 2002, p. 24).

(ii) The Internet is becoming dominant among other distance-education media

Distance education has existed in some form or another since the 1800s. However, accompanying the growth in Internet usage (see trend 23), "today's distance education focus has dramatically shifted toward network-based technologies (in general) and Internet-based delivery (more specifically)" (Kinley, 2001, p.7). Today, the Internet is being used more than other continuing education delivery strategies, such as Interactive Television (ITV), correspondence, and live-remote location combinations (Hickman, 2003). Not only is online learning more common now, but it increases 40% annually. One reason for the growth is the fact that digital media are transferable, storable, and widely accessible (Pond, 2003).

The UCEA Distance Learning Community of Practice (2002) recently collected a baseline survey of distance enrollments by medium. The average enrollment in university-level independent study courses was 4,725, with 56% of course credits delivered in print, 25% online, and 19% granted by passing waiver exams. In 2002, Brigham Young University Independent Study had 24,351 university-level enrollments. Of those, 32% were delivered online and 68% on paper—an increase in web-delivered courses since 1998, when only 15% were online (BYU IS, 2003).

(iii) The distinction between distance and local education is disappearing

As universities digitally enhance more courses, the distinction between distance and local education is becoming blurred. Digitally enhanced courses provide students in traditional classrooms with more opportunities for independent study: "Even in a conventional 'face-to-face' system, students spend much of their time working on their own. It may always have been so, but the increase in resources for individual learning and especially those through the new technologies has provided students with far more powerful tools for independent learning" (Rumble, 2001,p.36). Clearly, distance students are not the only ones who benefit from "distance" courses. In fact, most online students live in the local vicinity of the institution offering their course.

As a result of online courses, many institutions struggle to define Internet students (Hickman, 2003). Traditional in-state, out-of-state, and international student distinctions are being eliminated, and the corresponding fee structures for the respective groups are breaking down. Currently, 74% of distance learning institutions do not charge out-of-state distance students out-of-state tuition, 91% do not charge international students more, and 71% do not charge more for distance courses than they do for on-campus courses (Brigham, 2003).

(iv) The need for effective course-management systems and Web services is growing

With all the growth in online education, student- and course-managing systems are becoming ever more crucial. Web services is "a relatively new term used to describe new software standards that allow for integration of different applications as well as the secure exchange of data over the Internet" (Crawford et al., 2003, p. 24). Web services ranked number seven on the EDUCAUSE strategic IT concerns list, number six on the list of issues becoming more significant, and number three on list of highest resource expenditures. EDUCAUSE predicted that "at some point, vendors will... offer a standard approach to data integration, interchange and interface" (Crawford et al., 2003, p.24). Instructional/course management systems were similarly ranked number nine on the IT issues most likely to become more significant in 2003-2004 (Crawford et al., 2003).

(v) There is an increasing need for learning and teaching strategies that exploit the capabilities of technology

Technological advancements have naturally caused distance educators to ask how "new technologies such as wireless, mobile laptop computing, personal digital assistants (PDAs), videoconferencing, video streaming, virtual reality, and gaming environments enhance distributed learning" (Crawford et al., 2003, p. 24). For many administrators and faculty members, "how" is the question. While many studies have shown no significant difference when comparing online with traditional courses, applying traditional teaching strategies at a distance often causes frustration (Dasher-Alston & Patton). Appropriately, then, developing distributed learning and teaching strategies for online education was ranked number eight on the EDUCAUSE list of IT strategic concerns (Crawford et al., 2003). Distance learning research should focus on delivery strategies that help solve the capacity constraints, economic concerns, and higher-education consumer needs outlined in this article.

Conclusions

In summary, many trends in higher education will influence the future of distance learning. Student enrollments are growing to surpass the capacity of traditional infrastructures, learner profiles are changing, and students are shopping for education that meets their needs. Traditional faculty roles, motivation, and training needs are shifting while workload, compensation, and instructional issues continue to deter them from distance learning participation. The institutional and organizational structure of higher education is changing to emphasize academic accountability, competency outcomes, outsourcing, content standardizing, and adaptation to learner-consumer demands. The Internet and other information technology devices are becoming more ubiquitous while technological fluency is becoming a common expectation. Funding challenges are increasing with fewer resources to meet expanding, lifelong-learning demands. Distance education is becoming more abundant, especially online, and location independent, increasing the need for effective course-management systems and teaching strategies that utilize technology.

References

1. Anderson, T. (2001, November/December) The hidden curriculum in distance education: An updated view. Change. 33(6): 28-35.
2. Brigham Young University (BYU) Division of Continuing Education (DCE) Unit Review. (2003). Unpublished report, Brigham Young University.
3. Carnevale, D. (2000) Southern educators seek to cut tuition rates for online courses. The Chronicle of Higher Education.
4. Crawford, G., Rudy, J. A., & the EDUCAUSE Current Issues Committee. (2003, November). Fourth annual EDUCAUSE survey identifies current IT issues. 12-26.
5. Finkelstein, M.J., Frances, C., Jewett, F.I., Scholz, B.W. (Eds.) (2000) The American Council on Education and the Oryx Press: Phoenix, AZ.
6. Hickman, C. J. (2003, March 29). Results of survey regarding distance education offerings. University Continuing Education Association (UCEA) Distance Learning Community of Practice, Research committee report.
7. Kariya, S. (2003) online education expands and evolves. IEEE Spectrum. 40(5): 49-51.
8. Kinley, E.R. (2001) Implementing distance education, the impact of institutional characteristics: A view from the department chair's chair. A Dissertation at the University of Nebraska-Lincoln.

9. Oblinger, D., & Kidwell, J. (2000, May/June) Distance learning: Are we being realistic? Educause. 31-39.

10. Roach, R. (2002, October 24) Staying connected: Getting retention right is high priority for online degree programs. Black Issues in Higher Education.

11. Rumble, G. (2001) Re-inventing distance education, 1971-2001. International Journal of Lifelong Education. 20(1/2): 31-43.

12. University Continuing Education Association (UCEA) Distance Learning Community of Practice. (2002, February). Independent study program profiles 1999-00.

6

Empowerment of Knowledge Through Distance Education

Introduction

Education is the only one phenomenon which touches all spheres of human life. There is no nation, no community and no individual who keeping away from the spell of education and made their mark in the world. It is education that determines the philosophy of a nation and mould up citizen in accordance with that philosophy.

Distance Education

Distance education has been defined as an educational process in which a significant proportion of the teaching is conducted by someone removed in space and/or time from the learner. Open learning, in turn, is an organized educational activity, based on the use of teaching materials, in which constraints on study are minimized in terms either of access, or of time and place, pace, method of study, or any combination of these. Distance education may be defined as a mode of education in which instruction is provided without any contact between teachers and students.

Distance Education in Professional Growth

The most appropriate definition given to a profession in the present socio-cultural context could be of Alvin Rosenblum(2001) as (i) education beyond the usual level, to continue for life, (ii) self-regulation; (iii) technical competence for which one is held morally responsible; (iv) self improvement and (v) service to humanity. Hence for a professional there has been a growing need to update knowledge and learn such professional skills to discharge both organizational and social responsibilities effectively. Perhaps with these objectives many of the professional programmes have been designed by the Indira Gandhi National Open University (IGNOU) to meet the growing demands of the professional education in the country.

Distance education for health professionals' training

India, like many other countries, was committed to the Alma-Ata declaration of 1978 to provide Health for All by2000 AD (HFAI2000). Training of health professionals was an essential prerequisite for the achievement of the goals of HFA/2000. HFA has been a serious concern in most of the developing countries, as the set goal has not been accomplished and strategies are being constantly designed and tried out to keep pace with the changing health scenario. In India, both the Government as well as the health administrators has expressed their serious concern even now about adopting alternative strategies for achieving this gigantic task. Even though four decades have elapsed after the development of concept of distance education, only a few countries have initiated Distance Education for training. In India, health courses offered through distance education are few and offered by a limited number of institutions. Examples include a 1991 course on Health and Family Welfare Management for District Health Officers offered by National Institute of Health and Family Welfare; PG Diploma as well as M.Phil. in Hospital Administration offered by Christian Medical College, Vellore in collaboration with BITS, Pilani, Rajasthan and Tulane University (USA); 4 A two year medical Laboratory Technician training Course offered by Christian Medical Association of India, Indira Gandhi National Open University (IGNOU) has launched a B.Sc. Nursing program for in-service diploma holder nursing professionals which have been successfully running for more than a decade. A PG Diploma in Maternal & Child Health (DMCH) for medical officers/private practitioners in collaboration with the World Health Organization has also been launched by IGNOUin recent years.

Justifications for Skills Development Through Distance Learning

The 21st century has been variously described as the 'knowledge era', as information technology exerts a profound influence on human interaction such that the world is converted into a global village.. Manjulika & Reddy (2002) also observed that nations that do not inherit skilled human resources and technological infrastructures are unable to develop knowledge industries and cannot participate in the global knowledge economy. Such nations stagger under the strain of widespread poverty, unemployment, increased social hardship as well as public unrest. In addition, the economy suffers continuous decline and basic human needs are increasingly unmet at both local and national levels. Thus, strategic planning and investments in education and training are specifically urgent measures for survival. It is already a trite notion that the traditional approach to educational provision can no longer meet the needs of this new milieu, therefore the need to expand the provision of vocational and technical education to equip people with practical skills and competencies has become an imperative. The ascendancy open and distance learning into the higher education provision brings with it other critical issues such as lifelong learning, and functional literacy. Therefore, the capacity of ODL to reach large audiences for academic and theoretical disciplines can effectively be translated to vocational and technical skills courses. As rapid technological developments bring about significant changes in the socio-economic reality of contemporary society and by, it is important for people at all levels to develop an understanding of the importance of vocational and technical training and its contribution to the quality of life. A necessary precondition for this is mass access by a wide cross section of the population to a body of knowledge and skills which will enable people to gain an understanding and appreciation of a variety of new job skills that are necessary for individual and corporate survival in today's society. Dodds (1996) had indicated that the open and distance learning system seems to be the most effective means of empowering large proportions of African people, because of its ability to widen access to quality education at minimal costs. The National Open University of Nigeria through its Centre for Continuing Education and Workplace Training which offers proficiency certificate and diploma level courses in vocational and technical courses is poised to meet this need. These short courses are directed at improving the skills, competencies and abilities of participants for enhanced workplace effectiveness and to enable them recognize and utilize investment opportunities around them for financial empowerment and personal development. The primary purpose of this study therefore is to investigate the opinions and expectations of students, facilitators, counselors and some intending learners regarding the effectiveness of practical skills development using distance learning approaches in Nigeria.

Distance Education as Tool for Knowledge Enhancement for Teachers

Initial teacher education and training is the programme of studies which leads to qualified teacher status according to the official standards of a country. It is the basic or first level of qualification for a teacher. It may be taken as a pre-service programme (before a trainee teacher begins work as a teacher) or an in-service one (while an untrained teacher is working as a teacher). Continuing professional development enables teachers to extend existing knowledge and skills and develop new ones. Some of this takes the form of long structured courses leading to formal qualifications (diplomas or bachelor's or master's degrees). Other forms are shorter, concentrate on skills in managing children's learning or curriculum change and do not lead to additional qualifications. In some countries, qualified and unqualified teachers alike participate in continuing professional development. It may be provided as in-service activities (on-the-job learning) or out-of-school courses of varying length (off-the-job or in vacations).

Some countries have used distance education to provide a route to initial qualifications for significant numbers of teachers, both new entrants to teaching and experienced unqualified teachers. The China Television Teachers College and the National Teachers' Institute in Nigeria have long experience of this approach and have become a recognized and institutionalized part of the regular education system in their countries. In a programme that reflects an official policy shift towards more school-based training, the Open University in Britain has run a school-based qualifying programme for graduates who want to enter teaching but have had no professional teacher training.

Second, initial teacher education is no longer seen as enough. Distance education is therefore also being used to raise the skills, deepen the understanding and extend the knowledge of teachers. Some programmes are broadly focused while others are targeted at specialist groups. Programmes are taken either by individuals or by groups of teachers who are encouraged to participate by their schools or their employers, as can be seen in these case studies. For example, a non-profit television station is taking the lead on supporting school groups in Brazil. In other cases, programmes are available for individual teachers who want to improve their skills and their status, often enrolling on an individual basis, and at their own expense. Indira Gandhi National Open University in India has a number of programmes of this kind of which its Certificate in Guidance is one. The University of South Africa also offers programmes on this basis. Their BEd programmes are for experienced under qualified teachers and also new entrants to teaching, which serve to meet individual goals as well as contributing to the policy goal of a graduate teaching force. Some programmes are aimed at the upgrading of teachers' qualifications required by official policy as new standards are set in a country (as in China).

Third, distance education can have a role in programmes of curriculum reform which aim to change either the content or the process of education. In South Africa, the Open Learning Systems Educational Trust is using radio to improve the teaching of English, and to support teachers in this work. In Mongolia, radio and print are used across large distances to re-orient teachers to official changes in curriculum and teaching methods within a country in transition.

Fourth, distance education has been used for teachers' career development. As they seek promotion, or aim for the next qualification level, or aspire to become a head teacher, or work in a teachers' college, or become an inspector, teachers need to acquire new skills. In general, distance education programmes have been developed with varied intentions: of widening access to teaching qualifications; of disseminating good practice; of strengthening the education system as a whole by reaching not only teachers but the wider community; in enabling school-based training and professional development and as a means of strengthening the links between theory and practice

Distance education been used to teach. support and develop teachers for many years: UNESCO was a pioneer through its UNRWA/ UNESCO Institute of Education which was training teachers for refugees forty years ago. While the success of programmes has varied, experience demonstrates that distance education can be used to enable teachers to learn and to gain qualifications The term 'open and distance learning' is used as an umbrella term to cover educational approaches of this kind that reach teachers in their schools, provide learning resources for them, or enable them to qualify without attending college in person, or open up new opportunities for keeping up to date no matter where or when they want to study. The flexibility inherent in open and distance learning, and the fact that it can he combined with a full or near full-time job, makes it particularly appropriate for the often widely distributed force of teachers and school managers. Some open and distance learning programmes lead to a qualification, others do not; some are addressed to individuals and others to groups; some are tightly organized and others essentially a way of making learning resources available to teachers. All fall under this one umbrella of open and distance learning.

Distance Education - Knowledge Development

The relative importance of the major determinants of development has been changing over the past decades and the shift is taking place from manufacturing to services and from capital resources to knowledge resources. Increasingly, the element of knowledge is considered to be the key to escape both poverty and marginalization which in essence is the vision of the Millennium Declaration. Addressing the Second Global Knowledge Conference (GKP), the President of the World Bank stated: Distance education for development.

"The world has to move a revolution which is built on knowledge, on technology and on information.., knowledge, if it is properly transferred, if it is made available to all, gives the greatest opportunity for people to advance themselves and to fight against poverty." This shift in knowledge-based sectors of development requires investment in human capital, particularly education. A number of research studies for developed and developing countries have affirmed that educational development, which indicates the application of knowledge and information and communication technology (ICT), has preceded economic development. Knowledge-based human resources that we possess in abundance, can be utilized for achieving better results in many areas like agriculture and industrial productivity, employment generation, infrastructure development, improved education, training and health care and effective governance.

Conclusion

Definitely distance education has an immense power to elevate all the inherent potential of human being in positive direction. Today's technological and competitive world everyone should excel not only in economical development but also in self esteem. This can be possible and practicable only through distance education.

References

1. Garg, S. & Panda, S. (2006) Four Decades of Distance Education in India, Viva Books Private Limited, New Delhi.

2. Jose Chander N. (1991), Management of Distance Education, Sterling Publishers Pvt. Ltd. New Delhi.

3. Koul Bakshish singh, B.N. and Ansari, M.M (1988) Association of Indian Universtities, IGNOU, New Delhi.

4. Kulkarni S.S (1986), "Introduction to Educational Technology", Oxford and I.B.H. Publishing Company, Calcutta.

5. Pillai C.R. Naidu, C.G (1997) Cost analysis of Distance Education New Delhi, IGNOU.

7

Challenges in Distance Education System

Education is considered to be the most forceful instrument of development. Therefore it must reach all people living in every nook and corner of the country. Distance Education helps the economically weaker section and the people who are busy with day to day livelihood as they do not have time and money to spend in school, colleges and universities to receive education or to increase their academic qualifications.

Challenging task of Distance Education in India

Backward classes and scheduled castes tribes do not get benefit of education. There is a difference between male and female education. The disparity in facilities is also there between rural and urban population. To remove this disparity emphasis is laid on Distance Education so that all citizens may get benefit of education without discrimination.

Education commission (1964-66) observed that the standard of education has fallen over the years. It varies from institution to institution and from urban to rural area. Indeed rapid growth of sub-standard institution has not only affected adversely the progress of the nation but has also been responsible for lowering the quality of education. A better suitable system is needed to provide better systems of education. It can provide adequate opportunities to student desirous of higher degrees and to industrial agricultural and other kinds of workers to improve and update their skills and knowledge relevant to the occupation.

Education is considered to be the most forceful instrument of change. Therefore, it must not only reach all people but should also be relevant. The existing system is considered to be traditional and outdated. It is unrelated to life, needs and aspirations of people. It promotes divisive tendencies on the basis of caste, sex, class, region, state and language. 'Distance Education' on the other hand is considered to be the most suitable. It is accessible to all sections of people and can provide useful courses to all kinds of learners. It can improve the quality of education and can go a long way in improving educational and professional standards.

Though Distance learning system is truly an alternative educational system to the formal system of education, it has to face a wide range of challenges inherent in it as given below:

Challenges of Programme Development

The task of development becomes difficult due to the high expectations about the quality, structuring and commitment to the objectives.

Developing programmes has to bring teams of personnel from different fields of specialization. The unhealthy competition set between the content experts, instructional methodologies and hardware technologists get in way of educational and commercial programme generating cells.

Challenge of Quality maintenance and standardization

The very concept of quality and standards varies from one specialist team to another. A hardware technologist may think that if the material preparing team has high expertise and instruments, the rest of the aspects can be managed without any difficulty. Similar may be the outlook by different team specialists, regarding their area of specialization.

Challenge of Content treatment

The package programmes from developed countries are utilized by the developing countries. UGC Higher Education programmes are mostly western and so they hardly appeal to Indian students. Impact of programmes on children's concept of language, cultural understanding, social phenomenon and priority in decision making have no appeal to the Indian context. As Mass-Media is the most powerful threat to the government, the government likes to wield full control and caution in the use of this media.

Challenges at Storage and Retrieval Stage

The usable packages in Distance Education Centre require repetitive reforming. Such a continuous revising system demands the storage and retrieval centers more than being store houses. The centre should provide facility for storing and retrieving the material for day-to-day work. It should work as a workshop and R&D unit.

Challenges of Programme communication

The time schedule of telecasting programmes in a non-instructional setting considers the convenience of the majority. In the case of instructional setting the system has to oblige the learners with the satisfaction of his needs. Some of the many possibilities are consideration of having repetitive telecast, compulsory recording units at regional and local centers, change in relay timings as per the local needs, communication through established media like newspaper and radio about programme schedules, and use of teletext notes for transport.

Challenges at the Receiver's Level

The immediate concern of distant education at receiver's level lies in developing positive attitude towards learning through the new media. Indian students are habitual in learning under the presence of teacher in face-to-face situation. They learn under fixed time scheduled courses. To develop a self-study habit and self-responsibility of learning, the learners should also develop a differential outlook towards learning through distance mode.

Challenges in Curriculum

A major weakness of the curriculum of the distance education lays in the courses where development of skills is also an important component as for example, science courses, vocational courses, technical courses, computer and engineering courses etc. Distance education faces a severe constraint with regard to skill development of its pupils. Distance education can also offer unconventional modular course of short-term duration for certificates diploma, degree, post-graduate diploma etc. Indira Gandhi National Open University has introduced such courses. This would make distance-education system emerge as a viable alternative in the present form of educational systems.

Challenges of Admission

The students available to distance education are mainly from the left-overs of the conventional system. Hence, this second level choice by distance education affects the status of this system. Besides the admissions to distance education system do not take into account whether the students have pre-requisite skills or learning through the distance – education system.

Challenges of Economy

The main emphasis of the economy of distance education has been on saving rather on the performance or quality of education. The distance education is being exploited by several universities for the formal system of education. The distance education centers generate extra revenue that is transferred to utilise in the formal education system, thus exploiting weaker sections of the students.

Hence, the revenue generated by distance education should be utilized for improving the quality of distance education.

Challenges of Organization structure

The organizational structure of distance education finds it difficult to bring about flexibility in curriculum, instructional approaches, evaluation techniques and organization of student services. Besides, the distance education institutes are non-vocational whereas formal education system is vocational. Research survey (Biswal, 1980) reveals the fact that Correspondence lessons were not well-written and assignments were not properly checked. Also the personal contact programmes were not organized in the spirit as a support system of distance education. To set right the above flaws, the support system is properly organized by establishing study centers with adequate staff.

Conclusion

The authorities of the universities running distance education courses should sharply ensure that only quality education should be provided through distance learning programmes. Provisions should be made for the proper library; laboratory and required study related essential equipments and materials for the students in coordination with other related universities running similar programmes or located in the same region. It would rather be more appropriate if an inter-university body is set up by the UGC or The International Council for Distance Education of India coordinated by government educational related authorities to monitor and review the distance education programmes run by different universities and to ensure smooth progress of distance education.

Bibliography

1. Aggarwal, D.D; "Methods of Distance Education", Sarup & Sons, 2007.
2. Adity Sharma; "Text Book of Distance Education", Surjeet Publications, 2005.

3. Manjulika, S & Venugopal Reddy, V: "Distance Education in India" Vikas Publishing House Pvt. Ltd; Bangalore, 2005.

4. Pradeep Kumar Johir; "Modern Distance Education", Anmol Publications Pvt.Ltd; New Delhi, 2005.

8

Challenges in Distance Education in 21st Century

Introduction

Every country has got social and cultural value system. Education reforms launched by various countries including India are based on few features like Globalization of curriculum and Universalisation of education. The four pillars, which constitute the framework of education, are

(1) "Learning to Know"

(2) "Learning to go",

(3) Learning to be" and

(4) "Learning to live together". Because of the economy and social changes, the demand, the demand for learning is on the rise.

The new challenges arising out of these kind of consortium or federation or partnership alliances approach is the delivery system of the assessment and evaluation system vis-à-vis credentials and credit sharing between institutions which are providing such a service which is visualized that no longer in turn of the century.

The partnerships in the 21st Century will be driven by students volumes and skill, learners' choice and autonomy, job mobility and people's knowledge and technology independence and universalisation of education, thus shaping a strategy for survival of all, removing the territorial barriers (1).

Open and distance learning system offers the promise of ushering in the knowledge society especially in the context of the developing world. Trends such as Globalization, Liberalization, Democratization of forms of governance, pervasive influence of science and technology and the convergence of information and communication technologies fuel the growth of open and distance learning systems. Open and distance learning has crucial significance in addressing critical educational challenges especially in developing countries. However, we cannot afford to rest on our laurels. The creation of infrastructure and development of programmes to meet the exponential demand for education provision would need massive investment. (2)

A Personal Vision of Open and Distance Learning in the Next Millennium

Open and distance learning will not survive the next century let alone the next millennium. Correspondence education, distance learning and later open learning have been features of the education scene that provide the bookends for the 20th century. (3)

Challenges to teaching and learning in the 21st Century

Access

Higher and further education, as well as workplace, faces the challenge of access and the provision of teaching and training materials. In the 21st Century there will be significant growth in student numbers; unmatched by similar growth in funding.

Cost

There are financial and human costs involved in the process of teaching and learning. Providing teaching and training costs money.

It is unfortunate that in embracing Open and Distance learning methods, some providers have placed additional burdens on the learners.

Flexibility

The contribution of those working in open and distance learning has been considerable and is poised to increase further. (4)

New Millennium Distance education

Since its inception, distance education has been at the forefront of adopting new technologies to increase access to education and training opportunities. Distance education operations have evolved through the following four generations:

(1) the Correspondence Model based on print technology;

(2) the Multi-media Model based on print, audio and video technologies;

(3) the Telelearning Model, based on applications of telecommunications technologies to provide opportunities for synchronous communications: and

(4) the Flexible Learning Model based on online delivery via the internet.

In a society, dependent on innovation, education and education systems are cornerstones. Each process of innovation is closely interlinked with rapid, demand – oriented access to required knowledge. The increasing interlinking of the world of work and the education sector, means new challenges for higher education institutions, in particular, under the aspect of flexibility, not only with regard to the acquisition of basic qualification (training, studying), but also with regard to "lifelong learning" by those in employment.

Need of Reforms in India's Distance Learning System

UNESCO, in the autumn of 1998, presented a proposal at the

World Conference on Higher Education, which was subsequently adopted as a vision for higher education in the 21st Century. The most important among them are:

1. The University participation rates
2. Access and Equity
3. Barriers governed by age, prior learning, social status and geography
4. Quality and relevance
5. Changing the current culture of instructional practices
6. Freeing classrooms from time-bound regimes
7. Re-examining the campus- based delivery system
8. Re-examining the role of academics
9. Becoming familiar with and practicing a greater use of technology to deliver learning.
10. Partnerships

Conclusion

Improving the effectiveness of Distance Education

Because Distance Education is perceived as an increasingly effective method of instruction, educational researches have examined the purposes and situations for which distance education is best suited.

Good distance teaching practices are fundamentally identical to good traditional teaching practices and “those factors which influence good instruction may be generally universal across different environment and populations. “Because distance education and its technologies require extensive planning and preparation. Several cost components factor into the design of a distance education system are as follows:

1. Technology

2. Transmission
3. Maintenance
4. Infrastructure
5. Production
6. Support
7. Personnel
8. Accessible training to students in rural areas.
9. Students may complete their course of study without suffering the loss of salary due to relocation.
10. Students are exposed to the expertise of the most qualified faculty.

Reference

1. Encyclopedia of Distance Education (Vol.1), Dr.D.P.Rai, Dr.D.P.Bajpai, Dr.Neelam Singh, APH publishing corporation 4435, 36/7, Ansari Road, Darya Ganj, New Delhi – 110 002. Pp 193-197.
2. The world of open and distance learning (Abdul W. Khan) V.Venugopal Reddy, Manjulika.S., Viva Book Pvt. Ltd., New Delhi. Pp.462 & 463
3. The world of open and distance learning (Geft Peter) V.Venugopal Reddy, Manjulika.S., Viva Book Pvt. Ltd., New Delhi. P.467
4. The world of open and distance learning (Fred Lockwood) V.Venugopal Reddy, Manjulika.S., Viva Book Pvt. Ltd., New Delhi. Pp.470 & 471
5. The world of open and distance learning (James C. Taylor) V.Venugopal Reddy, Manjulika.S., Viva Book Pvt. Ltd., New Delhi. P.475.

6. Encyclopedia of Distance Education (Vol.1), Dr.D.P.Rai, Dr.D.P.Bajpai, Dr.Neelam Singh, APH publishing corporation 4435, 36/7, Ansari Road, Darya Ganj, New Delhi-110 002. Pp. 198-202.

9

Capacity Building Among the Distant Learners

Introduction

'Capacity' the term refers to the possession of a skill or a cluster of skills that enables an individual to perform a task successfully. This broadly perceived denotative meaning of this term drags us to inferentially conclude that it ought to pervade and percolate deep in all fields of life whether it is academic or social or economic or spiritual to the extent of considering it a pre-condition for victorious living in the competitive world of survival and spiraling excellence for either fulfilling the biological or psychological gratification of needs. If the dictum that it is a pre-requisite for excellence is accepted, the field of education cannot escape from imbibing the capacities among its stakeholders, none other than the learners, whether they are in the regular mode or distance mode and hence the need to capacity building among the distant learners.

The Inclusive Nature of Capacity Building

"I think, therefore I am", promulgated Descartes asserting the grandeur of humanism in an age of imperialistic dogmatic rulings. Today the time is ripened to say, "I am skilled, therefore I am". Though the peripheral perspective of the above maxim has a painful innate pragmatic philosophical impact 'An unskilled would perish', it has to be blatantly swallowed in as this has become the order of the day in the world of privatization and globalization.

Capacity building is much more than imparting training and it aims at

1. Human Resource Development - the process of equipping individuals with the understanding, skills and access to information, knowledge and training that enables them to perform effectively.
2. Organizational Development, - the elaboration of management structures, processes and procedures, not only within organizations but also the management of relationships between the different organizations and sectors.

Hence capacity building doesn't set its limit to mere skill development rather it inclusively aims at developing the whole personality of the individual and the organization in which he is a functional member by whose tasks the society and the family enjoys multi-coloured feathers on their caps.

Developing Distant Learners' Capacity – Rationale

Any learner is a dignified learner and licensing discrimination on the basis of the mode of learning is unjust and unwarranted from any corner. Though time, resources, teaching machinery, testing that include both theory and practice are ample for the regular mode of students wide-opening the channels of capacity building, it cannot lay an excusing ground to nurture the expected capacity among the distant learners, for the awarded degree is treated on par with excellence of regular-mode students and the distant learners are not deprived of any employment opportunity on this learning-mode ground. The fact that distant learners too become teachers, engineers, officers, and administrators, just like regular-mode of learners, justifies the rationale to build capacity among them amidst their limited feasibility and encountered hurdles.

Triple-twined Didactics of Capacity Building

An analytics on understanding the process of capacity building would off-shoot three basic 'Who' questions and drive us to find answers for the same which would provide a crystal view of the same. The three raised questions 'who should be given capacity building?', 'what should be given to capacity building?', and 'why should be given?' are answered in brief and diagrammatically presented as given below:

Capacities to be built

Listing out all the capacities to be developed among the distant learners would be too long and teaching all among the learners would be an attempt to shoulder the weight of the globe like Hercules.

Nevertheless to identify and pay attention to a few chosen important skills among the distant learners would strategically help achieve the purpose and make it successful within the parameters of educational framework.

Three Levels of Capacity Building

Capacity building among the distant learners to harvest maximum benefits should start at the individual level and then implemented at the institutional level and finally at the strategic/planning level. The first priority among these three levels should be upon the individuals because ultimately it is these individuals who are to be capacitated and the whole functioning and success of the system depends on these trained, gifted individuals in professional capacities.

Tangible Resultants of Capacity Building

"Man is a pleasure seeking animal", defined Sigmund Freud long back. Hierarchy Needs theory of Abraham Maslow arranges in order the drive to fulfill still the higher need when the lower need is fulfilled. Robert M. Gagne's learning theory serializes the learning activities and asserts the need to possess certain capacities for doing a learning task at each stage. These rudimentary psychological theories of learning focus on the need to develop skills for attaining mastery learning. Building capacity, using the social medium of education, efficiently and systematically will lead to the development of human potential and in turn that would lead to human security and development, by which a man derives pleasure and leads a satisfactory and grudge-free life.

Conclusion

Living becomes a winning not by birth but by learning. A learner has to win for academic success. A man has to win for successful living. Distant learners to win both in the arena of academics and life, capacity building is essential and let all the individuals and the mechanism concerned open up new vistas in this direction and make living making for themselves, for others and the nation.

Reference

1. Chris Kyriacou, 2005, *Effective Teaching in Schools: Theory and Practice,* Nelson Thornes Ltd., UK.
2. Victor M. Hernandez-Gantes et al., 2009, *Teaching English Language Learners in Career and Technical Education Programs,* Routledge, New York.
3. www.businessdictionary.com/definition/capacity-building.html
4. http://moodle.citylit.ac.uk/file.php/capabilities.pdf

10

Barriers to Learning in Distance Education

With the progress of time, education has gained huge importance. Its impact has been so massive that every individual is getting compelled to pursue studies. Taking the importance of education into perspective, many learning institutes are coming up with various educational techniques that can help individuals to work and study at the same time from the comfort of their home.

The concept of distance learning is gaining a lot of demand in India with each passing year. Distance learning is an excellent method of reaching the adult learner. Because of the competing priorities of work, home, and school, adult learners desire a high degree of flexibility. The structure of distance learning gives adults the greatest possible control over the time, place and pace of education; however, it is not without problems. Loss of student motivation due to the lack of face-to-face contact with teachers and peers, potentially prohibitive startup costs, and lack of faculty support are all barriers to successful distance learning.

Significance of Distance Education

In distance learning, students and teachers will find themselves playing different roles than is the norm in traditional education. The teacher is no longer the sole source of knowledge but instead becomes a facilitator to support student learning, while the student actively participates in what and how knowledge is imparted. More than any other teaching method, distance learning requires a collaborative effort between student and teacher, unbounded by the traditional limits of time, space, and single-instructor effort.

Technology has also changed the face of education. Advances in telecommunications technology has opened up the possibility of personal and group interaction in distance education.

Student Barriers to Distance Learning

Problems and barriers encountered by the student fall into several distinct categories; costs and motivators, feedback and teacher contact, student support and services, lack of experience, and training. More so than traditional students, distance learners are more likely to have insecurities about learning. These insecurities are founded in personal and school related issues such as financial costs of study, disruption of family life, perceived irrelevance of their studies and lack of support from employers.

A second area of concern for the distance student is the perceived lack of feedback or contact with the teacher. Because there is not daily or weekly face to face contact with teachers, students may have trouble in self-evaluation.

These barriers can be mitigated through technological methods such as e-mail. Video conferencing and electronic mail can be integrated into the delivery of the course to provide the missing interactivity. It is important that the student receive prompt feedback in any institutional setting, particularly in distance learning where the learner is impaired by the lack of casual contact with the teacher and other students. This is especially important for those students who live outside metropolitan areas. They may not have access to reliable telecommunications, computers, and postal mail. The frustrations resulting from problems with communication between student and academic institution are factors of which distance education planners should be well aware.

A third area of concern for distance students is the lack of support and services such as providing tutors, academic planners and schedulers, and technical assistance. The isolation that results from the distance learning process can complicate the learning process for adult students.

Another problem encountered by students is the lack of student training, particularly in reference to technical issues. Many adult students are not well versed in the uses of technology such as computers and the Internet. Using electronic medium in distance learning can inadvertently exclude students who lack computer or writing skills. These skills are required if computer technology is used. Students will typically be offered volumes of electronic-based information. Using this information will be a problem for some non-technical students. They must be taught how to manage, not only their study time, but the materials presented as well.

If students are undertaking distance learning courses that require knowledge of computers, then the students must be taught, at a minimum, the fundamentals of operating the system of choice of the distance-taught course. If distance learning is to be successful, technical barriers must be made a non-issue.

Organizational Barriers in Distance Learning

Organizational problems, especially infrastructure and technology problems, also present challenges. Faculties who teach distance education courses need organizational and administrative support from the institution.

Technology considerations are self-evident but are the most easily solved. Technology problems include; financing new technology, telecommunications, hardware issues, course production and technology, and Internet problems.

A primary concern for both learning institutions and students is availability of funds. When technology is used, the costs increase substantially for both the student and the institution. Universities must consider the initial costs as well as the continuing costs of installing, maintaining, using, and upgrading technology to support distance services. Telecommunications and connectivity costs such as those needed to use the Internet, are ongoing costs. "It's about a collaboration between teachers and technology that overcomes the restrictions of time and space, enabling students to learn more in less time, and with far less overhead."

Some students, particularly those without home computers with modems could have difficulty communicating with the university or teacher. Lack of adequate hardware and the subsequent cost barrier of obtaining equipment could place undue hardship on some remote students. However, implementing other communications systems (phone mail, etc.) could help overcome this barrier.

Course Considerations

The last area of concern lies in the distance courses themselves. Institutions must consider course standards, curriculum development and support, course content, and course pacing in developing distance learning programs.

Many believe distance courses are inferior to traditional courses. Careful attention must be paid to the quality of the material presented in distance courses. Curriculums and assessment materials must be developed that equal that of the traditional classroom if distance courses are to receive the respect they deserve. Maintain the same course content, learning objectives, standards, and credits for all sections, regardless of method of delivery.

Summary and Conclusions

The dramatic growth of the adult learner population is making distance learning an increasingly popular choice of learning techniques. Further study of student demographics and motivators will help target the adult learner population and will help institutions develop course materials and techniques appropriately. Close scrutiny of the intrinsic problems in distance education will help overcome problems encountered by students and faculty. Understanding and mitigating technology problems are important, especially with the rapid expansion of technology. Further research into course development techniques will help learning institutions understand which methods work best in the distance learning classroom.

References

1. Lockwood F (1997), Developing *Self Instructional Material for Open, Distance and Flexible Learning,* Pre ICDE Conference Workshop Report, Pennslyvania State University.
2. *Marrs, L.* (1995, June). *An analysis of distance education and educational technology. Offices of Continuing Education and Information and Telecommunication Services.* Bellingham, Washington: Western Washington University.
3. Rowntree Derek (1994), *Preparing Material for open, distance and flexible learning: An Action Guide for Teachers and Trainers,* Kogan Page, London.

11

Virtual Reality in Distance Education

The advancement of ICT has urged the evolution in educational field in various facts. The applications of technology in Teaching-Learning process are wide. ICT enabled learning is the "Need of the Hour". Virtual Reality is a computer generated simulation of a real or imagined environment or world. Virtual Reality field a greater application in distance education as it can provide Interactive learning through Multi-Sensory and experiential as a learning approach. ICT enables to sustain students motivation and also improves the achievement Virtual Reality finds wide application in Engineering, Medical and Science teaching.

Introduction

"By using VR in education material now considered too difficult for many students and taught even to advanced learners only at the college level could be mastered by most students in middle school and high school." -NASA Software Technology Branch.

Virtual Reality offers educators a truly new and innovative way to teach and engage students. Virtual Reality can best be described as a cutting-edge technology that allows students to step through the computer screen into a three dimensional, interactive environment. By putting on a special headset and glove, it places students inside of a simulated environment that looks and feels like the real world. Integrating Virtual Reality into everyday learning will revolutionize teaching and learning processes.

A helpful analogy to better understand the nature of the Virtual Reality is that of a child exploring a forest for the first time. Virtual Reality allows students to be fully involved in their education, instead of merely passive observers, focusing first and foremost on the learning needs of students. Understanding virtual reality-based learning means understanding the shift from text-based education to multi-sensory, experiential learning. The conventional wisdom about Virtual Reality is that it is an impressive learning tool, but only possible in the "future," because it is too expensive. The truth today however, is that Virtual Reality systems are now run by the same personal computers already in schools and homes.

Learning in Virtual Reality

1. Balances ideas with concrete information to facilitate sensory-intuitive learning
2. Uses visual aids: 3-D objects, video, and pictures along with verbal information
3. Provides demonstrations to accommodate different learning styles
4. Allows hands-on activities to facilitate active learning
5. Provides open-ended problems and exercises

Student Learning in Virtual Reality

Virtual Reality is exceptionally suited to take advantage of student learning preferences. They prosper when they can learn actively, through direct, hands-on engagement with readily apparent learning objectives.

1. Students start with high level of motivation to learn.
2. Students today are more self-directed and independent.
3. Students want to participate in decision-making.
4. Students quickly grasp the practical use of the content when it is presented to them
5. Time is an important for students. Attention spans of today's students are different- students quickly lose interest in learning

Experiential Learning In Virtual Reality

"I hear and I forget. I see and I understand. I do and I remember." – Confucius

The Five Basic Assumptions of Experiential Learning

1) Learning is most effective when it is an active discovery process
2) Students will learn more when they control the learning process
3) Learning is most effective when thought and action are integrated
4) Students need a safe environment to experiment with ideas
5) Realistic learning is more effective as a learning device

Virtual Reality learning guides the learning and discovery process as a collaborative effort between the program and the student. Students discover underlying principles and master necessary behaviours through active experimentation. Virtual Reality learning programs allow for more interaction by the student resulting in more personalized learning. Learning in Virtual Reality can also be understood as an every-day field trip where students are "taken" somewhere to better understand ideas and processes.

Important Features of Virtual Reality-Based Self-Directed Learning

1. Individual responsibility
2. Individual discovery

3. Individual pacing
4. Successful learning based on specific learning objectives
5. Providing a variety of activities and accompanying resources
6. Organized learning in discrete steps
7. Immediate confirmation of mastery

Visual Learning in Virtual Reality

The human being is a very visual creature. The human mind can only read 100 bits/characters per second. However, visually it can absorb the equivalent of 1,000,000,000 bits per second. Half of the human brain is dedicated to visual processing. Using Virtual Reality is the most natural way for us to learn aside from actually seeing, hearing, and doing. Because Virtual Reality presents information to us three-dimensionally (our brains think in three dimensions), we are able to process the information naturally and efficiently. We also retain more of the information presented to us, which is very important for learning purposes. We accept visual messages very quickly. This is increasingly true of students bombarded with images throughout their lives, from sources such as television, video games, and movies. Virtual Reality is a student-friendly solution to the reams of text and figures that now pass before their eyes on computer or in textbooks. It is a true paradigm shift from other forms of learning because it allows all the human senses, especially the most communicative one, vision, to interact with information.

Virtual Reality and Teachers

"Virtual Reality is a giant step towards "perfect learning"

From a teacher's perspective, Virtual Reality creates a structured environment that focuses students on specific learning objectives, similar to good teaching. Because the students are immersed in Virtual Reality with a headset, there are no distractions. Students respond positively when information is presented in varied formats.

Teachers select Virtual Reality programs to complement existing curriculum plans. In selecting a Virtual Reality program, teachers identify the learning goals and sub goals of the program to integrate it into their curriculum plan where they have similar or identical goals specified. Virtual Reality can help ensure that all students have similar experiences to facilitate learning and discussion. All learning experiences are social, and it is an ideal way for teachers to use Virtual Reality to enrich the larger classroom and learning process.

Virtual Reality in Distance Education

In Distance Education students depend upon only on the self-learning and the written study material. During which they may face a lot of problems. If they use Virtual Reality to learn they may have hands on experiences and many of their problems could be solved.

Conclusion

It would appear that the expansion of VR is set to have a massive impact upon society. The use of VR research and development in various industrial and scientific sectors could provide solutions to many questions, which may benefit from the use of research through VR technology. While the future of VR looks into developing its uses further, it must be noted that VR technology, due to its expense and accessibility will, for the time being be restricted to those who can afford it or access it. However, medium such as the internet will help to develop and increase the accessibility of VR throughout the population and into the next generation.

12

Technology – Enabled Distance Learning

In conventional teaching educational technology is a supplement to the teacher and used by the teacher to make the content of the course more persuasive. In distance education, however, technology is a substitute for the teacher. The essential of distance education is that replaces the interpersonal communication between the teacher and the taught and replaces it with a personal form of communication mediated by technology. International trends in educational technology reveal that technologies providing information through single medium are being pushed to back ground by those who can provide information in multimedia. This is enabled by the convergence of technologies. Learners are resorting to portable devices that can provide them with the information and two way communication facilities. The technologies capable of fulfilling such requirements of the new paradigm in learning whereby learners learn actively and independently. Information communication technology is a major factor in shaping the new global economy and producing rapid changes in society. Within the past decade, the new technological tools have fundamentally changed the way people communicate and do business. They have produced significant transformations in industry, agriculture, medicine, business, engineering and other fields. They also have the potential to transform the nature of education where and how learning takes place, and the role of students and teachers in the learning process. Embedding information technology in teaching-learning process is a major initiative in all branches of education; ICT has particularly important role to play in developing provision for bilingual learners. This is concerned with exploring new ways of working with bilingual learners as well as facilitating more established techniques. The increased use of ICT to deliver and enhance aspects of educational provision is now an emerging practice for all learners belonging to rural and geographically remote areas thus having advantages in overcoming geographical barriers. The recent trends in technology are resulting in the exchange of information anytime, anywhere and are thus making learning creative and flexible. In the context of Distance Education, technology implementations are appreciated in all spheres. This is so, because it is an alternative method to establish didactic relation between 'learner-tutor' and 'learner-learner'. Hence, its uses in distance education are seen vicariously. This paper throws a light of certain technologies which is put in use for distance learners.

Introduction

Technology has also changed the face of education. Advances in telecommunication technology have opened up the possibility of personal and group interaction in distance education. In a rapidly growing information society, technology plays a pivotal role in all aspects of our life, and thereby covers the learning phenomena — both academic and non-academic fields. In the academic arena, technologies are not only used as tools for support services but also embedded in instructional design of self-learning materials for assisting learners in their learning activities. In the context of Distance Education, technology implementations are appreciated in all spheres. This is so, because it is an alternative method to establish didactic relation between 'learner-tutor' and 'learner-learner'. Hence, its uses in distance education are seen vicariously. This paper throws a light of certain technologies which enables distance learning.

E-learning

E-learning is naturally suited to distant learning and flexible learning, but can also be used in conjunction with face-to-face teaching, in which case the term blended learning is commonly used. E-Learning pioneer Bernard Luskin argues that the "E" must be understood to have broad meaning if e-Learning is to be effective. Luskin says that the "e" should be interpreted to mean exciting, energetic, enthusiastic, emotional, extended, excellent, and educational in addition to "electronic" that is a traditional national interpretation. This broader interpretation allows for 21st century applications and brings learning and media psychology into the equation .In distance education especially, some programs require students to attend some classes or orientations, and many are delivered completely online. In addition, several universities offer online student support services, such as online advising and registration, e-counseling, online textbook purchase, student governments and student newspapers. In distance learning students and teachers will find themselves playing different roles than is the norm in traditional education. The teacher is no longer the sole source of knowledge but instead becomes a facilitator to support student learning, while the student actively participates in what and how knowledge is imparted. More than any other teaching method, distance learning requires a collaborative effort between student and teacher, unbounded by the traditional limits of time, space, and single-instructor effort.

Mutimedia

Multimedia presentation of educational content is overtaking instructions presented through a single medium. Educational effects get heightened through multimedia and as it is based on the principle that a variety of media provide experiences that overlap and reinforce the value of each other. Through this technology a distant learner acquires information in multiple forms and also has the scope for manipulation of certain parts of the content. Learning through multimedia is individualized, according to the pace and style of the learner, which is beneficial both for the gifted as well as slow learners.

It is more effective because several senses of the learner are involved. Multimedia presentation also helps in pacing the flow of instructions, repeating and reviewing it. In order to embed the digital revolution within the university courses, multimedia programmes of increasing quality are being designed (Baird, 2003).A collection of multimedia resources helps the teachers as well as the learners as an electronic library for ready reference. The advantages to integrating lessons with well-designed multimedia applications are abundant. Studies show that well-developed multimedia instruction:

1. **Increases motivation** through immediate feedback, multisensory involvement and greater enjoyment of learning.
2. **Increases involvement** as more senses and activity are required of the student, more learning and progress occurs.
3. **Ensures instructional consistency** because instruction progresses as mastery is achieved.
4. **Reduces learning time** by as much as 50 percent.
5. **Increases retention** of content over time
6. **Enables students to have more privacy** allowing them the experience of trial and error, failing tests and asking embarrassing questions without disclosure.
7. **Allows multiple access** so students can use programs when they need and want them and at a variety of places.

Web-based Learning

Today web based learning is a trend that has got well trenched in all the learning societies. Virtual educational institutions are not only common but with their immense popularity as reflected by the huge enrollments are challenging the conventional ones. Mainly the scope for individualized learning at a convenient place and pace appeal to today's lifelong learners. Today there are number of web based course management tools that help teachers and educational administrators in designing and developing on line courses. Distance education can be considered useful tools for delivering knowledge remotely and allow users to create their own instructional paths by using different technological alternatives and by deeply involving users themselves within the informative contents. Distance learners can better learn by managing, manipulating and organizing the information by their own. The possibility of the learners to perform a search of informative contents through links is a function allowed by web. This characteristic of web system makes the distance learners feasible to build a particular learning environment.

Educational Informatics

Educational informatics is an interdisciplinary activity that has received recent impetus by rapid developments in the use of the Internet as both an information environment and an environment for learning and teaching. It has two main areas of concern: first, to understand the effects on people of using digital information resources, services, systems, environments and communications media for learning and education; second, to contribute to the development of practical knowledge of relevance to diverse forms of learning/education using information and communication technology and digital resources. The kind of resources that may be looked upon in this manner could cover lesson plans, learning objectives, teaching methods, classroom management, and so on which is beneficial for distant learners.

Podcasting

Podcasting as an educational technology is a relatively new technology. Since the last few years it gained popularity because of its potential for providing multimedia services over the internet and it is today a useful tool for educational purposes. It offers facility for providing multimedia instructions. These facilities are available over the internet, which with the help of certain technologies for play back can make it available on personal computers. Today podcasts are recorded for students and teachers use them for their professional development .Podcasts are prepared even by the learners and shared with their teachers and peers by putting it on the internet. Learning is thus personalized, active and a creative experience for students.

Submitting assignments, viewing demonstrations, hearing lectures without going to classrooms are possible through this technology Podcasts delivered over the internet support on-demand learning and frees students from the compulsion of attending classes for distance learners. Similarly it can be used for training people far away. The main advantage of this technology is that it is a portable learning tool, allowing anywhere, anytime access to learning materials through multimedia. Discussion and interactivity are possible with the exchange of podcasts. Lectures need not painstakingly noted down as they can be down loaded and stored in the hard discs. Thus students can have a repository of learning materials and learners can access more educational content that ordinarily provided in a classroom with a heterogeneous group of learners. Teachers can rope in experts in different fields and prepare podcasts with their help so as to enrich learning experiences.

Web Quests

Web quest is an inquiry-oriented activity wherein the information with which the learners interact comes from the resources on the internet. Teachers can integrate the use of web quests as it helps in engaging their students in problem-solving activities. Teachers have used web quest as a tool to motivate their students and it has helped them in investigation of central, open-ended questions. Using web quests, students are able to develop individual expertise and are also able to participate in final group process. The students are eventually able to transform newly acquired information into more sophisticated understanding. The web quests can be used by the students in a manner where students are inspired to find a richer thematic relationship, facilitating towards contributing a real world of learning and finally reflect in their own meta-cognitive processes. Web quests also demonstrate the use of the research method as a form of education. This way the teacher can provide integrated problem assignments with clues and links to other resources. The teacher not only teaches them but also serves as a facilitator for them and can provide a helping hand to the students in evoking their complex creative behavior and help them to select their own decision procedure. Thus a teacher's role becomes that of an advisor and facilitator and encourages the learner to stimulate and cooperate instead of simply examining the student's knowledge.

Conclusion

Societal needs are also changing, bringing increased needs for lifelong learning and learning on demand. There are increasing pressures to provide affordable access for more students to postsecondary education. Under severe financial constraints, universities are being called on to deliver the very highest quality of education in more efficient ways than ever before. The predominant face-to-face, contact-hour model of instruction has been effective in the past, but it cannot be scaled to accommodate larger numbers of students without increasing instructional hours, physical plant and capital resources. Alternative delivery methods are made possible by technology, and these, combined with new capabilities for student services and communication, may lead to a technology-enabled, learner-centered and learner-controlled paradigm of learning. Distance education programmes can be enriched and made more attractive, effective and satisfying by using a variety of technology relevant to the content for learning

Reference

1. Phye, G., (2000). "Engaging Technology and learning opportunities: Technology Assessment tools". American Educational research association, New Orleans.
2. Baird,J.(2003).Learning and teaching with technology: principles and practices.London:Kogan page
3. Amar Nath Rai (2005), Distance Education Open learning Vs Virtual University concept, printed in India at Tarun Offset, Delhi

13

Student Support in Open and Distance Learning for Tvet

Introduction

In the delivery of technical vocational education and training (TVET) through distance education, student support plays the pivotal role. Whether provided to an individual student or group of students, student is necessary and complementary to the print material supplied. Student support includes all those activities which help students progress through the course. Many distance education practitioners have written extensively on the scope of student support in open and distance learning. They have all emphasized that student support services are integral to the overall working of ODL.

Areas of Student Support

Student support in TVET through distance education can be broadly categorised into two areas. The first is the administrative support and includes activities, which support students in marking enquiries, admission, pre–study advisory series, record- keeping, information management, non-academic aspects of assessment, library services and other administrative aspects. The second is the academic support, which consists of defining the course, explaining concepts, exploring the course, providing feedback, providing hands-on practical experiences, developing leaning skills, following up students' progress through the course, extending the boundaries of the course and sharing the excitement of learning (Simpson, 2000).

Tutoring

Tutoring brings ODL closer to face – to – face teaching of conventional universities. But skills of tutoring required in distance learning are much more complex and sophisticated than those required in conventional universities. Distance learning promotes independent learning and active participation of the learner: the two fundamental pillars of education. According to Simpson (2000), a distance tutor has to perform a combination of the following functions:

1. ***Defining the scope of the course*** - In distance learning, the course materials provided to students define the syllabus. It is, therefore, tutors who define the scope of the course.
2. ***Explaining the course***- A tutor explains the course through individual tutoring or small group discussions. The tutor has to be aware of different resources such as audio, videotapes, CD –ROM and other media support available for a particular course that could provide a variety of expositions for understanding the content. Unlike a conventional tutor who provides elucidation of the course, the distance tutor is the mindful that elucidation is the responsibility of the course materials and the distance tutor's responsibility is to facilitate learning.
3. ***Developing study skills***- Having strong study skills enable a distant learner to take full advantage of printed and other resources available. The course materials themselves, which are perceived difficult by many students, can't help the students develop study skills necessary to use the materials

to their best advantage. Therefore the responsibility of helping students develop that skill falls on the shoulders of the tutors.

4. ***Assessing students***- In distance education, generally the course material includes a number of self – assessment questions. There are, however, some double about their effective use by students. A tutor can informally ask question to assess students, discuss the answer and frame a supplementary question. Tutors also carry out formal assessment through assignments, which are marked either manually or by computer. Assignments provide an opportunity for invaluable feedback to students.

Technology and Student Support

Bates (1995) has proposed an ACTIONS model for the selection of media and technology for teaching, which is also applicable in the selection of technology for students support.(The acronym ACTIONS strands for access, costs, teaching/learning, interactivity and user-friendliness, organizational issues, novelty and speed).

Audio- Based Technologies

1. ***Radio*** has long been one of the most important forms of audio technology by many higher education institutions such as University of Nairobi. Many of the ODL institutions such as India Gandhi National Open University in India (IGNOU) and Open University of UK (UKOU) have used radio for student support. The radio programmes both take up crucial concepts from those covered in the print and clarify them; they provide an alternative perspective in which to view a concept which is already covered in the printed course material. Radio programmes are not interactive, and they cover only the theoretical part of the course. They do not help in developing hands- on practical skills.

2. ***Audio cassettes*** have been used by almost all institutions providing some form of distance education. Audio cassettes are much more flexible than radio programmes since they

can be listened to by students at their convenience. Moreover a student can listen to part or all of a program on a cassette as many times as he or she wishes. In some countries, audio cassette, are supplementing radio programmes. At the UKOU, the number of hours of radio broadcasts has decreased over the years, but the supply of audio cassettes has increased in the same period. Like radio programmes, audio cassettes also have their limitation in TVET programmes.

3. ***Telephone*** has been used occasionally to offer student support, but telephone support tends to be individualistic and expensive since calls are very expensive in many countries. Telephone support could occur student and tutor. One of the advantages of support through telephone is its immediacy. The disadvantage is lack of visual contact and absence of body language. Student support through telephone has the limitation of being restricted to only cognitive aspects of the course, through it has been found to be as effective as face-to- face student support.

4. ***Teleconferencing*** also known as audio- conferencing, is popular in countries such as Australia, Canada and India where distance between tutor and student can be great. In this mode, the tutor sets the agenda of the conference and at the other end, which is generally a study centre, a number of students sit across a table with a loudspeaker attached to the telephone. For a conference call to be successful, it has to be structured with the tutor seeking comments from each student by name, rather than from the whole group. Teleconferencing has been used by the University of the West Indies satellite project, (UWIDIET) in program of continuing education. The University of the South Pacific has also used audio links of this kind to support students in island states. Otaga University has used radio to link a number of regional centers for audio conferencing in its program of continuing professional development.

5. ***Voice conferencing*** is the combination of a telephone and computer to provide a complex voice mail service. By making

a telephone call to a number set up by the course provider, students can select from a menu of services provided, which can be available even on weekends and holidays.

Video-based Technologies

1. ***Television*** has been widely used by many distance education institutions to support students, particularly in developed countries. Like radio, it reaches a fairly large number of students' homes. Moreover, unlike radio, television program permit the richness of full symbolic representation. Developing countries have not been able to use television as much because production costs tend to be higher and broadcasting authorities tend to be reluctant to use air time for small audiences.

2. ***Video cassettes*** are a powerful resource for providing student support in ODL. They do use television, but not the air time. Like audio cassettes, they can be used by students at their convenience, either at home or at the study centers individually or in groups. In TVET program, video cassettes play a significant role because they can be used to demonstrate equipment, tools and/or the processes to be used in the tasks being learned. The University of Victoria in Canada used video to support students taking a certificate course in computer-based information systems.

Computer-based technologies

In many countries, computers are being used in a variety of ways to provide student support.

Computer conferencing is generally orchestrated by the tutor and involves posting a directional message, like a message on a notice board, which can be accessed by students at their convenience by logging on to a computer either at home or at a study centre. Students can then contribute to the discussion by posting their own messages. They can respond to each other's contributions and the tutor can intervene at any time. In computer conferences the tutor normally takes the role of stimulator and boundary setter. The tutor summarizes the discussion at regular intervals and posts more questions for discussion. Learning through computer conference is a self – directed, self- managed and self-motivated process.

E-mail communication has also become very common. Students use either their own computers or those at a study centers or an Internet café to send e-mail messages to peers or tutors to seek clarification on any topic of the course.

Conclusion

There are a variety of approaches that have been successfully used to provide student support in TVET program through distance education. No single approach is sufficient to meet varying demands of students and industry. The student support mechanisms have to provide for cognitive as well as psychomotor and attitudinal aspects of learning in TVET program. The technology available to distance education has the potential of providing quality student support required for delivering TVET program and has been successfully used by many distance education institutions.

References

1. Bates A.W. Technology, *Open Learning and Distance Education.* London: Routledge, 1995.
2. Reid, J. "Managing Learner Support." *In Open and Distance Learning Today.* London: Routledge, 1998.
3. Rumble, G. "Student support in Distance Education in the 21st Century: Learning from service Management." *Distance Education,* 21 no. 2 (2000): 216-235.
4. Simpson, O. *Supporting Students in open and Distance Learning.* London: Kogan Page, 2000.
5. Tait, A. "Planning Student Support for Open and Distance Learning". *Open Learning,* 15, no.3 (2000): 287-299.
6. Wright, S. "Supporting Learners in the Workplaces." *In Open and Distance Learning for Nurses.* London: Longman, 1989.

14

Role of Ict in Distance Education

introduction

In 1994, Sir Geoffrey Holland, Vice-Chancellor of the University of Exeter, stated that "by the year 2020 every education and training programme leading to a qualification or a credit towards one will be available in three modes: full time, part time, and through distance learning." (Wild 1994). The access to knowledge and skills to all people regardless of gender, age, race or location is enormously important. Education and training must be all-inclusive and reflect the vastly diversified present economy and various fields of human-power needs.

Distance education, also called distance learning, has existed for centuries. It involves obtaining knowledge outside of the traditional avenues of attendance at learned institutions. Distance education can play a crucial role in the economic development of a country by meeting human resources as per its needs. This system can cater to the requirement to those who are on the job. Their knowledge can be updated through continuing education programmes. Due to the low level of education among the labor force in developing countries like India, its work efficiency and productivity is also low particularly in primary sector of the economy. The quality of the labor force is a very important consideration, when we look at the human resource development in a country. This is influenced by the development of education and training and the availability of professionals and facilities like doctors, teachers, hospitals, schools and colleges etc. In terms of quantity, this is very low in comparison to those who complete secondary and higher secondary education. Besides quantitative expansion of tertiary and professional education in the country, one of the important tasks of distance education has been to upgrade the quality of both instruction and output at the secondary and higher stages of education. Though, it is not an easy task through formal system alone. For a better result we should use the ICT in the field of distance education.

Information and Communication Technology (Ict)

Information and communication technologies (ICT) have become commonplace entities in all aspects of life. Across the past twenty years the use of ICT has fundamentally changed the practices and procedures of nearly all forms of endeavour within business and governance. Information and communication technology (ICT) is a force that has changed many aspects of the way we live. If one was to compare such fields as medicine, tourism, business, law, banking, engineering and architecture, the impact of ICT across the past two or three decades has been enormous.

Within education, ICT has begun to have a presence but the impact has not been as extensive as in other fields. Education is a very socially oriented activity and quality education has traditionally been associated with strong teachers having high degrees of personal contact with learners. The use of ICT in education lends itself to more student-centered learning settings and often this creates some tensions for some teachers and students. But with the world moving rapidly into digital media and information, the role of ICT in education is becoming more and more important and this importance will continue to grow and develop in the 21st century. This paper highlights the various impacts of ICT on contemporary higher education and explores potential future developments.

The impact of ICT on *what* is learned

Conventional teaching has emphasised content. For many years course have been written around textbooks. Teachers have taught through lectures and presentations interspersed with tutorials and learning activities designed to consolidate and rehearse the content. Contemporary settings are now favouring curricula that promote competency and performance. Curricula are starting to emphasise capabilities and to be concerned more with *how* the information will be used than with *what* the information is.

Just as technology is influencing and supporting what is being learned in schools and universities, so too is it supporting changes to the way students are learning. Moves from content-centered curricula to competency-based curricula are associated with moves away from teacher-centered forms of delivery to student-centered forms. Through technology-facilitated approaches, contemporary learning settings now encourage students to take responsibility for their own learning.

Role of ict in distance education

The convergence of powerful computers with telecommunications technologies, over the past three decades has precipitated a fundamental shift in human history: the so called Information or Knowledge Revolution in the last decade of the previous century. Technological developments in Digitization and Telecommunication have led to fundamental changes in the production, storage and dissemination of materials and information. The focus in the information age or knowledge era is on these new digital information and communication technologies (lCTs). These are proving to be more powerful than previous technologies because of their ability to integrate multiple media into simple educational applications, interactivity, flexibility of use and connectivity. Not only text but a full range, of media including graphics, speech, sounds, still and moving pictures can all be stored and conveyed. It is 'now possible to combine elements of all these components in a single package (i.e. multimedia) instead of using a variety of components such as printed text, audio/video cassette, broadcasting, etc. (i.e. multiple media).

Education seems unlikely to escape the influence of such significant technological developments especially as the cost of access to ICTs continues to fall. The number of institutions adopting ICTs and introducing online courses has been growing. Undoubtedly this is leading to the ascendance of distance education as a popular mode of education being adopted by both distance teaching institutions as well as conventional institutions offering campus bound face to face education. It can be said that the adoption of ICTs has opened up new fundamentally different options for higher education both in how to run the business of higher education as well as in methodologies of teaching and learning. More institutions are involved in distance education today than at any other time in history. Distance education has truly moved to the centre stage today.

The uses of ict in distance education

Educational institutions have been offering programs at a distance for many years and there has been a vast amount of research and development associated with establishing effective practices and procedures in off-campus teaching and learning. Use of the technology, however, has extended the scope of this activity and whereas previously off-campus delivery was an option for students who were unable to attend campuses, today and many more students is able to make this choice through technology-facilitated learning settings. The scope and extent of this activity is given in some of the examples below.

a. School broadcasting
b. Teleconferencing (audio conferencing; audio-graphic conferencing, videoconferencing;)
c. computers and the Internet
d. Television and Radio programs

Conclusion

To conclude, ICT is the foundation for e-learning. Without ICT there would obviously be no e-learning. In distance education, ICT is the enabler for most means in imparting education. Hence, the requests by students to have more face-to-face seminars rather than online teaching should not be catered to. Furthermore, the findings from this research proved that attitudes toward ICT are more of the selfish nature of the adult students. If traditional teaching is preferred, then being a full-time student would be the solution.

15

Learning Technologies in Distance Mode

Introduction

Current developments in digital communications and the convergence of telecommunications technologies exemplified by international standards such as audio, video, graphic and data communication are created wonders in learning through distance mode. Therefore, as we look at distance learning technologies today and look to the future, it is important to think in terms of integrated telecommunication systems rather than simply video vs. audio, vs. data systems. More and more institutions that teach at a distance are moving toward multi-media systems integrating a combination of technologies both synchronous and asynchronous that meets learner needs. Therefore, while in the 1970's and 1980's many distance education institutions throughout the world used print as a major delivery medium, by the year 2020 many institutions will probably have adopted telecommunications-based systems for the delivery of distance education. This does not necessarily mean that print will no longer be used in distance education. It is more likely that print will be used as a supplementary medium in most telecommunications-based systems, and better ways of communicating information through print will be investigated and incorporated into the design of study guides and other print-based media.

In order to describe the technologies used in distance education "The 4-Square Map of Groupware Options" that was developed by Johansen et. al. (1991) which is based on recent research in groupware was selected. This model seemed most suitable to our purpose because we see distance education moving from highly individualized forms of instruction as in correspondence education, to formats that encourage teaching students as a group and collaborative learning among peers. The 4-Square Map of Groupware Option model is premised on two basic configurations that teams must cope with as they work: time and place. Teams or groups of people who work together on a common goal deal with their work in the same place at the same time as in face-to-face meetings, and sometimes they must work apart in different places and at different times as in the use of asynchronous computer conferencing. They also need to handle two other variations: being in different places at the same time as in the use of telephones for an audio teleconference, and at the same place at different times as in workplaces, study centers or laboratories. Based on these configurations, the four square model classifies four types of technologies that support the group process: Same Time/Same Place, Different Time/Different Place, Same Time/Different Place, and Same Place/Different Time. These four categories are used for describing technologies that currently support distance teaching and learning.

While the four square model discuss the major distance education technologies currently being used, this model does not lend itself very well to discussing new and future developments in integrated telecommunications. Since these integrated systems incorporate many of the features that we classify separately in the four square model.

Same Time/Same Place Instruction

Same Time/Same Place group interaction is the most familiar

format of face-to-face meetings. Certain objectives in distance education programs can only be met by meeting face-to-face. The British Open University, which teaches entirely at a distance, brings students on campus during the summer to participate in laboratory experiments. When course objectives require the careful demonstration, observation, practice and feedback of life threatening procedures such as a surgical procedure, it is important to organize face-to-face meetings. In a face-to-face setting accepted practices are only modified slightly to accommodate electronic media. Basic technologies that facilitate a face-to-face meeting involve an overhead projector, a flip chart, electronic blackboard or a projection system that displays computer screens via a LCD monitor. At the more sophisticated end are desk top workstations for each group member who runs on special software that helps the group to brainstorm, generate ideas, rank solutions and vote. Also, a record of the group process can be produced at the conclusion of the groups' activities. IBM's Decision Conference Center in Bethesda, Maryland employs such sophisticated groupware to facilitate group decision making processes. However, innovative approaches are now being adapted to the design laboratory work at a distance by using technologies, as in the dissection of a fetal pig experiment that was designed by the University of Maine using a combination of two-way interactive television; videotape and group work at sites.

Same Time/Different Place Instruction

There are two kinds of Same Time/Different Place Instruction: 1. a meeting through a telecommunications medium or teleconferencing where participants who are separated by geographic distance can interact with each other simultaneously, and 2. the use of non-interactive media such as open broadcast television and radio to instruct a vast number of students at the same time without the ability for the students to call back and interact with the originators of the program. Teleconferencing can be classified into four separate categories depending on the technologies that they use: audio teleconferencing, audio graphics teleconferencing, video teleconferencing and computer conferencing. There are two types of computer conferencing: synchronous computer conferencing when two or more computers are linked at the same time so that participants can interact with each other and asynchronous computer conferencing when participants interact with each other at a time and place convenient to them. Asynchronous computer conferencing is described under Different Time/Different Place instruction. The four major types of teleconferencing vary in the types of technologies, complexity of use and cost. However, they have several features in common. All of them use a telecommunication channel to mediate the communication process, link individuals or groups of participants at multiple locations, and provide for live, two-way communication or interaction. One advantage of teleconferencing systems is that they can link a large number of people who are geographically separated. If satellite technology is used for the teleconference, then, there is no limit to the number of sites that can be linked through the combination of several communications satellites. In order to participate in a teleconference, participants usually have to assemble at a specific site in order to use the special equipment that is necessary for a group to participate in the conference. The only exceptions are audio teleconferences which can link up any individual who has access to a telephone, computer conferences that can link up individuals, their computers and modems at home, or direct broadcast satellites that can deliver information directly to participant's homes. However, if more than two people are present at a participating site then it is necessary for the participants to gather at a location which is equipped with teleconferencing equipment in order to participate in a teleconference. This may restrict access for some learners. In terms of control, participants will have control over the interaction that takes place in a teleconference only to the extent that the instructional design allows for it. However, if the teleconference is taped for later review, students will have more control in the use of the conference. The unique advantage of teleconferences is that they provide for two-way interaction between the originators and the participants. Teleconferences need to be designed to optimize the interaction that takes place during the conference. Interaction needs to be thought of not only as interaction that occurs during the teleconference but pre- and post conference activities that allow groups to interact. Monson (1978) describes four design components for teleconferences: humanizing, participation, message style and feedback. Humanizing is the process of creating an atmosphere which focuses on the importance of the individual and overcomes distance by generating group rapport. Participation is the process of getting beyond the technology by providing opportunities for the spontaneous interaction between participants. Message style is presenting what is to be said in such a way that it will be received, understood and remembered. Feedback is the process of getting information about the message which helps the instructor and the participants complete the communications loop. Monson (1978) offers excellent guidelines for incorporating these four elements into teleconferencing design. The symbolic characteristics and the interfaces that are unique to each medium are discussed with the description of each technology.

Conclusion

Current developments in digital communications and the convergence of telecommunications technologies exemplified by international standards. The 4-Square Map of Groupware Option model is premised on two basic configurations that teams must cope with as they work: time and place. Teams or groups of people who work together on a common goal deal with their work in the same place at the same time as in face-to-face meetings, and sometimes they must work apart in different places and at different times as in the use of asynchronous computer conferencing. Thus the four square model classifies four types of technologies that support the group process: Same Time/Same Place, Different Time/Different Place, Same Time/Different Place, and Same Place/Different Time. These four categories are used for describing learning technologies that currently support distance teaching and learning.

References

1. Arger, G. (1990). Distance education in the third world: Critical analysis of the promise and reality. *Open Learning, 5* (2), 9-18.

2. Barnard, J. (1992). Multimedia and the future of distance learning technology. *Educational Media International, 29* (3), 139-144.

3. Brew, A., & Wright, T. (1990). Changing teaching styles. *Distance Education, 11* (2), 183-212.

4. Clark, R. E. (1989). Evaluating distance learning technologies. In *Paper presented at the Invitation of the United States Congress* Office of Technology Assessment, Washington, DC

16

Integrating Information and Communication Technology (ICT) in Open and Distance Education

Definition of Distance Education (DE)

Distance education, or distance learning, is a field of education that focuses on the pedagogy, technology, and instructional systems design that aim to deliver education to students who are not physically "on site".

DE elements

1. Student: the core of DE
2. Community: private / public organization for-profit / non-profit
3. Communication: radio, television, Internet, etc.
4. Content: diverse courses.

Five generations of DE

1. Correspondence
2. Broadcast radio / television
3. Open universities using combined approaches
4. Interactive teleconferencing
5. The current generation of online-based classes

Factors Promoting the DE

Economic trend

1. Lifelong learning is becoming a competitive necessity
2. Higher education, more chances of job
3. Changing career demands, the retraining

Academic Trend

1. Knowledge and information are growing exponentially and the need of knowledge proliferation is more eager than ever

2. Universities cater diverse courses to match learners' specific needs.

Technology Trend

1. Technological devices are becoming more versatile and ubiquitous.

2. Technology is being used more competently by more people from all nationalities, age groups, and socio-economic levels.

Factors restricting the distance education

(1) The funds

1. For institutions: continuing costs of installing, maintaining, using, and upgrading technology to support distance services.

2. For students: computer, associated software and charges to the Internet service provider

(2) The system of evaluation

a. Distance education has difficulty in controlling cheating because of the lack of teacher control.

b. With the development of technology, the system of evaluation will be improved.

In India

The Indira Gandhi National Open University uses print, recorded audio and video, broadcast radio and television, and audio conferencing technologies.

Open and distance learning

Open and distance learning is defined by the Commonwealth of Learning as "a way of providing learning opportunities to all sections of society"

Learner-centered Environment

The National Research Council of the U.S. defines learner-centered environments as "pay careful attention to the knowledge, skills, attitudes, and beliefs that learners bring with them to the classroom."

Distance education, or distance learning

A field of education that focuses on the pedagogy, technology, and instructional system designs that aim to deliver education to students who are not physically "on site" in a traditional classroom or campus

Distance education denotes...

1. Physical distance between the teacher and the Learner

2. Time distance between preparation and delivery of the lessons or learning material.
3. Time distance between preparation and delivery of the lessons or learning material
4. In other words: distance learning is the process of creating an educational experience of equal quality for the learner to best suit their outside the classroom

Advantages: Distance learning is a flexible form of learning where a student can study from home, work, on the move or wherever else is convenient

Definition: "Diverse set of technological tools and resources used to communicate, and to create, disseminate, store, and manage information." These technologies include computers, the Internet, broadcasting technologies (radio and television) and telephony.

Technologies used in communication

The types of available technologies used in distance education are divided into two groups: synchronous and asynchronous.

Synchronous technology is a mode of online delivery where all participants are "present" at the same time requiring a timetable to be organized

Asynchronous technology is a mode of online delivery where participants access course materials on their own schedule. Students are not required to be together at the same time.

Types of distance education courses

1. Correspondence conducted through regular and electronic mail
2. Internet conducted either synchronously or asynchronously
3. Telecourse / Broadcast, in which content is delivered via radio or television.

4. CD-ROM, in which the student interacts with computer content stored on a CD-ROM
5. Pocket PC/Mobile Learning where the student accesses course content stored on a mobile device or through a wireless server
6. Integrated distance learning, the integration of live, in-group instruction or interaction with a distance learning curriculum
7. Online tutoring

   E-learning / online-learning.

Effectiveness of ICT in Open and Distance Learning

1. the need to reduce the cost of imparting education,
2. to introduce need based educational programmes to a large number of people and
3. to reduce time required for sanctioning new programmes by adopting new flexible nature of administration.

Through the extraordinary pace of software development, enriched teaching and learning with enhanced graphics, interaction, animation and visualization.

ICT used by IGNOU

1. Broadcasting
2. Television channels like Gyan Darshan (GD) and
3. The educational radio Gyan Vani

Other Devices

SITE: Satellite Instructional television Experiment.

INSAT-1B: Indian National Satellite

Conclusion

More courses, degrees, and universities are becoming available through distance-education programs. Internet is becoming dominant among other distance-education Medias. The area of education which is growing fast today in the open and distance education as a result of technologies expansion. D.E becomes accessible to all meaningful only when old and new technologies are integrated.

References

1. Cetron, M. J., & Daview, O. 2003. 50 trends shaping the future. Special Report Published by the World Future Society.
2. De Alva, J. K. 2000, March/April. Remaking the academy, P32-40.Dunn, S.
3. 2000, March/April. The virtualizing of education. The Futurist. 34(2): 34-38
4. Hawkins, B. 2003. Distributed learning: Promises and pitfalls. 2003 UCEA 88th
5. Gallagher, S. 2002. Report—Distance learning at the tipping point: Critical success factors to growing fully online distance learning programs. Eduventures, Inc.: Boston MA
6. Making the Grade: Online Education in the United States, 2006,
7. Merriam, s., Caffarella, R., & Baumgartner, L. (2007). Learning in Adulthood, New York: Wiley.
8. Moore, Michael G.; Greg Kearsley (2005). Distance Education: A Systems View (Second ed.). Belmont, CA: Wadsworth.

17

Incorporating ICT in Distance Education: A Challenge

Introduction

ICT is useful to a learner so far as it increases the range of available alternatives in a strategy of learning. ICT can prove effective not just because they involve more than one senses but because they add to the possibilities of a learner going for grouping, image-fixing organizing categorizing and associating. ICT has drawn attention of learners as many different media as possible are evoked as being essential to a particular learning package for no better reason than that exists.

Distance Education

Distance education is defined as education or training courses delivered to a remote location via audio, video, or computer technologies. Courses conducted exclusively on campus, as well as classes conducted exclusively via written correspondence, are not included in such a definition of distance. The rapid proliferation of new courses and programs, colleges and universities are taking advantage of the Internet to enhance the admissions process and give possibility students the opportunity to ask online.

Ways to Ensure Distance Learning Success

Distance learning students must take a far more active role in learning and accessing information than traditional students in face-to-face classrooms. Written messages or posts from the professor and classmates replace other means of direct communication, and course materials are posted online. Rather than simply sitting through a class and jotting notes, students must take the initiative to download and read lectures and course materials.

1. Read the Syllabus and Use it as a Roadmap
2. Turn in All Assignments Complete and on Time
3. Follow Online Resources Carefully Week by Week
4. Search for One New Idea in Every Class Session, Assignment, and Reading
5. Contribute to Discussions
6. Never Procrastinate
7. Consider How Your Experience Fits Into the Discussion
8. Set Long-Term Goals

Does Ict-enhanced Distance Education Really Work?

The educational effectiveness of ICTs depends on how they are used and for what purpose. And like any other educational tool or mode of educational delivery, ICTs do not work for everyone, everywhere in the same way.

Problems and Challenges In Distance Education

The acceleration in distance education brought on by the development of sophisticated computer network tools is pushing discussion and action on a variety of challenges faced by distance educators. Due to a number of challenges and obstacles, it often requires a high degree of commitment on the part of the learner.

Balancing the combination of work and education

Most of the Open and Distance education students are older, have jobs and families. The task of balancing all of the above responsibility is truly challenging for most of them.

Study habits

The students' everyday environment is very distracting for most of the students. The openness of the online distance program gives students the freedom to do their learning process whenever they like but most of the time, procrastination is the culprit. Unfocused view of their learning goals also will make the students act irresponsibly towards their learning.

Recognizing and mastering strengths and skills

In online distance learning, technology is the main conduit which information and communication flow. A computer with internet access is usually needed for this process and its application will need the user to master certain level of acquirement. The students will also need to have some basic writing skills and a go online distance command of English language. Unfortunately, not all of the students possess the above-said skills.

Lack of motivation

Motivating themselves as well as maintaining and increasing self-esteem is a major challenge. The motivational factors are absent due to lack of contact and competition with other students. The lacks of immediate support of a teacher who is able to motivate will also affects the learners.

Lack of interaction with peers

Most of the time, learners will learn most effectively when they have the opportunity to interact with other students. Sadly, forming of the study group is not easy. This is caused by the difference in the usage of time between students.

Library facilities

Most of the library only opens during office hour and the learners would not be able to go to the library during office hour due to demanding works at the office. This will definitely cause problems to students who want to gain access to the reference material. Library database program such as the OPAC will also require the students to have proper training and skills in order to maximize the usage.

Technological Literacy - Including Computer Literacy

Instructors will need focused training in order to make effective use of the technologies involved. There might be audio/video tape material, television-aided learning, overhead projectors, computer referencing and computer-assisted instruction using the internet. Some students might feel uncomfortable with these learning strategies due to lack of skills and knowledge in using those strategies.

Program Evaluation and Accreditation

Mechanisms need to be developed for faculty evaluation of programs originating at their institutions. Successful programs need to be reevaluated before implementing them in a different cultural environment in this increasingly global village.

Losing the Content in the Technology

There is a need to avoid simply providing information, rather than instruction; or of simply transmitting lectures through this new medium. Avoid focusing on the technology rather than the instructional design and support.

Alienating Instructors

Faculty should be involved in the whole process, and should

understand that while one goal may be to reduce costs; this will not be at the expense of faculty jobs. Distance education technologies are not alternatives to teaching.

Non-Native Language Instruction

Many of the tools available, whether on the Internet or not, have severe limitations in their ability to accommodate non-native language instruction.

Institutional Support for Distance Learners

Academic institutions must remember that course content is just one element of the education they provide. If distance learners are being sought, they will need to be provided with similar support to that received by on-campus users. This includes everything from *full* library support to academic counseling.

Copyright Issues

While few researchers raise the issue explicitly, all are aware that many questions of copyright in an electronic environment remain unanswered. It is important to make sure that the necessary clearances have been obtained as needed to achieve the goal of education.

Conclusion

In order to overcome these distance education challenges, learners must first plan and manage themselves effectively in order to balancing work, family and study. They have to apply smart time management. They must be more responsible and have a focused view towards learning and improve themselves in areas they are lacking because not all skills will be taught by the tutor. They need to motivate their own self by setting achievable goals and have a positive attitude. They have to make an effort to interact with peers and tutors frequently.

Reference

1. Sharma R.A. (2009), Technological Foundation of Education, R. Lall Book Depot, Meerut

2. Garrison Randy (2000), Theoretical Challenges for Distance Education in the 21st Century: A Shift from Structural to Transactional Issues, International Review of Research in Open and Distance Learning, ISSN: 1492-3831, Vol. 1, No. 1

3. Hawkins,R., "Ten Lessons for ICT and Education in the Developing World"; available from (2002), http://www.cid.harvard.edu/cr/pdf/gitrr2002_ch04.pdf;

18

Factors Affecting Quality in Distance Education

Introduction

While distance education has been in existence for at least hundred years, the medium has changed from pencil and paper correspondence courses to real-time internet courses. But regardless of the medium, distance courses have common characteristics and likewise, have similar problems. The literature review examines the different types of distance education and significance as a learning method. Student demographist is presented and their relevance to distance learning barriers established. Lastly, the nature of student, faculty, organization and course curriculum and their respective impact on distance learning are explored.

Definition of Distance Education

Distance education or distance learning, is a field of education that focuses on the Pedagogy, technology, and instructional systems design that aim to deliver education to students who are not physically "on site".

Three Generations of Distance Education

The medium for,

1. The first generation was written and printed material. While writing had been in use for centuries, the introduction of new printing techniques enabled low cost production of text books.
2. The second generation was marked by the setting up of the open university of the UK in 1969. This was the first time that a deliberately integrated multiple media approach had been used for distance education. It developed large quantities of high-quality, specially designed materials.
3. The third generation uses information and communication technology (ICT) as its basis, offering two-way communication in various forms (text, graphics, sound, moving pictures) either synchronous or asynchronous. In both cases it can facilitate greater interactivity between tutor and student, between student and student and between student and learning resource of various kinds.

Significance of Distance Education

Technology has changed the face of education. Advances in telecommunications technology has opened up the possibility of personal and group interaction in distance education. Both computer and audio conferencing permit the introduction of class discussions without the group meeting face-to-face. Phone calls and electronic mail replaces personal office visits. Distance education is already a fact of life for most universities and an increasing number of community colleges, knowing the intrinsic problems and overcoming them will be critical to successful implementation of distance programs on a larger scale in the future. More than any method, distance learning requires collaborative efforts between student and teacher, unbounded by the traditional limits of time, space, and single-instructor effort.

Barriers in Distance Education

Problems and barriers encountered by the faculty, teacher and student fall into several distinct categories.

Student Barriers

Insecurities About Learning

Distance learners are more likely to have insecurities such as financial costs of study, disruption of family life, perceived irrelevance of their studies and lack of support from employers about learning.

Lack of Feedback or Contact

The distance student is the perceived lack of feedback or contact with the teacher. Lack of communication between student and the institution.

These barriers can be mitigated through technological methods such as e-mail. Computer conferencing and electronic mail can be integrated into the delivery of the course to provide the missing interactivity.

Lack of Support and Service

The distance students have the lack of support and services such as providing tutors, academic planners and schedulers, and technical assistance.

No Individual Consideration

Distance learning institutions provide equal educational opportunity to all, but careful consideration did not given to the special needs of the students.

Lack of Student Training

Many students are not well versed in the uses of technology such as, computers and the internet. They must be taught how to manage, not only their study time, but the materials presented as well.

Faculty Barriers

Lack of Support

The biggest problem for distance programs is the lack of support by the faculty. Faculty roles must change the most in administering distance learning programs. This can be difficult adjustment for some teachers. They must change teaching styles to that of a mentor, tutor, and facilitator. There are a number of reasons for this lack of support.

Lack of Basic Skills

The advent of computers, telecommunications and the worldwide web provides an unprecedented opportunity for faculty and students to learn in a co-operative environment. It does not offer immediate feedback and also does not help in building oral communication skills.

Threat to Tenure and Human Resource Staffing

Depending on the school and the academic department, courses taught as a part of a distance program may not always count toward tenure considerations, thus causing a disincentive for participation by some non-tenured faculty.

Organizational Barriers

Lack of Support

Faculties who teach distance education courses need organizational and administrative support from institution to be responsible for managing the program.

Technology Problem

It includes financing new technology, telecommunications, hardware issues, course production and technology, and internet problems.

Non Availability of Funds

When technology is used, the costs increase substantially for both the student and the institution. Universities must consider the initial costs as well as the continuing the costs of installing, maintaining, using and upgrading technology to support distant services.

Staff Training Costs

Institutions must also plan to have competent computer staff to support Internet use. These staff must then be kept up-to-date on the newest, fastest, cheapest technology available; therefore, ongoing staff training costs must be considered.

Lack of Communication

Some students, particularly those without home computers with modems could have difficulty communicating with the university or teacher. Lack of adequate hardware and the subsequent cost barrier of obtaining equipment could place undue hardship on some remote student

Common Barriers

Limited External Motivations

In traditional on-campus college program, external motivations are found everywhere: attending a class room with professors who can see, remind and even reprimand in person, as well as being surrounded by other students who are also pursuing their education. While taking classes online, these external factors are not present to use as a crutch.

No "College Experience"

In distance education students does not enroll like a traditional on-campus college program so they will not have the typical college experience.

Text Book Shipping

Taking classes through online, distance education students have to order the text books from an online book store. It adds an extra expense to the students.

Increased Computer Usage and Dependence

Learning through online almost depends on computer. It does not suitable to all type of learners.

It Leads to Social Isolation

The feelings of alienation and isolation reported by distance students. This problem must be mitigated by institutions providing a sense of involvement between the student and the institution.

Juggling Between Job and Studies

Distance learning is only fruitful if we manage both job and studies with equal sincerity. It needs lot of efforts at both fronts.

Course Considerations

Institutions must consider course standards, curriculum development and support, course content and course pacing in developing distance learning programs.

Factors Affecting the Cost of Open and Distance Learning

1. The number of learners enrolled.
2. The size of the curriculum.
3. The number of years over which courses are offered without change.
4. Containment of course development costs.
5. Sharing course development costs.
6. Technology choice.
7. The level of students support.
8. Working practices.
9. Labor market practices.
10. Structural practices.

Conclusion

More courses, degrees and universities are becoming available through distance education programs. Internet is becoming dominant among other distance education Medias. But also the above presented factors affect the distance education program. Close scrutiny of the intrinsic problems in distance education will help overcome problems encountered by the students and faculties.

19

Development of Self-instructional Materials for Effective Learning in Distance Education

Introduction

In the facilities of education starting from school to university level, distance education is an innovative dimension. Distance education, or distance learning is a field of education that focuses on the pedagogy, technology and instructional system designs that aim to deliver education to students who are not physically "on site" in a traditional classroom or campus. It has been described as "a process to create and provide access to learning when the source of information and the learners are separated by time and distance, both".

Self-instructional Materials (Sim)

The self-instructional materials include printed self-instructional materials, audio and video (broadcast and cassette mode), Telephone, computers, video discs, teleconferencing etc. However, printer material is the major medium of instruction in most of the distance education programmes. Attempts have been made by most of our universities to produce printed material on self-instructional format. As regards distance education institutions, the attempts are being made from conventional format to SIM format. The self-instructional materials must carry out all the functions a teacher would carry out in conventional situation guiding, motivating, intriguing, expounding, explaining, discussing, provoking, reminding, asking questions, discussing alternating answers, appraising each learner's progress, giving appropriate remedial or enrichment help and so on.

Textbook Vs Self-instructional Materials

It is very important to understand the major differences between a textbook (normally used by a learner in a conventional system of education) and a SIM (study material supplied to a learner in an open and distance learning system of education). *Lockwood,* (1997) made a comparative study of traditional textbook and self-instructional materials.

Characteristics of the Sim

According to Self-Instructional Course Units- Handbook-5'(1989),*IGNOU,* the following are the major characteristic features need to be kept in view for writing the self-instructional materials.

a. Self-explanatory: The content should be presented in a style so that a learner can go through the material without much external support. It should be self-explanatory and conceptually clear. For this purpose, the content is analyzed logically (system approach) before it presented. This order maintains the continuity and the consistency of self-content. Thus, the SIM promotes self-learning on the part of the learner.

b. Self-contained: Efforts should be made to make the text self-sufficient and the learner should not search for another sources or even a teacher. For this, the scope of the content of the unit should be visualized with the essential details. So that the unit can cover every information required by the learners and keeps away all that is not necessary.

c. Self-directed: The study material should aims at providing necessary guidelines, hints and suggestions to the learners at each stage of learning. The self-directed material is presented in the form of easy explanations, sequential development, illustrations, and learning activities, etc... The material performs the role of a teacher who can guide, instruct, moderate and regulate the learning process in classroom situations. Thus, the course material should direct the entire process of learning.

d. Self-motivating: The study materials should arouse curiosity, raise problems, relate knowledge to familiar situations and make the entire learning as meaningful for them. The sense of reinforcement should be strengthened at every stage and retention.

e. Self-evaluative: As the learners remain separated from the distance institution and the teachers, the study materials should make provisions for feedback as well. To ensure optimum learning, the learners should know whether they are on the right track. Self-evaluation in the form of self-check questions, exercises, etc., provides the learners with the much-needed feedback about their progress, reinforces learning and motivates them for learning. The self-evaluation course writer should develop a built-in evaluation system by giving appropriate number of self-check exercises, activities and check your progress questions.

e. Self-learning: Self-instructional materials must be based on the principles of self-learning. Therefore, a unit should provide the learners study guide, directions, hints, references, etc., to facilitate their independent learning. To make the content comprehensible, it is supported by simple explanations, examples, illustrations, activities and so on.

Development of Self-instructional Material

Development of study material on SIM format is a challenging task and is quite different from the material mean for formal education. There need to plan an effective instruction is imperative for the successful distance learning. This is because the instructional designer, the author(c), and the student are often separated by distance. As much as possible, teaching by distance should stimulate the student's intellectual motivation and contain all the necessary learning instructional activities that are capable of guiding through the course objectives. Therefore, the course/self-instructional material should contain all that which the syllabus prescribes.

Essentials of an Instructional Plan

1. Instructional goals
2. Objectives for each goals
3. Test items for each objective
4. Instructional activities for each objective or cluster of objectives
    a. Type of instructional activity
    b. content
    c. Means of presenting instructional activity

Modularization of Instruction

Modularization is done by selecting, re-arranging or organizing material and activities and breaking them into smaller sub-units. In order to promote better understanding, the instructions are given in such a way that students know what specific objectives they are supposed to reach. Each sub unit may have optional activities from which students choose accordingly, all enabling them to reach the same objectives. Through such instruction, the students can direct themselves through learning activities, with minimum assistance from the teachers. They can work at a particular rate that suits them.

Role of Instructional Activity

The current competency level of students needs to be considered in order to inform the level and type of activities. The activities built into the course are the instrument that can be used to measure the effectiveness of the instruction. Therefore, self-instructional material should be interactive, interesting and relevant. The nature of instructional activities used in SIM materials depend on the domain of learning that they reinforce in the text, that is cognitive, affective and psychomotor. Students may be encouraged to gain, apply and communicate (orally or in writing) the knowledge acquired. The provision of exercises in the form of assignments, projects, and tutorial feedback is necessary.

Role of Ict in Developing Sim

The effect of multimedia computer changes the present teacher-oriented system to a learner-oriented one on creating individualized learning environment. Multimedia is not a product but a combination of technologies. The variety of information can be added with graphics, text, video and animation can clearly demonstrate the complex process easily in education.

Conclusion

Teaching-learning material is an important as anything else in the teaching-learning process. Everything of the society including values of life need to be reflected in the materials. Only the right type of material can modify the behavior of the learner and making him a fit person for the society. This paper has discussed about the characteristic features of the SIM, essentials of an instructional plan, need for modularization of instruction, role of instructional activity and the uses of ICT in developing SIM.

Refernces

1. Anil Kumar, IGNOU, *Journal of Distance Education,* 57-61, New Delhi.
2. Siva Kumar. P., *Application of ICT in Education, Neelkamal* publication pvt.Ltd, Hyderabad, 2009.
3. DermotMoore, Annemaric Bates and Jean Grundling, *Instructional Design*, chapter 8,71-82.
4. Lockwood.F., *Materials Production in Open and Distance Learning,* 1994. London,

5. Lusunzi,*Building Self-Instructional Materials in distance Education*, Distance Education Unit, Botswana.

6. Priyanjan Karthik, *Audio Visual Aids and Education*, 2nd edition, Dominant publishers and Distributors, New Delhi, 2008

20

Challenges in Distance Education in 21st Century

Introduction

The terms *open learning* and *distance education* represent approaches that focus on opening access to education and training provision, freeing learners from the constraints of time and place, and offering flexible learning opportunities to individuals and groups of learners. Open and distance learning is one of the most rapidly growing fields of education, and its potential impact on all education delivery systems has been greatly accentuated through the development of Internet-based information technologies, and in particular the World Wide Web.

Present trends in open and distance learning

It is more than ever clear that open and distance learning will be an important element of future education and training systems. It is approaching acceptance within mainstream education and training in such a way that it will make up part of the repertoire of most educational institutions in the future. The emergence of new forms of distance learning based on new information and communication technologies; in particular those supported by the Internet and using the World Wide Web, have significant pedagogical, economic and organizational implications.

Furthermore, there is a significant trend towards intensifying globalization. Institutional and inter-governmental co-operation is increasing, and the global classroom has been realized in quite a number of projects, particularly in connection with emerging global communications networks. Governmental leadership concerning network development and access will be essential in this sphere.

Web-based learning

The Web potentially offers a worldwide forum in which to teach courses. One can assume, for example, that each student at any time has an excellent encyclopedia at his or her disposal. Course material can be dynamically updated. Course text, examples and exercises can be interactive in the sense of immediately illustrating equations with graphs, changing parameters and seeing the results, linking to other web-sites according to the interests of the student. The Web-based learning model is essentially free from limitations of space and time while it reaches students around the world with great ease.

In addition, the Web-based learning model offers students a wealth of information that was never possible in the classical model. For example, the student who suddenly becomes interested in what kind of music was composed during Newton's lifetime could link to that information, even though the instructor may not know how to answer such a query. The possibility of linking to information worldwide in a multitude of formats creates a remarkably rich medium for learning. Web-based courseware is not merely an electronic duplicate of the original course material.

Internet usage and Web-Based Education

Taking the huge scale of the Internet into account, the creation of mechanisms designed for effective navigation of the Internet, and the collection, analysis, exchange and distribution of information for the specific use of education acquires great importance. However, despite the outstanding progress made in some countries in the creation of universal information retrieval systems and specialized information systems for education, neither set of systems taken separately can provide a complete service. It has usually been found that only 2 or 3 out of 20 current Internet-applications are used in most educational institutions. Further, this situation arises from a lack of information rather than a lack of finance.

The application of the Internet in education is understood as the use of various Internet-technologies for the solution of various educational tasks, namely, teaching, learning and management of the educational process. The systematic analysis of experiences as they have hitherto been identified and defined in using the Internet in education provides an opportunity for comparison and generalization.

Advantages of New Technologies

It represents a new type of educational materials which takes full advantage of the emerging Web and multimedia technologies in order to achieve an effective yet enjoyable learning process. Thus, complex concepts are introduced in innovative ways. Full linking to vast resources available worldwide introduces new levels of value to the courseware. A web-based course is envisioned as a dynamically-evolving resource that will prove beneficial to both students and instructors alike.

The richness of modern Web and multimedia technologies allow for unlimited creativity when it comes to electronic courseware development. Such richness offers educators new opportunities to develop very interesting course material while it also poses a substantial challenge in that it requires faculty to rethink their own course offerings in the light of the new technologies.

Challenges in Distance Education

1. Time constraints were another limiting factor that hinders the depth and width of the study.

2. The committee was not able to get in time relevant, up to date and enough literature to conduct the study.
3. With scattered students, dispersed part-time tutors, far-flung logistics, reliable-communication services, time sensitive communication services, time sensitive production and distribution of learning materials, and detailed student records, successful distance education programme's require management team with above average skills in organization, logistics and problem solving. This management team need not be large, but it must be capable.
4. Students who enroll in distance learning courses do so for convenience. They are either time bound due to work or travel schedules or location–bound due to geographic or family responsibilities.
5. Distance learning is student–centered learning; thus knowing the characteristics and demographics of the distance learners helps us understand the potential barriers to learning.
6. Problems and barriers encountered by the student fall into several distinct categories; student support and services, alienation and isolation, lack of experience, and training. Distance learners are more likely to have insecurities about learning and these insecurities are founded in personal and school related issues such as financial costs of study, disruption of family life, perceived irrelevance of their studies and lack of support from employers.
7. The concern for the distance student is the perceived lack of feedback or contact with the teacher. Because there is not daily or weekly face-to-face contact with teachers, students may have trouble in self-evaluation. These barriers can be mitigated through technological method such as e-mail, computer conferencing and electronic mail can be integrated into the delivery of the course to provide the missing interaction.
8. It is important that the student receive prompt feedback in any Institutional setting particularly in distance learning

where the learner is impaired by the lack of casual contact with the teacher and other students. This is especially important for those students who live outside metropolitan areas. They may not have access to reliable telecommunication, computers and postal mail.

9. Area of concern distance students is the lack of support and services such as providing tutors, academic planners, schedulers, and technical assistance. The isolation that results from the distance learning process can complicate the learning process for adult students, support for distance learners should not be overlooked when planning distance programme's, students need tutors and academic planners to help them complete courses on time and to act as a support system when stress becomes a problem.

10. A problem area is the feeling of alienation and isolation reported by distance students. Students of all kinds want to be part of a larger school community, and simply of "a correspondence" course. The "distance" aspect of distance learning takes away much of the social interactions that would be present in a traditional learning environments.

11. A problem is prevalent with newer distance students. If distance learning Institutions is serious about providing equity of educational opportunity to all, then careful consideration must be given to the special needs of students undertaking distance education for the first time. Of particular importance is the design of study materials for distance students.

Conclusion

The distance education is changing with an alarming speed, particularly as educational processes become increasingly globalize in terms of physical reach and scope of courses and programme's of study offered. In distance learning students and teachers will find themselves playing different roles than is the norm in traditional education.

More than any other teaching method distance learning which exercises new mode of delivery, requires a collaborative effort between student and teacher unbounded by traditional limits of time, space and single instructor effort. Distance education as a provision will undoubtedly help the learners to enhance the acquisition of new knowledge and skills to lead a better life.

21

Career Development Through Distance Education

Distance education is 'an emergency system 'which may attract talented and imaginative academics and noon-academics as it provides outlets for their talents but may fail to retain them for long. Success in such distance education experiences may invite them back to the professions they originally came from and professions. Such possibilities are open in fields like education, broadcasting, educational television, publishing and printing, education communication etc.

Therefore, it needs to display a 'career' i.e., the various possible, or existing, stages of professional growth which follow one another successively providing the careerist ample opportunities for developing the career-system(Distance education) and his own personal career within the domain of distance education. This, by implication, is a question of asking whether or not' distance education' is a discipline by itself.

It is to say here that any professional training in distance education worth its name should highlight "those progressive stages towards greater professionalism" which should enable it to be seen both as a career and a discipline. Providing full fledged professional training in distance education is a positive and necessary step in this direction.

Procedure for Training Distance Teachers

Many people are involved in the whole process of distance education. So far as the activities in a professional training programme for distance teachers are concerned, two major types of people, viz., those who are engaged in the programme. Businesses used to partner with employees to carry out employees' career planning and development. Times have changed. Now, businesses are coming to view career development primarily as the employee's responsibility. If you are concerned about your career, as you should be during these turbulent economic times, then take complete ownership of it. But now-a-days in this busy and demanding world, our career can be developed through distant education.

Distance Education

Distance Education system is basically a correspondence course in which teaching processes are imparted with modern technologies like audio discs, online videoconferencing, satellite broadcasts through radios and other online internet facilities along with traditional postal correspondence services without attending regular classes.

Importance of Distance Education in India

After independence, India had made tremendous progress in the field of education, though mostly quantitative in nature. Earlier, education was available only to the elites in society, and a large majority of poor and marginalized people remained illiterate. Political considerations have an important role in the expansion of higher education, especially at the state level. These considerations have led to fast expansion of higher education in our country, which in turn, have adverse impact upon its quality. Therefore, in order to insure access and education of a reasonably good quality, we must think of some alternative system capable of supplementing the role of conventional system, and distance education is one of such alternatives.The success of these courses led to the establishment of Indira Gandhi National Open University, which is now rated as one of the best distance courses university in the world.

Correspondence education is a piece and part of open learning. Distance education system is also known by some other common names like Correspondence Courses, Correspondence Education, Distance Education and External or Private Appearance etc. This system of education is suitable for the persons who wanted to enhance their qualifications but were not in a position to attend classes on a regular basis. Now at present, India has two types of distance education institutions. They are:

1. Correspondence courses institutions.

2. Open Universities.

So we can say that distance education mode has become very popular and common in India, because it is catering to a wide range of aspirants (students), who are willing to upgrade their educational qualifications for various reasons.

What is A Distance Learning Education Program

Distance learning can be defined as an education program imparted by an university beyond the barriers of its campus and taken by a student outside the walls of an university. Distance learning program is a medium that connects students to the universities of the world.

Distance learning is imparted through the electronic media and study materials supplied by the University for a Particular Course. It helps people to upgrade their educational qualification even when they are tied up in their working schedule. Some business houses also use distance learning to train their employees as it is less time consuming, less expensive and adds to the human resource enrichment of the business house.

Every coin has two sides and distance learning program is not an exception to the rule. It may fail to motivate a student to study resulting in no good for the candidate, this shows registering yourself is not sufficient, you must also have a drive in yourself to continue with the study. The success of distance education also depends on the success of the technology. And without a good support system and infrastructure the distance learning may be a failure.Such distance courses proved a boon for the service persons as well as others desirous of pursuing higher education. Thus we can say that distance learning is a boon for today's busy and demanding world but it also demands a significant level of maturity from its students.

As Good as A Classroom

Distance learning is a course that can be undertaken by an individual in the privacy of their own home. Distance learning today has become on par with traditional classroom learning in the sense that technology has enabled maximum interactivity between the student and the educator. The certificates bestowed do carry significance, the educators provided are proficient in their work and the interaction enabled is as good as one can get in a traditional classroom.

Convenient and Cost-effective

The various options available to an individual are to take lessons by mail, the internet or by telephone. Some distance learning programs even organize regular meetings with the educators. The course fees are also very reasonable, as you just pay for setting up the hardware, software and the study material. Since the student does not have to relocate or commute on a daily basis, time and money is saved while allowing the student to carry on with his or her personal obligations.

Synchronous Distance Learning

The virtual classroom is the latest in distance education. In this type of distance learning you get a similar experience of traditional classroom learning whereby students connect with their educator in real time through email, telephone or chat. The hardware required is a computer and an internet connection or a telephone connection. This is good for those who learn in an interactive classroom-like atmosphere, but do not have the time or resources for the same.

Asynchronous Distance Learning

This type of distance learning provides the student with coursework, assignments and objective exams that can be completed at the student's own pace, but within a stipulated time period. The course curriculum is shared through both text and online. Email, forums and printed materials are also used. This kind of learning requires the student to have the ability to learn on his or her own by reading or listening to the respective media. The student can take longer time on topics he or she is weak at, and can skim through quicker on topics that he or she understands well. Thus there is a freedom to progress at one's own pace.

Why Distance Learning is Convenient

First, distance learning home school programs have helped parents to bring dynamic learning experiences into their home via the Internet. Also while these home school credits meet high school requirements, they are often able to earn college credits at the same time. This benefit puts them ahead of the curve in how long it will take them to earn their college degree. And most often you'll find that distance learning courses are less expensive than tuition at a local private school. With distance learning, parents and students find that they are not restricted to physical locations. For example, in some rural communities and small towns where there may not be access to a school without driving a pretty significant commute, distance learning gives parents of these children different options to consider.

Through distance learning a student can view lectures and participate in group discussions via a private chat room on the Internet. Technology has helped distance learning to advance to the point of convenience. It is no longer a slow process of snail mail to get assignments or exams.

With the right guidance, from their teachers, distance learning students can do just as well as those students who study on campus. Teachers are responsible for student's performance to an extent, and are constantly communicating with students, and inspiring them to perform better. Thus students are motivated and also do not feel left out or neglected. With distance learning, children become persistent and self-disciplined, since they have to rely primarily on themselves, though a strong support system is available.

Time Management Skills for Distance Learning

As a mature, professional, student who is studying a course or qualification by distance learning, managing your time effectively is critically important. As a busy professional, it is vitally important to manage your time. You don't have to perform at "genius" level. If you work hard and as efficiently as you reasonably can, you are doing well.

One of the most effective ways of managing interruptions, disturbances, and unexpected activities, is to take preventative, pre-emptive, action. This is the time management equivalent of "prevention not cure", as promoted by those in the Quality Management field. In time management terms, this is taking action to prevent other people and other events from causing you difficulties. One simple example of how this approach can make a major difference is in thinking, in advance, of all the people that are likely to interrupt you, or to ask to see you, and, instead of waiting for them to decide when they want to come to visit you, email you, or telephone you, or ask you to come to them, you plan when you want to see them, or email them before they email you, or telephone them when it is convenient to you.

Follow this approach on a weekly and monthly basis for the weekly and monthly lists. Prioritize jobs and activities, and eliminate, discard, activities which are not of any use to you. Then concentrate on the important jobs first. Managing your time effectively is not easy. It is a task in itself, a discipline that has to be learned and applied consistently. But it can make a tremendous difference to your life, at work, at home, whilst studying, and at leisure. These can be work related activities, but can also include study time, relaxation time, relationship time, and, as important as any of the others, time simply for you.

Some of the Benefits of Distance Learning

1. Distance Education and Correspondence mode of higher studies has become popular among the persons aspire for career advancement and opportunity.
2. Distance Education and Correspondence course of study through advanced electronics mode along with postal correspondences help the students of remote areas of their residence and working place to pursue advance study for increased job opportunity.
3. Career aspirants and self-esteemed students or working persons can be able to increase their education level through Distance Education for career prospect
4. Distance Education mode of course offer scope for independent study from home or working place through well designed and interactive course and study module to help for successful career prospect.
5. Distance Education helps the aspirants to adopt advance technology based study through internet wave based communication system for advancement of their career prospect along with advance study.
6. Distance Education mod of study help the students to interact with teacher through telephones, email and online chat with instant and close touch with teachers for clarification of any topic of their study.
7. Distance Education mod of study help the students to interact with teacher through telephones, email and online chat with

instant and close touch with teachers for clarification of any topic of their study.

8. Distance Education and Correspondence study may be helpful to the aspirant housewives to enhance their qualification by studying at home in their leisure time of house responsibilities and also to avail any employment opportunity in any disciplines of their interest.
9. Distance Education and Correspondence study is open to all ages of persons residing or working at any places.
10. Distance Education and Correspondence method of study is becoming popular way of advancement of qualification and career for time and place flexibility specially for working professional and students of remote places.
11. Distance Education system provided by some of the Universities or Institutions have their support centers located at various cities to help for students' counseling in addition to online interactive facility.

Last but not the least, the students and aspirants of higher study for their qualification enhancement and career prospect should verify the approval of the Institution by the Joint Committee of Distance Education Council of Indira Gandhi National Open University,

Tips to Help You Face the Challenges of Distance Education

First you need to set your own goals depending on the kind of routine you follow. It is very important to break the assignments and lessons in appropriate section and make sure that you complete the said section in the set time span. Just because the education can be gained at your own convenience don't lengthen the time span of your course. Just don't carelessly play around with the study material. Even though there are no traditional classes or any kind of deadlines to complete the assignments you have to make sure that be serious with your study. Take one silent corner of your house where you can study peacefully without any kind of extraction or disturbance.

How to Initiate A Distance Education Course - 9 Points to Consider

If you're thinking of taking up a distance education course for the first time, there's a fair bit to think about and do. Here are 9 of the most important - yet simple - steps to take How to initiate a distance education course? That's the question you may be asking yourself if you've come to the conclusion it would be a good idea to get qualifications in a particular area, or maybe just increase your knowledge of the subject, but you've no idea how to get started.

Here are Nine General Points to Cover:

1. Have a think about what it is you want to achieve, and make a list

It's okay if it only consists of a single line, such as "Learn to speak enough French to get by on holiday". The reason for doing this is to avoid choosing a course you don't really need. For example, you might want knowledge on how to sell your house without the help of a realtor. It's unlikely you need a full real estate learning program. But you might want a course that covers how to improve the curb appeal of your house as well as the legalities you need to cover. And it's likely that you'll need something that tackles any local laws that apply, or at least refers you to a place you can find the information you need. The answer to considerations like these will determine the course you need to look for.

2. Research the program you need to follow

Where to look for your distance education course? Online is an obvious contender. Or try magazines devoted to the subject you're interested in. Such courses will appear in the classified advertisement section, or, if they're really popular, somewhere among the editorial. They'll usually be smallish box ads (though not necessarily: Linguaphone have been known to take out much larger display adverts).

3. Decide whether accredited distance learning programs are what you need to look at

Accreditation will be of greater or lesser importance depending on what you're aiming to achieve. If it does happen to be important, make sure the accrediting body is well regarded. It may be worth doing a little digging on the internet to establish this.

4. Arrange the time

Unless you live alone, following distance learning programs can mean negotiating with family members, rescheduling parts of your life, and possibly making resolutions to get up early or stay up after everyone else has gone to bed so you can study.

5. Try approaching your boss if your course is in any way work-related

If you're trying to improve your work prospects, ask if there's any chance of help with the costs, some free time at work to study (some employers have a program for these things), and perhaps some flexibility in your attendance if you need to be elsewhere for exams, etc. (Promise, you'll make the time up later, although if you work for a great company, this may not be necessary.)

6. Sign up for the course

There's a natural human tendency to question whether we're doing the right thing, whether this wouldn't all just be a waste of money, or to imagine that our life is going to be disrupted beyond belief if we start doing something new. Bur none of these things are true. Or we may wonder what will happen if we fail. Well, you have to be spectacularly bad to fail. Exams assume you aren't going to be 100%, and pass marks in some subjects are as low as 65%. Besides, online colleges aren't out to fail you. They want you to keep coming back for more, and to tell your friends.

7. Be prepared for periods where you feel somewhat less than motivated

No article on how to initiate a distance learning course would be complete without mentioning that after about four weeks of hard work, you'll hit the occasional slump in enthusiasm. It's important to have some mechanism to keep you going.

One strategy is to itemize your goals-or dig out your list from point 1 above—then writes next to each why it is vital you achieve them. Keep that image in your head, or repeating your goals to yourself. You may not end up firing on all cylinders, but you will have reminded yourself, as NASA famously said, that failure is not an option. It will be enough to keep you going

Reference

1 Shashi Prabha Sharma(2003) – Teacher Education, Principals, theories and Practices- Kanishka Publishers, New Delhi(Page No.419-420)

2. Y.K. Sharma(2004) – Comparative Education- A comparative Education of Educational System Kanishka Publishers, New Delhi(Page 256-260)

3. Deighton, Lee (1991) - Encyclopaedia of Education, MCMillan Company and Free Press Vol-II(Page No.153)

4. Trivedi, R.S(1989) –Reading of Teacher Education- Sardar Patel University, Vallabh Vidhyanar.(Page No.69)

22

Blogging in Distance Education

Distance Learning - A Paradigm Shift

Distance learning, in the older paradigm, can be as simple as postal correspondence and telephone communications. Due to the technological advances of the recent past, a great deal of excitement and hope has been generated for the use of distance learning in education. Rapid advances in computer and telecommunications capabilities have made possible the development of learning modules that include elements such as video transmission, e-mail, the Internet, and the World Wide Web. The progression of long distance learning from pen-pals, college correspondence courses, teleconferencing over speaker phones, teleconferencing via modem, transporting still pictures along with interactive audio, to the latest technology of two-way, full audio, full video communication has implications for public education.

Technological advances have created a paradigm shift in education and the definition of distance learning, as described by James Morrison (1996), who states that telecommunications, software, and the Internet eliminate walls and boundaries. Distance education is becoming a common practice as evidenced by the number of universities that offer distance education programs, the number of businesses offering distance learning and training programs, and the number of distance learning projects K-12 that are being created or are currently in use.

The History of Distance Learning

Some of the earliest distance learning on record dates back to 1728 and offered to teach students how to write in short hand through lessons sent to their homeweekly.These simple, practical lessons were commonly taught through the mail throughout the 1700's and 1800's and allowed anyone to gain valuable job skills even in they lived well-away from major centres of education and commerce. The refinement and expansion of postal systems in the U.S. and abroad brought about the true beginnings of distance learning. By the 1960's, distance learning had grown tremendously and distance learning universities comparable to size to traditional universities had developed.

Today, distance education is offered through a variety of formats. Radio, television, telecommunications, and especially the Internet have come to play an integral role in expanding the minds of students around the world. With the wide distribution and accessibility of computers, distance learning has become faster and more prevalent. Of course, traditional universities are not without online options as well, as it is estimated that almost 96% of them offer some kind of online coursework and that millions of students across the nation are enrolled. With the ever increasing accessibility of computers and the internet, little is known as to how online learning will evolve in the coming years. Given the growing popularity of this type of learning one thing is for sure, however, that distance learning is a resource for students that will be around for years to come.

The importance of technologies in Distance Education

As the emerging technologies of distance learning begin to break down the walls of the traditional classroom and begin to build bridges around the world, the future work of educators must be characterized by a spirit of inquiry and continuous learning that involves educators, students, and all other stake holders .These action guidelines can be used to manage the change process and to effectively address the issues of excellence, equity, and access that will inherently complicate the implementation of distance learning as a commonplace tool in education. The effective use of distance learning technologies is a potential bright spot in current educational reform movements.

Teachers are at the core of the success of distance learning technologies. Any reform effort should value the experience and professionalism of educators. The growth of distance learning technologies will be dependent upon training and professional development being offered to educators. Educators, in turn, will have the resources to manage and to embrace the changes brought about by distance learning.

The various technologies used in distance learning

Voice - Instructional audio tools include the interactive technologies of telephone, audio conferencing, and short-wave radio. Passive (i.e., one-way) audio tools include tapes and radio.

Video - Instructional video tools include still images such as slides, pre-produced moving images (e.g., film, videotape), and real-time moving images combined with audio conferencing (one-way or two-way video with two-way audio). ***Data*** - Electronic-mail, fax, real-time computer conferencing, and World-Wide Web applications.

The concept of Blogging

The term “blog” is a combination of the words “web” and “log. It is a web site that contains an online personal journal with reflections, comments, and often hyperlinks provided by the writer .Blogs are displayed in reverse chronological order. Most blogs are mainly textual, but images and audio files are increasingly included. Blogs generally have a conversational style of writing and focus on particular area of interest. Recently, blogs have evolved, producing spin-offs such as video blog (vlog), photograph blog (photoblog) and sketch blog (sketchblog). Blogs are considered to be part of Web 2.0, which is a second generation of Internet based services that emphasize online collaboration and sharing among users. Unlike traditional websites which are passive, read only documents, blogs are active and allow feedback and comments from readers, fostering a two-way communication. Another unique characteristic of a blog is its trackback feature. Trackback allows readers to post a response on their own blogs and link it back to the original posting.

The exponential growth and popularity of blogs is due to a number of factors. First, blogs are easy to create, modify and update. Blog publishing is as simple as writing an email. Secondly, blogs provide a platform for self-expression. The dynamic nature of blogs, and the ease of collaboration, adds to their appeal. Finally, blogs are versatile and cater to diverse interests and uses, such as group blogs, family blog s and corporate blogs. In addition, Edu Blogs have also emerged in educational circles (Williams and Jacobs, 2004).

Effectiveness of Blog in Distance Education

Blogs are used in education for a variety of reasons: as a conventional tool, as a tool to create knowledge, for developing a community of practice, and for knowledge management. A review of literature by Luehman (2008) reports that blogs allow self-direction, provide opportunities for reflection, invites perspective making, allow knowledge brokering, and support identity development. In Distance education settings, blogs are used as a tool for constructivist approach to learning and foster collaboration and meaning making in a social environment. Professional development of educators as a reflective practitioner is an important aspects of the numerous affordances the blog offers. The use of blog can also be analyzed from the use and gratification perspective, which says that people used media strategically and choose a particular medium based on how it meets their specific needs or goals (Katz, Gurevitch and Haas, 1973).

1. Blogs help to keep students involved, interested and motivated.

2. Blogs empower the students and give them an avenue to let their voices be heard and noticed.
3. Blogs help students to reflect.
4. Blogs allow the students' work to be searchable and sharable.
5. Promote critical and analytical thinking.
6. Be a powerful promoter of creative, intuitive, and associational thinking.
7. Promote analogical thinking.
8. Be a powerful medium for increasing access and exposure to quality information.
9. Blogging is a type of asynchronous tool. An asynchronous tool is one where participants are communicating at different times and places.
10. Students have time to reflect and provide meaningful answers.
11. Blogs benefits to such as discussion boards are student debates where learners have to negotiate and provide evidence for their posts, threaded discussions where students are communicating making connections and looking deeper into the matters.
12. Blogs are more learner-centered.
13. Students who are shy also provide responses because of the less intimidating environment
14. Social, collaborative construction of a meaningful knowledge.
15. Teaching becomes conversational than a lecture.

Conclusion

As blogs are becoming increasingly accepted as an important technology tool, blogs can be effectively used for education and, in particular, distance education. According to Williams and Jacobs (2004), blogs have the potential to be a transformational technology for teaching and learning. Blogs promote effective interaction and pave way for web publishing and updating their knowledge of current affairs. Blogs create a good rapport between the teacher and the learner. It removes all the inhibition involved in the formal teaching learning setting. As the world move towards are integrated knowledge society, there will be an increasing need for the populace which is not just literacy enhanced but be equipped to understand and effectively utilize ICTs.

References

1. Downes, S. (2004). Educational blogging [Electronic version]. *Educause Review, 39(5),* 14-26.

2. Educause Learning Initiative (2005, August). *7 things you should know about blogs.* Retrieved October 15, 2006, from http://www.educause.edu/eli

3. Effland, R. (2005, April 24). *Scans resolve mystery over King Tut's death.* Retrieved December 2, 2006, from http://homepage.mac.com/reffland/blogwavestudio/index.html

4. Eide Neurolearning Blog. (2005, March 2). *Brain of the blogger.* Retrieved December 1, 2006, fromhttp://eideneuro learningblog.blogspot.com/2005/03/brain-of-blogger.html

5. Farrell, H. (2003, September 15). The street finds its own use for things. *Crooked Timber.* Retrieved December 1, 2006, from http://www.crookedtimeber.org/archives/00516.html

6. Kim, K. & Bonk, C. J. (2006). The future of online teaching and learning in higher education: The survey says... [Electronic version]. *Educause Quarterly, 29(4),* 22-30.

7. LaMonica, M. (2006, December 1). Futurist: To fix education, think Web 2.0. *CNET News.* Retrieved December 3, 2006, from http://news.com.com/Futurist+To+fix+education%2C+think+Web+2.0/2100-1032_3-6140175.html.

8. Lenhart, A. & Fox, S. (2006, July 19). Bloggers: A portrait of the Internet's new storytellers. *Pew Internet and American Life*

Project. Retrieved December 1, 2006, from http://www.pewinternet.org/

9. Prensky, M. (2001). Digital natives, digital immigrants. *On the Horizon, 9(5),*1-2.

10. Richardson, W. (2006). *Blogs, wikis, podcasts, and other powerful web tools for classrooms.* Corwin Press, Thousand Oaks, California

11. Dan McDowell on Technology (2006, November 8). *Teacher Magazine, 18(2),* 46. *Technorati.com.* www.technorati.com

23

Barriers of Learners in Distance Education

Distance learning is an excellent method of reaching the unreaching. Because of the competing priorities of work, home, and school, the students desire a high degree of flexibility. The structure of distance learning gives students the greatest possible control over the time, place and pace of education; however, it is not without problems. Loss of student motivation due to the lack of face-to-face contact with teachers and peers, potentially prohibitive startup costs, and lack of faculty support are the barriers of successful distance learning. This paper explores about distance learning and barriers of the learners.

While distance education has been in existence for at least four decades, the medium has changed from pencil and paper correspondence courses to real-time Internet courses. But regardless of the medium, distance courses have common characteristics and, likewise, have similar problems. This literature review examines the different types of distance education and its significance as a learning method. Student demographics are presented and their relevance to distance learning barriers established.

Definition of Distance Learning

Greenberg (1998) defines contemporary distance learning as "a planned teaching/learning experience that uses a wide spectrum of technologies to reach learners at a distance and is designed to encourage learner interaction and certification of learning". Teaster and Blieszner (1999) say "the term distance learning has been applied to many instructional methods: however, its primary distinction is that the teacher and the learner are separate in space and possibly time". Desmond Keegan (1995) gives the most thorough definition. He says that distance education and training result from the technological separation of teacher and learner which frees the student from the necessity of traveling to "a fixed place, at a fixed time, to meet a fixed person, in order to be trained".

Learners' Barriers in Distance Education

Problems and barriers encountered by the student fall into several distinct categories; costs and motivators, feedback and teacher contact, student support and services, alienation and isolation, lack of experience, and training. More so than traditional students, distance learners are more likely to have insecurities about teach (Knapper, 1988). These insecurities are founded in personal and school related issues such as financial costs of study, disruption of family life, perceived irrelevance of their studies and lack of support from employers. These pressures often result in higher dropout rates than among traditional students (Sweet, 1986).

A second area of concern for the distance student is the perceived lack of feedback or contact with the teacher. Because there is no daily or weekly face to face contact with teachers, students may have trouble in self-evaluation. Keegan (1986) believes that the separation of student and teacher imposed by distance removes a vital "link" of communication between these two parties. The link must be restored through overt institutional efforts so that the teaching-learning transaction may be "reintegrated" (Keegan, 1986, p. 120). Citing Tinto (1975), Keegan hypothesized that students who did not receive adequate reintegration measures such as electronic or telephone communication, would be less likely to experience complete academic and social integration into institutional life. Consequently, such students would be more likely to drop out (Sheets, 1992).

These barriers can be mitigated through technological methods such as e-mail. Computer conferencing and electronic mail can be integrated into the delivery of the course to provide the missing interactivity. Because both are essentially asynchronous, they continue to leave the student in charge of setting his or her own work times — a critical success factor for the distance student. It is important that the student receive prompt feedback in any institutional setting, particularly in distance learning where the learner is impaired by the lack of casual contact with the teacher and other students.

A third area of concern for distance education students is the lack of support and services such as providing tutors, academic planners and schedulers, and technical assistance. The isolation that results from the distance learning process can complicate the learning process for adult students. Support for distanced learners should not be overlooked when planning distance programs. Students need tutors and academic planners to help them complete courses on time and to act as a support system when stress becomes a problem. Technology costs and considerations can be a source of budgeting problems; however, student support for distance learners should take precedence.

A fourth problem area is the feelings of alienation and isolation reported by distance students. Students of all kinds want to be part of a larger school community, and simply a member of a "correspondence" course. For many traditional students, this is an important part of their social lives.

The "distance" aspect of distance learning takes away much of the social interactions that would be present in traditional learning environments. This problem must be mitigated by institutions providing a sense of personal involvement between the student and the institution. One way to help solve this problem is through the use of tutors that communicate with students either electronically or by phone. Students believe that having a good tutor is vitally important in helping them get the most out of a course and achieve a credit (Meacham & Evans, 1989). Geographical isolation has been identified as one of the major problems for distance students (Meacham and Evans 1989). In addition to the practical problems of contacting academic and administrative staff, obtaining study materials and borrowing library books, distance students suffer from the disadvantage of being unable to interact with other students and are often denied the perception that they belong to a scholarly community. This may lead to feelings of inadequacy and insecurity, and a lack of confidence in their own abilities (Wood, 1996).

A fifth problem is prevalent with newer distance students. If distance learning institutions are serious about providing equity of educational opportunity to all, then careful consideration must be given to the special needs of students undertaking distance education for the first time. Of particular importance is the design of study materials for distance students.

Study materials must take into account the significant proportion of students who enroll with little or no experience of distance study. These students are at risk of dropping out unless they develop study survival skills as rapidly as possible (Wood, 1996).

Another problem encountered by students is the lack of student training, particularly in reference to technical issues. Many adult students are not well versed in the uses of technology such as computers and the internet. Using electronic medium in distance learning can inadvertently exclude students who lack computer or writing skills. These skills are required if computer technology is used. Students will typically be offered volumes of electronic-based information. Using this information will be a problem for some non-technical students. They must be taught how to manage, not only their study time, but the materials presented as well.

While undertaking distance learning courses the students require minimum knowledge of computers, that should be taught to them in a abstract manner which would ensure distance learning and to erase the barriers in learning through distance education.

Conclusions

Although distance learning is not new, it has not received respect in the academic community because of the number and seriousness of problems presented here. The dramatic growth of the adult learner population is making distance learning an increasingly popular choice of learning techniques. Further study of student demographics and motivators will help the target adult learner population and will help institutions develop course materials and techniques appropriately. Close scrutiny of the intrinsic problems in distance education will help to overcome the problems that encountered by the students.

Reference

1. *Anglin, G.* (Eds.). (1991). Instructional Technology Past, Present, and Future. Englewood, Colorado: Libraries Unlimited, Inc.

2. *Chou, P.* (1994). Guide to managing a telecourse/distance learning program. Suisun, California: Learning Resources Association.

3. *Coldeway, D.* (1986). Learner characteristics and success. Distance Education in Canada

4. *Cookson, P.* (1989). Research on Learners and Learning in Distance Education: A Review. American Journal of Distance Education, 3(2), 22-34.

24

Emerging Challenges in Higher Education- A Scenario in Nagaland

Abstract

In the context of developing countries, education has been considered as a very important instrument of social change. Compare to other institutions in society, higher education has a much bigger share as a foundation head of change. It nurtures the competency of future leadership in the student who hold in potential to develop the society. India is witnessing unprecedented expansion of higher education and mushroom growth of colleges and universities. Modern times are known as the most turbulent times. Social, economic, political and technological conditions are fast changing and this change will have far reaching impact on future. Change will be unprecedented and unparallel. The future shape of things is too complex to envision with precision. Auden calls this as "advent of anxiety". We are trading on new era that can be called "World Revolution". Change has been occurring which reach to the very foundation of human life and society. Higher education represents the stage of education that succeeds secondary education. It includes the system of institutions that provides for general and professional courses and also engages in research activities. It also prepares the younger generation to take part in different developmental programmes in the emerging society by creating different professionals and specialists in different lines of work. Therefore, it can be rightly be said that higher education produce efficient manpower and promotes economic development at a faster level. It is an evident that there is tremendous growth in higher education in the country since independence. However, simply increasing the number in higher educational institutions with their enrolment capacity is not enough, because this will not accomplish the development goals of the nation. What seems to be more important is the simultaneous awareness to the quality of the educational system— its access to those who desire, and equity measures that ensures fair and impartial treatment to the disadvantaged section of the society.

Introduction

Higher education should acquire and maintain quality. Quality in higher education produces knowledgeable persons and in this modern world, 'knowledge is power'. Every organization has a unique culture which is influenced by lots of external and internal factors. The main benefit of quality culture is that it provides an institution a solid front in a competitive higher education world. Higher education in India is facing two major challenges: one is quality and one is access. India is far behind in access rate to higher education from not only developed countries but from many small Asian countries too. Despite having the largest higher education system, the quality in education in general cannot be claimed to be the best. Higher education would be strengthened not only to satisfy the needs of the students but making them more enjoyable but also combat possible competition from foreign universities.

A brief introduction about Nagaland

Nagaland is a hilly state located in the extreme north-eastern region of India with its capital at Kohima. The state shares common boundaries with Myanmar in the East, state of Assam in the West; Arunachal Pradesh and a part of Assam in the North with Manipur in the south. Nagaland became the 16th independent state of Indian Union only on 1st December 1963 by an amendment in the constitution of India. A portion of the present day Nagaland was a district in Assam – the Naga Hills district. Later in 1958 it was merged with Tuensang area of NEFA (North East Frontier Agency) to form the NHTA (Naga Hills Tuensang Area) which, eventually in 1963 was made into a State). The Distinctive identity of each tribe in terms of Tradition, custom, language and dresses is apparent to the visitors. About 95% of the state's population is Christian and there are good many number of churches located in all over the state. For this reason Nagaland is popularly known as the "The most Baptist state in the world".

An Educational scenario in Nagaland

The education system of Nagaland is very well organized. It offers the quality education so as to make people self-reliant. Education is highly desirable and most wanted by many people in Nagaland. Nagaland is regarded as the state of knowledge seekers. The people of Nagaland are very well aware of the role of knowledge in nation building. So, they look forward for higher education. According to a 2011 census, the literacy rate of Nagaland figured 80.11%. It is said that the Universities play a very important role in making the future of a nation. Both the Universities of Nagaland have occupied an important place among the other institutions of higher education in India. These play a significant role in offering good quality education and opportunities to the people of Nagaland. These are providing education in various fields like humanities, commerce, social sciences, art & culture, information and technology etc. The universities of Nagaland work for the growth and prosperity of Nagaland in all the fields. The main aim of these universities is to make the people realize their responsibilities towards the nation. These carry the message of unity and strength in the nation.

Universities in the state

The state has one central university. It is the Nagaland University situated at Kohima. It is regarded as the highest seat of learning for the students, teachers as well as the researchers. It was established on 6 September 1994. There 48 colleges which are affiliated with the university and around 26 departments spread over to 3 campuses. These are Kohima, Lumami and Medziphema. Its main campus is Lumami. Each campus has a separate administrative as well as academic unit. All are offering training and education to the people in almost all the fields including Humanities, sciences, commerce and many others. The University Grants Commission of India has provided affiliating university status to Nagaland University. The Nagaland University offers affiliation to minority institutions. Another pioneer university in Nagaland was established under the Global Open University Act 2006 of the Government of Nagaland. It is Global Open University. It is mainly associated with the task of providing vocational and job oriented education. The government has taken many bold steps for strengthening the activities of this university. There are twelve (12) secular Colleges and one professional College for Teacher Education directly under the Department. Each of these Institutes is headed by a Principal, assisted by a Vice Principal. The following are some particulars in respect of the Colleges under the Department.

Table-1 Details of degree colleges in Nagaland

Sl.No.	Name of Institute	Year of Establishment	Streams
1.	Kohima Science College, Jotsoma	1961	Science
2.	Fazl Ali Govt.College,Mokokchung	1959	Arts & Science
3.	Dimapur Govt. College, Dimapur	1966	Arts & Commerce
4.	Wangkhao College, Mon	1983	Arts
5.	Sao Chang College, Tuensang	1973	Arts & Science
6.	Zunheboto College, Zunheboto	1980	Arts
7.	Phek Govt. College, Phek	1981	Arts & Science
8.	Mount Tiyi College, Wokha	1974	Arts
9.	Nagaland College Of Teacher Education, Kohima	1975	B.Ed
10.	Kohima College, Kohima	1967	Arts
11.	Peren College, Peren	1987	Arts
12.	Yingli College Longleng	1992	Arts
13.	Zisaji Presidency College, Kiphire	1997	Arts
14.	Pfutsero College, Pfutsero	1982	Arts

All these Colleges were started through private initiative and were privately managed for a good number of years, before they were taken over by the Government. The endeavor of the government is to make higher education in Nagaland colleges more accessible and affordable to the economically weaker sections and the rural students and to create employment opportunity through higher education in Nagaland colleges.

Table 2. Total number of colleges in Nagaland

Universities	Teacher Training Colleges	Arts & Science Colleges	Polytechnic	Others
2	3	48	1	6

The Challenges and issues on higher education

Poor quality of Higher Education has a multiplier effects and puts the whole system beyond redemption. As rightly observed by K.Hannumantappa, the main challenges and issues of concern in the coming Decades and Beyond are-

1. Access and adaptation
2. Administration, Accountability and Governance
3. Knowledge Creation And Dissemination
4. The Academic Profession
5. Private Resource and Public Responsibility
6. Diversification and Stratification
7. Economic Disparities
8. Political and Academic Forces
9. Resource Crunch and Societal Needs
10. Vocationalisation.

The constraints

There are five constraints on the system

1. Philosophical constraints
2. Cultural constraints

3. Economic constraints
4. Operational constraints and
5. Managerial constraints;

The strains

While the system works under the five-fold constraints, it is also subjected to five-fold strains that further diminish its capability as an instrument of development the youthful human resource of the country.

1. Systemic strains,
2. Demographic strains
3. Developmental strains,
4. Political strains and
5. Ethical strains

Squeeze

Higher education in India is, thus, subjected to pull and pressure of various constraints and strains. They apply a relentless squeeze on the system leading to deleterious consequencies like the following:

1. Immobilization
2. Stagnation and
3. Routinisation

Thus, it gives false sense of survival. We cannot afford to keep our system of higher education in such a state especially when the demands on higher education for tomorrow's India are changing fast in their range and quality.

Problems of higher education are

1. No quality research
2. Poor salary
3. Interests in science and management studies
4. Poor funding etc

Remedies

The Indian socio cultural system has proved its resilience and capacity to renew time and again. There is no reason why our higher education system should not show the same response in moments of crises. We need to muster our moral, spiritual and material strength to manage the crises of squeeze in our higher education today.

Step like the following can provide remedies to the ailment caused by the squeeze.

1. Moratoria
2. Prioritization
3. Selective excellence
4. Alternative modalisation
5. Social insurance

Suggestion for quality in higher education

5. Accountability of institution
6. Mobilization of resources
7. Improvement basic infrastructure

Conclusion

Education is an important aspect of level of ling for fuller life, in poor countries it has definite effect on human productivity, and constitutes an important form of investment. Human productivity is highly complex, open to different interpretations. Education is one of the basic needs. It is also contributing to opportunities for new partnership for research and teaching with agencies and institution across the globe. Changing demographics longer lives, longer working days larger urban area, more diverse population and more frequent migration affect higher education.

25

Endeavour Transformation in Management of Indian Higher Education

Introduction

India has the third largest higher education system in the world after China and the United States of America in terms of enrolment which is around 11.6 million(2006-2007). In terms of the number of institutions, India is the largest higher education system in the world with 416 Universities and 20,677 Colleges. After the X Five Year Plan period (2002-2007), there will be a tremendous pressure of number of additional students will be knocking at the doors of higher education institutions in the country. There are also new challenges of management and regulation being faced by these institutions, which require serious attention, both at the institutions in the public sector and also those in the private sector now growing fast pace.

Two observations have to be made at the outset of any statement on higher education in India. First, education, in general, and higher education, in particular, plays a key role in the realization of India's extraordinary potential and aspirations for economic and technological development. Secondly, preciously because of this potential and its implications for individual advancement, there is an extraordinary demand for higher education among India's young. Here this paper makes an attempt of explaining some of the innovative methods in Management of Indian Higher Education.

Governing Goals of Higher Education

It is necessary to recognize that the present approach toward higher education is governed by the "National Policy on Education" of 1986 and program of Action of 1992 was based on the two land marks reports.

The reports are namely the "University Education Commission" of 1948-49 popularly known as Radhadrishnan Commission and "Education Commission" of 1964-66 known as Kothari Commission. These two landmark reports in fact laid down the basic framework for the National Policy for higher education in the country. The most important and urgent reform needed in education is to transform it, to endeavour to relate it to the life, needs and aspirations of the people and thereby make it the powerful instrument of social, economic and cultural transformation necessary for the realization of the national goals. For this purpose, education should be developed so as to increase productivity, achieve social and national integration, accelerate the process of modernization and cultivate social, moral and spiritual values.

Expansion in Higher Education Institutional Capacity

The extent of higher education is generally measured by enrolment ratio in higher education. Three alternative methods are used to estimate extend of access to higher education namely *Gross Enrolment Ratio* (GER), *Net Enrolment Ration* (NER) and *Enrolment of Eligible* (EER). The GER measure the access level by taking the ratio of persons in all age group enrolled in various programs to total population in age group of 18 to 23. The NER measures the level of enrolment for age specific groups namely those in age group of 18-23. While the EER measures the level of enrolment of those who completed higher secondary level education. Three alternative sources namely *Selected Education Statistics*, (SES) *National Sample Survey* (NSS) and *Population Census* (PC) provide data on number of student enrolment.

Quantity Expansion in the Excellence in Indian Higher Education

Equity is to be ensured through equitable access to the deprived socio-economic strata of the society. The quality of teaching and learning experience through use of information pathway is to be enhanced. Setting up of new Universities and colleges aided by the Government to increase enrolment of women students by building hostels for women in metropolitan cities, semi urban and rural areas and access to good institutions and facilities. Implementing, more provision of fellowships for women students, hostel facilities and creation of more infrastructures by the Universities, to bring more women students in the realm of Higher Education and imparting of good training in fields like special education by the institutions, which may not be conventional academic in nature, may be looked at with different perspective.

Quality Expansion in the Excellence in Indian Higher Education

In order to facilitate the growth of excellence in institutions with potential, Academic ambience in all Universities needs to be improved in great deal. Quality and excellence are the watch-word in today's liberalized environment. Development of Multi-skills and Transforming Learning patterns, application of Information and Communication Technology (ICT) in Quality Framework, Development of Internal Systems of Quality Assurance and the Performance Based Quality Assessment Approach are to be developed with due emphasis and arrangements for appropriate monitoring.

Faculty Development in the Excellence in Indian Higher Education

There is a need for provision of fully staffed, equipped and functional Academic Staff Colleges in all the Central Universities.

Professional development of teachers in higher education needs to be a continuous and an on-going process for maintaining quality. Vacancies in the sanctioned teaching posts must be urgently filled up all over the country. Principals of colleges should be given training program in innovative leadership. Exchange of faculty members across the borders should be done for developing managerial skills. The facility of going on sabbatical leave for improving subject knowledge and skills should be extended to teachers of colleges as in the case of Universities. The Universities and colleges are to participate in promotion of Indian Higher Education abroad and to attract as many foreign students as possible to study in India.

Research and Development (R &D) in the Excellence in Indian Higher Education

Scientific base in all the Universities needs to be strengthened to attract talented students. Developing a creative framework for combining the strengths of scientific laboratories, private initiatives and universities are to start advanced institutions for undergraduate and post graduate science education. Twining with Research and Development institutions and industries for symbiotic program, Promoting cross flow of teachers and Scientists through interchange between Universities and diverse research laboratories at both National and International level and expanding links with international Educational and Research institutions for enriching the students and faculty with upgrading scientific infrastructure in Universities are to be implemented.

Infrastructure Development in the Excellence in Indian Higher Education

To make proper investment for removing the backlogs relating to maintenance of physical infrastructure and of equipping classrooms with modern conveniences, audio-visual equipments and quality seating arrangements for students are to be developed. The University Libraries and Laboratories should have the capacity of having journals and laboratory equipments with the rise of cost of books.

Innovations in laboratory teaching need to be encouraged. Also the sports facilities in Universities and Colleges need to be strengthened.

Use of Technologies in the Excellence in Indian Higher Education

Information and Communication Technology has tremendous potential to extend and augment quality in higher Education. In collaboration with corporate houses, a laptop initiative can be put in place for post-graduate and research Scholars. This will greatly enhance equitable access to knowledge base. Uploading equipment for each Central University should be established.

Conclusion

Considering both the multitude and magnitude of the difficulties that Indian Higher Education faces, it would be easy to be overwhelmed by the problems and to despair of finding solutions. The tremendous potential of India's booming industry and technology and the considerable progress made in higher education and research in recent decades is much easy to reach a state of exuberance. Having built up a modern system of Higher Education and research virtually from scratch since independence has been a major achievement and should be a solid predicator of future growth.

Bibliography

1. Anna Lee Saxenian ," The New Argonauts: Regional Advantage in a Global Economy", Cambridge, MA. Harvard University Press, 2006.
2. J.B.G. Tilak, "The Dilemma of Reforms in Financing Higher Education in India." Higher Education Policy, 1997.
3. Pawan Agarwal, "Higher Education in India: The Need for Change ", (ICIER Working paper No.180). New Delhi: Indian Council for research on International Economic Relations, June 2006.

4. "Varieties of Learning: An Interface between Higher Education and Training", Commonwealth Department of Education Science and Training, August 2002.

5. "Regulating Higher Education", (Published in three parts), Indian Express, New Delhi Edition on July 14th, 15th and 16th, 2005.

26

Enhancing Employability Through Innovative Curriculum Integrating Humanities and Information Technology

Introduction

This paper describes a new curriculum, which aims to balance the traditional approaches of humanities with the approach of Information Technology Studies (IT). Students will develop general humanities knowledge through meeting the degree requirements for humanity studies, and a set of Information Technology skills aligned to the job requirements of knowledge industry with emphasis on domain. According to the industry, the employability level in engineering/technical education is around 20 percent, while it is only 10 percent for arts and science. The present system concentrates only on transfer of knowledge and not on domain skills. By skills, everyone thinks it is only communication and soft skills. The area that is ignored is the domain skill, which is what the industry rues about. Hence domain skill oriented special IT modules need to be developed and blended with arts and science curriculum. The backbone of this innovative curriculum is the sequence of domain modules, one every semester that aims to integrate all three dimensions of the knowledge industry job requirements, the information technology, the process and the domain-with an emphasis on domain skills. The domain modules help students to explore and develop their employability by building a competency of industry specific skills throughout all three years. We describe the background for how we arrived at this curriculum and the curriculum design for this integrated innovative curriculum.

Employability is key to the Higher Education agenda. Recent employability studies and research indicate that good practice is often seen as embedding one or two employability features only. Our aim in developing an Employability Framework for faculty of humanities was, rather, to take a holistic approach. We wished to enhance the employability of humanities students by the integrated embedding, throughout courses, of a comprehensive set of features. Our Employability Framework defines employability and specifies essential and additional curriculum features that should be present in courses if they are to enhance students' employability.

The principles underpinning the Employability Framework

Employability definitions are on a continuum from those related to job acquisition (First Destinations) to those related to student attributes and continual personal development. Our definition focuses on the enhancement of lifelong employability, reflecting research on the graduate attributes sought by employers: industry savvy, intelligent, flexible, self-aware lifelong learners with communication, interactive and team working skills, who add value to and transform organisations.

We believe that the way to have maximum impact on students' employability is via the integrated embedding of aspects likely to support that employability throughout curriculum. This:

1. Demonstrates commitment to and valuing of employability (Harvey et al 1999, 2001, 2002)
2. Encourages student engagement (Drew, 2001)

3. Supports the transfer of learning (Neath, 1998, Lave and Wenger, 1991) - this is further explored in section 4 below 'The Employability Framework.
4. Supports the widening participation agenda by ensuring equity of provision and engagement with a diverse student population (CHERI, 2002; Morey et al, 2003, HEFCE 1997; Forsyth and Furlong, 2003).
5. Integrates course and central employability provision (Harvey et al, 2002).
6. Ensures the development of employer contacts and employability resources (Harvey et al 1999, 2001, 2002).
7. Ensures that quality processes are applied.

It is our view that add-on modules or focussing on selected aspects of employability cannot address all the above. We define 'embedding' in the following way: there are learning outcomes (LOs) relating to all the Employability Framework features, within modules and through all programme levels; there are learning and teaching methods that support those LOs; those LOs are validly assessed, with assessment criteria and feedback enabling the improvement of employability attributes. We define 'integration' as interrelating and aligning all the Employability Framework features (Biggs, 2003), for example a course might use Personal Development Planning (PDP) or work experience as a vehicle to pull together all those features.

The Employability Framework

The Employability Framework advocates pulling together such features to maximise impact on students. It is based on the following definition: *'enabling students to acquire the knowledge, personal and professional skills and encouraging the attitudes that will support their future development and employment'*[1] (Sheffield Hallam, 2002).

We see 'employment' as referring to a wide range of potential work activities: paid employment; self employment; creative and artistic work; work in or for the community; family or domestic responsibilities; other lifestyle choices.

The Employability Framework draws on the literature on constructivism and on the work of Biggs (2003) who suggests that courses with elements that are clearly aligned with each other are most effective in helping students create meaning (Biggs, 2003). It draws the literature on experiential learning (Kolb, 1984), on the nature of skilled behaviour (Elliot 1991), on reflective practice (Schon, 1987), and on Lave & Wenger's work (1991) that highlights the 'situated' (ie context dependent) nature of learning. The critical concepts underpinning employability are *transformation*, the enhancing and empowering of students through knowledge and attribute acquisition, and the *transfer* of this to other contexts. Our Employability Framework is underpinned by a distillation of theoretical work about transfer (Thorndike, 1906; Pea,1989; Detterman and Sternberg, 1993; Neath, 1998) and transformation (Harvey & Knight,1996; Astin, 1985), mediated by our own development work, evaluations and research.

The literature indicates that transfer is not automatic, but that it is dependent on context (happening more readily within rather than across 'domains', eg team skills used on the sports field may transfer more readily between sports than into business contexts) and on 'skills of transfer' (being able to analyse contexts, see connections and adapt performance). The essential features of our Framework, aligned and integrated, address both transformation and transfer: the development of skills required to acquire and apply knowledge; their use in contexts mirroring external settings; the development of 'skills of transfer' (reflection on using knowledge and skills between contexts; reflection on own performance and action planning in Personal Development Planning; career management skills); the ability to autonomously adapt to situations. These are summarised in the Employability Framework.

Framework features seen as essential for all courses

1. Progressive development of autonomy.
2. Skills development (intellectual; subject; professional; Key Skills).

3. Personal Development Planning (PDP).
4. Inclusion of activities reflecting external environments.
5. Reflection on the use of knowledge and skills between contexts.
6. The development of career management skills.
7. Engagement with learning from work (LfW).

Additional features that may be appropriate, depending on the nature of the course

1. Preparation for professions.
2. Engagement with enterprise.

The curriculum framework has two objectives: "(1) to provide skills and competencies to job seekers through appropriate training programs that are directly connected to existing jobs for immediate employment; and (2) to empower institutions to offer relevant programs in line with job demands,"

ITES/BPO Job requirements

BPO nations across the globe face the problem of talent crunch as they attract more work than they can handle. Pro-globalization officials, economists and businessmen agree that the BPO industry is the key to arresting the growth of joblessness in the India. The BPO universe—of which the call-center industry is a subset-helps the economy in two ways: it reduces unemployment and earns foreign exchange for the country. Industry identifies call centers as the fastest and most immediate job-generator.

BPO curriculum module for an English literature course as an example

In BPO organization, like any other organization, career opportunities exist across various facets of the business - extending from the core contact center to support functions like HR, legal, marketing, quality, administration etc. Opportunities specific to the contact center industry include customer support, telemarketing, technical support and multilingual support. The enhanced curriculum on Training for BPO Jobs need to provides the necessary skill-enhancement to the users in order to take on the responsibilities for various job positions within the BPO industry.

Conclusion

As explained above for English literature discipline, Curriculum can be drawn in consultation with industry – High quality practice modules to mirror what is done in the industry for various other humanities courses – Chemistry in alignment with pharmaceutical industry, Physics in alignment with electronics industry, Tamil literature in alignment with media industry leveraging IT that is pervasive across industries.

The business model is to provide various reskilling and up skilling programs in order to make graduate students employable or self-employable. To convert human population in to human potential and make them more employable in their area of expertise.

References

1. Aspden, L., Helm, P., & Thorpe, L. (2003) "Capturing learners' experience with e-learning: preliminary findings" In J. Cook & D. McConnell (eds) Communities of practice: *Research Proceedings of the 10th Association for Learning Technology Conference (ALT-C 2003).* Held 8th – 10th September 2003, The University of Sheffield and Sheffield Hallam University, UK.

2. Aspden, L. and Helm, P. (2004) "Making the connection in a blended learning environment" *Educational Media International – Special Issue: Distributed Learning Environments*, Vol 41 (3).

3. Astin N, A.W. (1985) *Achieving Educational Excellence*, San Francisco, Jossey-Bass

4. Biggs, J. (2003) Teaching for Quality Learning at University. Buckingham. SRHE and Open University Press

5. Bowers-Brown, T. Stevens, A. Leman, J., Harvey, L. Drew, S. and Bradley, S. (2004) *A report of the Employability and Personal Development Planning (PDP) Survey Findings.* Sheffield Hallam University, Centre for Research and Evaluation. Available at http://www.shu.ac.uk/research/cre/A%20 report%20of%20the%20Employability%20and% 20Personal% 20Development%20Planning.pdf , Last visited 2.4.04
6. Centre for Higher Education Research and Information (CHERI) (2002), *Access to What: analysis of factors determining graduate employability.* Bristol, HEFCE. Available at http:// www.hefce.ac.uk/Pubs/RDreports/Downloads/report16.htm Accessed 10 May 2003.
7. Detterman , D K and Sternberg, R, J (Eds) (1993) *Transfer on Trial: Intelligence, cognition and instruction.* New Jersey, Ablex Publishing Corporation.
8. Drew S. 'Students' perceptions of what helps them learn and develop in Higher Education' in *Teaching in Higher Education,* Vol 6, No 3, 2001
9. Enhancing Student Employability Co-ordination Team (ESECT 2002). Available at http://www.ltsn.ac.uk/genericcetnre/ index.asp?=17641. Last visited 30.3.04
10. ESECT (October 2003) *Enhancing Student Employability Conference.* Derby
11. Forsyth, A. and Furlong, A., *Socio-economic disadvantage and experience in higher education.* Report for Joseph Rountree Foundation, May 2003. Available at http://jrf.org.uk/ knowledge/findings/socialpolicy/563.asp Accessed 10 July 2003. Harvey, L. and Howard, H. (1999) *Graduate Employability Audit,* December. Cardiff Cyngor Cyllido Addysg Uwch Cymru/Higher Education Funding Council for Wales.
12. Harvey, L. (2001) *Work Experience and Employability Plans 2000-03,* Report for Higher Education Funding Council for Wales, January 2001.
13. Harvey, L. (2002) *Work Experience and Employability Plans 2001-03,* Report for Higher Education Funding Council for Wales, January 2002.

14. Harvey, L. and Knight, P. (1996), *Transforming Higher Education.* Buckingham, Open University Press and SRHE.

15. Harvey, L. and Locke, W., with Morey, A. (2002) *Enhancing Employability, Recognising Diversity: Making links between higher education and the world of work.* July. London, Universities UK.

16. Higher Education Funding Council for England (HEFCE) (1997) *The Participation of Non-traditional Students in Higher Education*, Research Series M8/97, June 1997

17. Kolb, D. A. (1984) *Experiential Learning.* Englewood Cliffs NJ, Prentice Hall

18. Lave, J. Wenger, E. (1991) *Situated Learning: Legitimate Peripheral Participation.* Cambridge. Cambridge University Press

19. Morey, A., Harvey, L., Williams, J., Saldana, A. and Mena, P., 2003, *HE Careers Services and Diversity: How careers advisory services can enhance the employability of graduates from non-traditional backgrounds.* Manchester, HECSU.

20. Neath, M. (1998) *The Development and Transfer of Undergraduate Group Work Skills* (unpublished PhD thesis) Sheffield Hallam University

21. Pea, R. (1989) 'Socialising the knowledge transfer problem' in *International Journal of Educational Research.* Vol. not known. pp224-50

22. QAA (2004) The Quality Assurance Agency for Higher Education. Available at http://www.qaa.ac.uk Last visited 25.11.04

23. Schon, D. A. (1987) *Educating the Reflective Practitioner.* San Francisco, Jossey Bass

24. SEDA (February 2004) *Supporting Staff to Enhance Student Employability Conference.* Leicester

27

Impacts of Globalization on Higher Education

Introduction

Globalization is a feature of changing world. It is no more a recent phenomenon in the world and since India is major player of twenty first century we are facing its socio-economic impacts. Initial enthusiasm for globalization as a beneficial set of processes has yielded to an understanding that the phenomenon is largely associated with increasing social inequality within and between countries as well as instability and conflict. Globalization has a multi-dimensional impact on the system of education. It promotes new tools and techniques in this area like E-learning, Flexible learning, Distance Education Programmes and overseas training. Globalization will mean many different things for education.

Since Lifelong jobs have been converted in to yearly contracts there is still possibility of even short duration jobs. Our education system should deliver such education and training so that professionals can adjust themselves as per market expectations. It has underlined the need for reforms in the educational system with particular reference to the wider utilization of information technology, giving productivity dimension to education and emphasis on its research and development activities. The benefits of globalization accrue to the countries with highly skilled human capital and it is for the countries without such specialized human capital. Developing and transition countries are further challenged in a highly competitive world economy because their higher education systems are not adequately developed for the creation and use of knowledge. Converting the challenges into opportunities depend on the rapidity at which they adapt to the changing environment. As part of globalization, the economic reform packages were introduced in India in the beginning of 1991. These reform packages imposed a heavy compression on the public budgets on education sector, more specifically so on higher education.

The Impacts of Globalization

The globalization of the economy and its concomitant demands on the workforce requires a different education that enhances the ability of learners to access, assess, adopt, and apply knowledge, to think independently to exercise appropriate judgment and to collaborate with others to make sense of new situations. Globalization is not the only factor behind the changes that are affecting education, and likewise it is not the only factor that motivates the local interest groups that formulate policy. Nevertheless globalization has posed challenges of a hitherto unknown nature to nation states, and much of the seemingly recent, never-ending change in education is a corollary of these challenges. The nature and complexity of the forces involved in globalization that any discussion of its impact upon education raises fundamental issues and should be a matter of considerable debate among educationists, researchers, and policy makers.

Schooling

As the major formal agency for conveying knowledge, schooling features prominently in the process and theory of globalization. Early examples of educational globalization include the spread of global religions, especially Islam and Christianity, and colonialism, which often disrupted and displaced indigenous forms of schooling. Recent postcolonial globalizing influences of education, over the last 200 years, have taken on more subtle shapes. In globalization, it is not merely the business transaction and political agreement, but also the shared consciousness of being part of a global system that bring nations and societies together. That consciousness is developed through transnational's movements of people and most recently over the last twenty years the spread of computer technology and media. The unalterable transformation of consciousness brought on by globalization impacts the content and delivery of education, as schools play a significant role in the process.

Indian Universities

India is one of the largest higher education systems in the world facing the crisis of, university of the poor, with continued expansion, deteriorating standards, limited resources, and political involvement. In this regard, it is important to note that recently, the Indian government has approved the Foreign Education Providers Regulatory bill (2010) that will allow foreign universities to open branches in India. When this bill becomes a law after approval in the parliament, foreign universities will be able to enter the education market. However, this raises some concerns among Indian politicians as many believe that there would be no control, over export and import of higher education, and the private institutions, from overseas would open branches in India, exchange of degrees and certificates that would go on without any restrictions. Some of politicians argue that Indian Universities are already at loss as more than 50,000 students of our country are studying abroad in U.S., Australia and U.K., where as a very small number of foreign students are seeking admissions in Indian Universities.

On the other hand, some politicians argue that the presence of foreign universities, within India would also undermine task of creation of knowledge and services for the community and for nation building, as Indian Universities have their special mission to provide traditional educational values, which perpetuate the caste system which severely impacts women along with teaching, learning and research. The Vedic values of Gurukul, are embedded in the higher education of India, to preserve the cultural heritage to keep our customs, rituals and spiritual touch of divinity alive.

Challenges of Globalization on Indian Higher Education

Globalization

As it is known globalization, no doubt, promises dramatic and rewarding change to the higher education systems of the developed countries. Whereas for the developing and the underdeveloped countries, where the system is facing the scarcity of resource, it threatens the stability needed to build the well performing system. Developing countries often have to adjust willingly or unwillingly both to the quickening pulse of international change, and accordingly, reform on several fronts simultaneously, which may not be possible under the given resource status of higher education.

Globalization - Challenge or an Opportunity

Two of the strategic and long-term questions that Globalization poses to the higher education system are:

1. 'Commoditization' - the use of knowledge as a purchasable and saleable good.
2. 'Alternative providers' with profit motive of higher education's landscape that are engaged in the transmission of knowledge using Information and Communication Technologies.

Higher education today, Globalization or no Globalization, is no more constrained by geographical boundaries. Innovative forms of translocation and transnationals education have become a possibility. Multi campus institutions, "franchised institutions learning centers providing university degree, off campus education, distance learning, internet based distance education, virtual universities merging of part studies to combine into a whole for obtaining national as well as international degrees are only few models as examples. As far as higher education is concerned, an enthused and well-informed student has umpteen choices, for the first time in the history of education, to access for a "global marketplace". Yet, the matter of the fact is, this access remains only as availability. Who can reach to it and how? What alternative provisions are made for those who cannot afford to reach is the crux of the matter.

Challenges of WTO and GATS

WTO was established on January 1, 1995 by replacing GATT at the Uruguay Round. According to European Commission "the GATS is first and foremost an instrument for the benefit of business". GATS has two components,

1. The framework of agreement containing 29 articles.
2. A number of Annexes, Ministerial Decisions etc.,

As well as the schedules of commitments undertaken by each Member government, which bind them to allow market access and/ or remove existing restrictions to market access. This agreement in general covers all the services including the education services. This is a first multilateral agreement, which provides "legally enforceable rights to trade in all services. Only the services provided entirely by the government do not fall within the GATS rule. Whereas the services provided either by the Government partially, or some prices are charged, as happens in Education or provided by the private providers shall fall under GATS rule. Some people argue that any institution that requires payment, like fees, should fall under GATS as it currently exists".

WTO on Higher Education in India

As far as the quality, access, relevance and equity of higher education are concerned little is yet known about the consequences of GATS. Also to the extent of GATS' influence on the national authority to regulate higher education systems, and unforeseen consequences on public subsidies for higher education. There is this fear of unknown with regard to impact of WTO and GATS on the

Higher Education sector that is haunting the minds of those concerned with higher education in India.

The impact of globalization and WTO & GATS on the Higher Education would be multidimensional, it would be on:

1. The higher education policy, programmes and its implementation.
2. The very system of higher education.
3. The structure, functions and structure-function relations.
4. The accreditation and assessment of higher education.
5. The role of regulatory bodies.
6. the individual institutional policy and programmes;
7. Finally on the acts and statutes of universities and state education acts.

No doubt, it is an opportunity for those who are aware of the benefits, who has the information, who knows from where to get the information, who has the where wit-halts to get this information and has the inquisitiveness to get more and more and take benefit from that. In India a very small percentage of population is getting all the benefits and yet demanding for more and more. It is a threat for those who are ignorant and has no information, and no means to get this information, and not even know from where to get this information and to the extent not even known that they do not have the information, and impact of this status on them. This group, which is large enough to ignore, would remain the sufferers. To convert the threat into an opportunity it is essential to concentrate on:

1. Urbanization of Rural areas i.e. provide all those facilities to rural mass;
2. Nationalization prior to Globalization;
3. Equalization of access and opportunities;
4. Decentralization of powers to the stakeholders;

5. Qualification of existing institutions to the international standards.

With these, preparation probably the impact of globalization would be positive.

Remedies

We propose that higher education institutions consider in their strategic planning the world-wide forces from economic and social perspectives. First, the challenge that most global educators are facing is to design visionary and new agendas to cultivate a re-vision of humankind with the view of generating the learners' intellect necessary to cope with the complexity of globalization as an evolving new reality. The emergence of globalization is making educators' task more challenging than ever it was. Second, it must be the utmost priority of the higher institutes to cater the needs and demands of diverse population of the global world. Third, higher education institutions need to look for all possible avenues and to foster their quality of education.

Finally, in this evolving global context, American higher education institutions need to creatively operate out-of-the-box attitudes and prepare themselves for new challenges of the 21st century and establish more networking, collaboration, cooperation and more importantly to embrace developing multidimensional scholarship.

Conclusion

We suggest that for higher education faculty and administrators, our university policies can greatly impact our international and national students to help them explore innovative perspectives to educate humankind for future global citizenship. Education toward a future where global cooperation is the social norm and the notion of universal citizenship is the foundation of a globalize world. Universities though pressured by market forces can and must lead in framing education policies to ensure that the common good of the world is our focus.

The objective of education is no longer simply to convey a body of knowledge, but to teach how to learn, problem-solve and synthesize the old with the new. The emphasis is less on community and equity, and rather more on individual advancement and the need to satisfy investors and influential consumers. Education has come to resemble a private, rather than public, good. Only focused aware actions by those in higher education can ensure the role of universities in the promise of a better life. Thus, there is an urgent need for setting up new agendas and curricula issues to address the challenges of higher education in a globalize world. It is important to note that global processes are putting immense pressure on educational practices world-wide.

References

1. Agarwal P., (2006), "Higher education in India: the need for a change", Indian Council for Research on International Economic Relations.
2. Ambani M., & Birla, (2001), Report on a framework for Reforms in Education, Government of India, New Delhi.
3. Guy Neave**,** **"**The Dark Side"**,** Globalisation: Threat, Opportunity or Both**,** ***R***eport presented to the IAU Administrative Board Meeting at its Mexico City meeting in November 2001).
4. Mushirul Hasan, (1998), "Knowledge, Power and Politics: Educational Institutions in India", Roli Books, New Delhi.
5. Rao U.R., (2003), "Revitalising Technical Education", AICTE Review Report, AICTE, New Delhi.
6. UGC Annual Report, 2000-2001
7. Google Search

28

Innovative Instructional Methods and Techniques in Higher Education

Educator's in today's classroom face increasing challenges which include the changing complexities of students needs. It is the careful planning if each steps in the entire process of education resources, man, machine and time that is primary. It is essential to develop unique and innovative strategies to connect with teacher flexibility, patience, open mindedness, positive attitudes and high expectations. As they would develop new technologies are invented with the hope of introducing welfare to the lives of human beings. Many people now prefer stay at home and access education through home based technologies like the internet.

Educational Technology

Education is to rear a child for her to keep constructing knowledge. Technology is the study of materials. When you put the two words education and Technology together it does not mean giving education through machine only which Teaching through a BB, Posters, Charts, PowerPoint, films, etc...On the other hand during

1974775 Satellites for Instructional Television Experiment (SITE) was undertaken with a borrowed American Satellite. In this fantastic experiment for a year 2000 TV sets were placed in many villages in six states of India.

Defining Assistive Technology

The phrase assistive Technology (AT) is widely used in the field of Education. Federal law defines assistive Technology devices as any item, place of equipment or product system used to increase maintain or improve functionally capabilities of Individuals with disabilities. Especially the selected software company published a range of cross curriculum productivity tools that support the concepts of universal. Design for learning (UDL) to help users of all age and levels of ability improve their reading and writing skills.

Additional Features which support UDL for inclusive settings

1. Read aloud Text - to - speech
2. Scanning paper document to be read aloud.
3. Dictionaries that can speak.
4. World Translation.
5. Speech maker.
6. Pronunciation Tutor.
7. Spell checker with a phonetic map.
8. Color coding of confusable words lists possible alternatives with audible definitions and sample sentences.

Constructivist Approach

For instance, we know that young children, understand scientific ideas if they are allowed to take a "hands - on - approach Being allowed to investigate and experiment with concrete objects helps children to think critically and gain confidence in their problem -

solving abilities. Constructivist is an Innovative one constructivism is a very popular idea relating to the learning and teaching of science.

The major constructivist assumption is that "all knowledge is constructed from previous knowledge, irrespective of how one is taught. Another major assumption of constructivism is that we as humans construct our own knowledge, as opposed to the idea that knowledge is somehow transmitted directly into our minds.

Two main principles of constructivism

1. Knowledge is not passively received
2. The function of cognition is adaptive and serves the organization of the experimental world, not the discovery of ontological reality.

1. Activating prior knowledge
2. Acquiring Knowledge
3. Understanding knowledge
4. Group activities.
5. Using knowledge.
6. Reflecting on Knowledge

The constructivist teacher could use the "concept mapping" strategy as described by Novak (1991). Concept maps are graphical two dimensional representations of a person's knowledge about a specific topic.

In this theory stresses the importance of considering what is already in the learners mind.

NCF 2005 recommends 5 guiding principles of curriculum construction. They are

1. Connecting knowledge to life outside the school.
2. Ensuring that learning is shifted away from rote methods.

3. Enriching the curriculum to provide for over - all development of children rather than remain text book centric.
4. Making examinations more flexible and Integrated into classroom life.

Nurturing an overriding identify informed by caring concerns with in the democratic polity of the country.

E - Learning

The trend of using e-learning as a teaching tool is now rapidly expanding into education. Although e-learning environments are becoming popular there is minimal research of the impact of e-learning on the teachers. E - Learning is the new wave of learning strategy. Though innovative use of modern technology, e-learning not only revolutionizes education and makes it more accessible, but also brings for mind able challenges for instructors and learners. E-learning makes knowledge and skills available immediately and reduces the learning time required to master even the most complicated topics.

Critical Pedagogy Approach

Teacher and student engagement is critical in the classroom, students are critical observers of their own conditions and needs, and should be participants in discussions and problem solving related to their education and future experiences and perceptions are important and should be encouraged to develop the mental skills needed to think.

Critical Pedagogy provides an opportunity to reflect critically on issues in terms of their political social, economic and moral aspects - what children learn out of school - their capacities, learning abilities, and knowledge base - and bring to school is important to further enhance the learning process. Critical pedagogy facilitates collective decision making through open discussion and by encouraging and recognizing multiple views.

Distance Education Strategies

Distance Education generally use one / or combination of the following 5 methods of teaching and instruction.

Instructor - led Training (ILT)

In this type of teaching method, students enter a virtual classroom and are taught by an instructor or a teaching assistant.

Electronic performance support system (EPSS)

These systems usually function as support programs and help applications and provide the students with vital information and materials when the need arises. The main job of these systems is to provide the support for the enhancement of the distance program.

Computer - based Training (CBT)

In this system, learning materials are usually delivered on CD-ROMs. The theory includes multimedia features such as video chips, sounds, animations, simulations.

Web - based Training

In fact there is not much difference b/w this system and CBT. The main difference lies in the fact that in this case, learning materials are delivered to students through the internet.

Collaborative Learning

This system is web based and requires collaboration and interaction between learners and teachers, mediated by technology, its interaction may be synchronous or asynchronous.

In the former cast, tag is conducted and controlled the instructor and through the implementation and the use of such facilities as chat rooms, shared electronic white boards, video conferencing and soon. Closely related to collaborative learning is the concept of computer, mediated communications (CMC). They allow audio & video communication and even file sharing, letter writing, fax, email.

Features of Distance Education Strategies

1. It is potentially free from time and location
2. In this system has great flexibility for access to teaching materials and also make it possible for the dearness to manage their own time.

Features difference between Distance Education Strategies and Traditional

Features	Distance Education Strategies	Traditional
Flexibility	Independent from time and location.	Time and location bound
Hidden Expenses	High	None
Ease of updating content and materials	Difficult	Quite easy
Feedback	Low and deferred	Class bound
Development of learners social skills and personality	Very low	Very high
Possibility of Individualization	Exists with the use of new technologies.	Very low depends on teacher.

Drawback

1. The most serious drawback for this approach is that in many developing countries and almost all under developed ones
2. These infrastructures either do not exist.
3. Lack of eye contact between teacher and learner.
4. The difficulty of controlling cheating in examination.

Conclusion

Computer / mass media technology in and of itself has no special power to enhance and facilitate learning. When embedded with instruction that addresses social and cognitive processes of knowledge construction, however, distance technologies may offer powerful learning opportunities. Therefore, if is recommended that any district and/or state designate a support team that is exclusive to this type of software program implementation. Along these same lines, if may also be beneficial for districts of states to conduct a random survey to determine the scope of technology capabilities. Personnel responding to technology issues and teacher and student security access capabilities.

The results from this brief assistive technology software utilization evaluation were clear. All participants were willing to continue utilizing the program after the trial ended but clearly stated that supports needed to continue. The use of assistive technology has become significant for all students (but especially for students with learning disabilities) in outcomes based education. By following these guidelines and avoiding the pitfalls mentioned, all educators will be proactive in creating an educational setting that will allow students to maximize their true potential.

The research tool (IELTH) focuses on gathering information about the mind set of teachers on how far e-learning improves their personal effectiveness in teaching, their teaching skills and helps in promoting their research and academic activities. E-learning is in the embryonic stage in the Indian higher educational scenario. This is the time to read the mindset of the teachers towards e-learning and accordingly the appropriate e-learning strategies may be evolved in the higher educational institutions. This research tool will be of immense use for the educational administrators, which will throw light upon the impact of e-learning on teachers of Higher Education.

Reference

1. RICE, K.L (2006). A comprehensive look at distance education in the K-12 context. Journal of research on Technology in education 38(4). P425 – 448.

2. National Assistive Technology Research Institute (NATR 1) (2005). [Assistive Technology state case studies] unpublished raw data.

3. Deepak K Srivastava, (2005) E-learning. A new way of education university news, l 43(26), June.
4. Krishna kumar. R and Rajesh kumar.M , developing a tool measure the impact of E-learning on the teachers of Higher education.
5. National curriculum framework 2005.

29

Innovative Methods in Management of Higher Education

Introduction

The Information Age demands transformational initiatives. The pursuit of technological transformation in higher education has become widespread in today's educational world with the extensive pervasiveness of global networks like Internet. The current focus of technological transformation in education seems to be centered on the use of the Internet and intranets, which is also referred to as e-learning. There is a growing awareness and commitment to prepare students for effective participation in the emerging global knowledge economy. E-learning can be used in this regard to assist students to acquire skills and familiarity with the tools of the knowledge economy while studying. E-learning also has the potential to create continental and other international networks and links utilizing the connectivity of e-learning. E-learning is further seen as having the potential to increase the success rate of students through more formative feedback, repetition, access to wider materials and contact with other students and teachers who can provide additional support. E-learning can thus increase the support and communication between teachers and learners both locally and abroad. E-learning can also provide new levels of flexibility in learning and teaching with students studying at their own pace, place, time and preferred ways of navigation. E-learning need to be implemented within a strategically developed framework based on a clear and shared vision and a central educational rationale.

Higher education is becoming a major driver of economic competitiveness in an increasingly knowledge-driven global economy. As higher education systems grow and diversify, society is increasingly concerned about the quality of programmers. E-learning comprises all forms of electronically supported learning and teaching. The information and communication systems, whether networked learning or not, serve as specific media to implement the learning process. The term will still most likely be utilized to reference out-of-classroom and in-classroom educational experiences via technology, even as advances continue in regard to devices and curriculum. E-learning is essentially the computer and network-enabled transfer of skills and knowledge. E-learning applications and processes include Web-based learning, computer-based learning, virtual education opportunities and digital collaboration. Content is delivered via the Internet, intranet/extranet, audio or video tape, satellite TV, and CD-ROM. It can be self-paced or instructor-led and includes media in the form of text, image, animation, streaming video and audio. Abbreviations like CBT (Computer-Based Training), IBT (Internet-Based Training) or WBT (Web-Based Training) have been used as synonyms to e-learning. Today one can still find these terms being used, along with variations of e-learning such as e-learning, e-learning, and eLearning.

Literature Review

E-learning services have evolved since computers were first used in education. There is a trend to move towards blended learning services, where computer-based activities are integrated with practical or classroom-based situations. Bates and Poole (2003) and the OECD (2005) suggest that different types or forms of e-learning can be considered as a continuum, from no e-learning, i.e. no use of computers and/or the Internet for teaching and learning, through classroom aids, such as making classroom lecture Power point slides available to students through a course web site or learning management system, to laptop programs, where students are required to bring laptops to class and use them as part of a face-to-face class, to hybrid learning, where classroom time is reduced but not eliminated, with more time devoted to online learning, through to fully online learning, which is a form of distance education. This classification is somewhat similar to that of the Sloan Commission reports on the status of E-learning which refer to web enhanced, web supplemented and web dependent to reflect increasing intensity of technology use.

In the Bates and Poole continuum, 'blended learning' can cover classroom aids, laptops and hybrid learning, while 'distributed learning' can incorporate either hybrid or fully online learning. By 2006, 3.5 million students were participating in on-line learning at institutions of higher education in the United States. According to the Sloan Foundation reports, there has been an increase of around 12–14 percent per year on average in enrollments for fully online learning over the five years 2004–2009 in the US post-secondary system, compared with an average of approximately 2 per cent increase per year in enrollments overall. Allen and Seamen (2009) claim that almost a quarter of all students in post-secondary education were taking fully online courses in 2008, and a report by Ambient Insight Research suggests that in 2009, 44 percent of post-secondary students in the USA were taking some or all of their courses online, and projected that this figure would rise to 81 percent by 2014.

Scope of E-Learning

E-learning is suited to distance learning and flexible learning, but can also be used in conjunction with face-to-face teaching, in which case the term Blended learning is commonly used. E-learning pioneer Bernard Luskin argues that the "E" must be understood to have broad meaning if e-learning is to be effective. Luskin says that the "e" should be interpreted to mean exciting, energetic, enthusiastic, emotional, extended, excellent, and educational in addition to "electronic" that is a traditional national interpretation. This broader interpretation allows for 21st century applications and brings learning and media psychology into the equation. Virtual classrooms and meetings can often use a mix of communication technologies. Participants in a virtual classroom use icons called emoticons to communicate feelings and responses to questions or statements. Students are able to 'write on the board' and even share their desktop, when given rights by the teacher. Other communication technologies available in a virtual classroom include text notes, microphone rights, and breakout sessions. Breakout sessions allow the participants to work collaboratively in a small group setting to accomplish a task as well as allow the teacher to have private conversations with his or her students. E-learning can also provide new levels of flexibility in learning and teaching with students studying at their own pace, place, time and preferred ways of navigation. E-learning can also be used to transcend geographical distances more effectively and it is also seen as a key strategy to counter the threat of national and international virtual institutes seizing traditional student markets. If managed well, e-learning can also increase access to education.

Issues in Implementing E-Learning

Along with the terms learning technology, instructional technology, the term Educational Technology is generally used to refer to the use of technology in learning in a much broader sense than the computer-based training or Computer Aided Instruction of the 1980s. It is also broader than the terms Online Learning or Online Education which generally refer to purely web-based learning. In cases where mobile technologies are used, the term M-learning has become more common. E-learning, however, also has implications beyond just the technology and refers to the actual learning that takes place using these systems. E-learning is naturally suited to distance learning and flexible learning, but can also be used in conjunction with face-to-face teaching, in which case the term

Blended learning is commonly used. In higher education especially, the increasing tendency is to create a Virtual Learning Environment (VLE) (which is sometimes combined with a Management Information System (MIS) to create a Managed Learning Environment) in which all aspects of a course are handled through a consistent user interface standard throughout the institution.

Conclusion

A growing number of physical universities, as well as newer online-only colleges, have begun to offer a select set of academic degree and certificate programs via the Internet at a wide range of levels and in a wide range of disciplines. While some programs require students to attend some campus classes or orientations, many are delivered completely online. In addition, several universities offer online student support services, such as online advising and registration, e-counseling, online textbook purchase, student governments and student newspapers. E-learning can also refer to educational web sites such as those offering learning scenarios, worksheets and interactive exercises for children. The term is also used extensively in the business sector where it generally refers to cost-effective online training.

Reference

1. Allen, I. E. and Seaman, J. (2008) Staying the Course: Online Education in the United States, 2008 Needham MA: Sloan Consortium

2. Allen, I.E. and Seaman, J. (2003) Sizing the Opportunity: The Quality and Extent of Online Education in the United States, 2002 and 2003 Wellesley, MA: The Sloan Consortium

3. Bates, A. and Poole, G. Effective Teaching with Technology in Higher Education San Francisco: Jossey-Bass/John Wiley, 2003

4. Crane, Beverley E. "Using Web 2.0 Tools in the k-12 Classroom" Neal-Shuman Publishers Inc., 2009, p.3

5. Diecker, Lisa; Lane, Allsopp, O'Brien, Butler, Kyger, Fenty (May 2009). "Evaluating Video Models of Evidence-Based Instructional Practices to Enhance Teacher Learning". Teacher Education and Special Education, 180–196. http://tese.sagepub.com. Retrieved 9/17/2011.
6. Downes, S (2005) E-Learning 2.0. Downes.ca
7. EC (2000). Communication from the Commission: E-Learning – Designing "Tejas at Niit" tomorrow's education. Brussels: European Commission
8. Graziadei, W. D., et al., 1997. Building Asynchronous and Synchronous Teaching-Learning Environments: Exploring a Course/Classroom Management System Solution
9. Harasim, L., Hiltz, S., Teles, L. and Turoff, M. (1995) Learning Networks: A Field Guide to Teaching and Learning Online Cambridge, MA: MIT Press.
10. Hebert, D. G. (2007). "Five Challenges and Solutions in Online Music Teacher Education".
11. Hiltz, S. (1990) 'Evaluating the Virtual Classroom', in Harasim, L. (ed.) Online Education: Perspectives on a New Environment New York: Praeger, pp. 133–169
12. Karrer, T (2007) Understanding eLearning 2.0. Learning circuit
13. Mason. R. and Kaye, A. (1989) Mindweave: Communication, Computers and Distance Education Oxford, UK: Pergamon Press
14. Nagy, A. (2005). The Impact of E-Learning, in: Bruck, P.A.; Buchholz, A.; Karssen, Z.; Zerfass, A. (Eds). E-Content: Technologies and Perspectives for the European Market. Berlin: Springer-Verlag, pp. 79–96
15. OECD (2005) E-Learning in Tertiary Education: Where Do We Stand? Paris: OECD
16. Tavangarian D., Leypold M., Nölting K., Röser M.,(2004). Is e-learning the Solution for Individual Learning? Journal of e-learning, 2004.

30

Challenges Facing and Resolving Human Disagreement

Introduction

Time and workplace stress due to conflicts crop up between employees when their attitude and abilities differ. Employee's personality development programs are the best solutions to reduce the differences right from the origin of the conflict and stress. Employee's personality development programs also help an organization by making the employee to give out maximum results. Free will of an employee is essential to self develop their behaviour. Personality development programs prepare an employee to think positive because negative thinking is one of the main reasons for workplace stress and conflicts. Positive thinking brings in the change in the employee's attitude and abilities. These days work related stress is increasing because of the veracity of organizations to overload their employees heavily. Similarly conflicts in a workplace have become unavoidable because of the negative approach of the employees. Conflicts arise mainly due to over work, improper communications, personality clashes because of lack of ability to get along with colleagues and many more such reasons. Human development programs for the employees are the positive solution to reduce stress and conflicts at workplace. Human development program need to be adapted in various phases to concentrate on different types of conflicts so that the conflicts are totally reduced.

Soft Skill Development to Change Adjusting Behaviour

It is important for the employers to know their employee's reactions for stress and conflicts to provide them the correct development program, because some will come out freely and some may get embarrassed and hide facts. Employers have options with personal development programs such as communication models and emotional intelligence. It is essential for the employer to know the thinking type and behaviour modes of their employees so that that the specific stress or conflict can be handled efficiently. Workplace stress and conflicts can be reduced by organizing personal development programs to develop the employee's physical and mental conditions. These programs will bring down the stress faced by both employers and employee. Sometimes in life people just forget to smile. Good personality development classes will bring out your best, whether it is your outward look or your inner self. It just teaches you to put your best foot forward, make use of your strengths, reduce your weaknesses and helps you to learn and acquire that skills you don't possess. When this happens your work improves and that is followed by less stress and even lesser conflicts in your work place. Just change yourself in a positive way and watch success come searching for you!

Deal with Workplace Tension and Conflict in the Work Place

Conflicts with co-workers can be one of the most difficult sources of workplace stress. There is a way to reduce that tension and the negative toll that these conflicts can have on your job satisfaction and efficiency however. Understanding the nature of the conflict and learning a few simple conflict-resolution skills can be really helpful in making your work environment a more productive place. Typically, we respond to conflict in very unproductive ways. Sometimes our responses can even be destructive. You might deny the conflict, change the subject, make excuses, put the situation off onto someone else or find someone blame. Even worse, you might react emotionally and become aggressive, abusive, hysterical or just downright scary. Learning the right way to manage conflict is very important. The skills involved in managing conflict are learned behaviours, but it is a set of skills that anyone can learn.

Avoid conflict by knowing what not to do

There are a few common office practices that can really get you in to trouble and should be avoided. Don't gossip, because it has a way of getting back to the person you targeted. Give credit when credit is due. Omitting credit will almost always result in a negative reaction. Don't act disrespectfully or rude towards co-workers. Make an effort to be kind and offer your thanks when it's warranted. And don't point out minor faults in a person's work, approach, style or voice. This will only make them angry or defensive. Try to keep your criticisms constructive if you absolutely have to say something. Treat others the way you would want to be treated.

Figure out why everyone's upset

You want to bring all of the issues out in to the open. In order to resolve a workplace conflict you have to understand what the real problem is. Don't withdraw or use other defence mechanisms that prevent the resolution of the bigger issues at play. Focus on the problem you're faced with, along with the actions and consequences. You want to address the issues head-on before they become even bigger problems.

Think before you act

Always think about things before reacting to a argumentative co-worker. Did you do something to provoke this confrontation? Is the answer is yes, stop it, acknowledge you were wrong, and make sure that the other person understands what your intentions were.

Choose your battles

Ask yourself how important this problem really is. Does it really affect you or is it something that has nothing to do with you? Is it an ongoing problem or a one-time incident? If this is a one-time incident or only a mild offense then let it pass without making a fuss.

Become an active listener

Active listening is a valuable skill that enables you to demonstrate that you truly understand what another person is saying. With active listening you restate, in your own words, what the other person has said to you. You should name the feeling that the other person is conveying and state the reason they are feeling that way. Being an active listener is a way for you to check if your understanding is correct. It feels good when someone makes an effort to understand you.

Watch your body language

You don't want to display defensive or hostile body language. This includes rolling your eyes, crossing your arms in front of your body, and tapping your foot. This won't help you to resolve the underlying issues.

Remain professional and calm

Disputes are going to happen if you don't get along with a co-worker. If you are confronted by that co-worker, try to remain calm and unemotional. Remember that two wrongs do not make a right. Don't start pointing fingers or try to mimic the other person's behaviour. Just let them say whatever it is they came to say, ask questions to get to the root of the problem and let this co-worker know you want to work together to make things right. It is always important to remain rational in these types of situations.

Use humour to diffuse the situation

Humour can make a tense situation blow over sometimes. Point out something funny about the situation. Never use self-deprecation or sarcasm as a form of humour however. You might mean it as a joke but these comments can come across as rude to someone else.

Take some time to cool down

Sometimes you need to take a time-out in these highly emotional situations. Stepping away from the situation for a moment will reel your emotions back in and allow you to see things more clearly. After you've calmed down you can decide what you want to do about this conflict, if anything.

Work as a team

Effective teamwork is important for any business. If you are working on a team project with your worst enemy, use it as an opportunity to come together and get the job done. You might be able to get rid of all of that animosity if you share a positive work experience with this person. Understand that there are many personality types out there and you won't get along with everyone. Strive to work with all of these personality types. You don't have to like them or take them out to lunch, but you do have to work with them. Make the best out of this situation so you can all do your jobs.

Don't be a tattle-tale

If your co-worker messes up, don't go running to your boss with the news. You should go through the proper chain of command and discuss the problem with your co-worker first. Talk to the person in a private setting instead of going to upper management. Doing this will avoid creating any unwanted, tense work relationships.

Keep the conflict between you and the other person involved

Don't complain to other co-workers about your issues with this other person. This is none of their business, and your conflict should not become an office wide event.

Write the right way

Watch your tone in emails and other written communications. These documents can often be taken the wrong way. Make certain that your tone comes across clearly. Avoid sarcasm, writing in all capitals, or using excessive exclamation points (interpreted as screaming in an email). Avoid cross email exchanges with co-workers that you don't get along with. Talk with them face to face so you can both resolve your issues in a more productive manner.

Don't hold a grudge when it's all over

This is very important if you want to have a pleasant work environment. You're not expected to be best friends, but you should be civil. Say hello and smile. What point is there in being mean and dismissive? The office should not be a tense or stressful place. Just get over it and move on. You'll be much happier in the long run.

Conflict is a natural part of life. You have probably been a part of some type of conflict before today and will more than likely find yourself in a similar situation in the future. What's important is that you know what to do when that time comes. With these conflict management strategies you will be prepared when the situation arises.

Establish and Maintain Good Relationships in the Workplace

You spend most of your time with them. With a single word, they can make or ruin your day. They know more about you than does your own mother. They're your co-workers and your associates, your bosses and your employees, your clients and your colleagues. In fact, all of your workmates have an enormous impact on your mood, stress level, and emotional well-being.

It's all too easy for relationships in the workplace to go sour. Unresolved conflict in a professional setting can cause stress for you and ultimately your loved ones. How many times have you anticipated escaping a bad day at work, only to arrive home in a mood so unpleasant that you took out your bad temper on your spouse, kids, pets, or friends? Simply put, if your day is ruined, so is everyone else's.

Prevent conflict and maintain a good working relationship with your co-workers

1. Your work relationships begin, not the first day on the job, but at the job interview. The interview is when you meet your future colleagues. Keep in mind that these are the people with whom you're going to spend most of your time. Be friendly - though they may be just fleeting faces to you now, they will notice you and remember you. This first interaction counts far more than you'd think.

2. While on the job, behave decently and respectfully towards everyone - from the mail clerk to the Head. This is recommended not merely because that modest-seeming mail clerk may very well evolve into the Head at some point, but because the cornerstone of good working relationships is a mutually respectful attitude.

3. Avoid social clique. Don't hang out exclusively with people in your own department, of your own age or socioeconomic class, or who share your interests or job classification. Branching out can be challenging. Yet if you avoid cliques, you avoid excluding and offending your co-workers. The Golden Rule has it right - welcome others and they will welcome you. You may even find that those with whom you assumed you had nothing in common are well worth getting to know.

4. In the event you witness a personal conflict, don't take sides. Matters of business are one thing - after all, your professional opinion is part of what you're paid for. But if you're thinking of insisting that Mark in Accounting must be lying because Joe in Human Resources happens to be your best golfing buddy, think again. It's better to remain neutral and let the combatants fight it out themselves.

5. If all else fails and conflict between you and a co-worker arises (and eventually it will), then absolutely, positively do not ignore

> it. It's tempting to brush over conflict and pretend it doesn't exist. But therein lies disaster. Turn the other cheek, and work-related conflict will bite you in the rear. Disaster lies, too, in aggressive confrontation, manipulation, revenge, and other assorted dominating behaviours. The key to resolving work conflict is to address it in a clear, straightforward, and sincere manner.

The above advice is a great beginning toward resolving conflicts in the workplace before they start. Remember that a good working relationship lets you do your job without hindrance and allows you to maintain your emotional health on the job, which reduces your stress level. A lower stress level on the job means better emotional health off the job. And better emotional health means happier family and friends. No doubt about it maintaining a good relationship in the workplace allows you to give the best of yourself to the people who matter to you most.

Conflict at Work

There's no doubt that more needs to be done to help employers resolve conflict in the workplace. Conflict costs employers time, money, employee commitment and reputation. According to Chartered Institute of Personnel and Development (CIPD), there were more than 115,000 employment tribunal applications in 2003 to 2004, a rise of 17% after two years of falling applications. A key finding from CIPD's research is that a significant amount of conflict in the workplace results from personal behaviour and identified bullying/harassment at work as a common cause of workplace conflict and one of the most difficult to manage. Organizations have to act to prevent these disputes and address problems that do happen as early as possible. The CIPD defines bullying as persistent behaviour against an individual that is intimidating, degrading, offensive or malicious and undermines the confidence and self-esteem of the recipient. Harassment is unwanted behaviour that may be related to age, sex, race, disability, religion, sexuality or any personal characteristic of the individual. It may be persistent or an isolated incident. It is essential to remember that it is not the intention of the perpetrator that is key in deciding whether bullying or harassment has occurred, but whether the behaviour is unacceptable by reasonable, normal standards and is disadvantageous or unwelcome to the person/people subjected to it. According to one estimate, bullying costs employers 80 million lost working days and up to £2 billion in lost revenue each year. It also accounts for up to 50% of stress-related workplace illnesses. The vast majority of employers have a policy that covers defining and encouraging non-discriminatory behaviour at work. Different organizations use different types and names for policies that cover these areas. 91% have a diversity/equal opportunities policy, 83% have a bullying/ harassment policy and 39% have a policy covering dignity at work.

Conclusion

The main challenge facing organization in resolving conflict at work is to encourage line managers to become more proactive in recognizing problems. They need to identify the problem early on so it doesn't escalate further. Some managers ignore the issue, hoping it will go away will only worsen the conflict at workplace. Another biggest challenge in tackling bullying at work is giving confidence to individuals to report bullying/harassment, providing independent support to both accuser and accused, as often the focus can be on one or the other but not both. Organization also need to change managers' attitudes so that they fully understand what behaviour is and isn't acceptable. Thus, a clear and effective policy that stated procedures and guideline to handle conflict or harassment will be useful for all type of organization to eliminate conflict at work.

31

Oer and Traditional Resources in Higher Education: Opportunity or Challenge

Introduction

In the world of globalization, like all other phenomenon, the concept of education has also undergone a radical change. Like economical equality, globalization also aims at educational equality. To achieve this educational equality and to increase the participation; irrespective of class, national and financial status, various new models are exposed to learners and researchers in higher education. Traditional education system being closed to nations had its own resources that were adequate to fulfil the requirements of the learners. In modern times, education, being global in its scope and framework is no longer closed to national requirements only. To fulfil the global requirements and to encompass the largest number of target learners OER i.e. open educational resources are introduced. So that crossing the boundaries of location, time and other constraints more and more learners can join the stream of higher education and add to quality research. Thus open educational resources can be categorized as a step ahead to traditional resources of education.

Present research paper elaborately discusses the status of transition in higher education and issues related to it. It reviews the traditional educational resources, their nature, scope and relevance. The paper records the reasons for the need of open educational resources, their scope and relevance. The paper concludes on the reflection whether OER and traditional resources complement each other pose a challenge to each other and the very spirit of education.

Higher Education: Notion and Issues

Alpesh Nakrani (Kadam, Lalwani, Jadhav, 2010, 28) finds higher education as, 'the apex of formal education. It can be broadly summarized as education beyond the school level. The objectives of higher education may range from primary objectives such as employability, enhancing the earning potential, seeking and advancing knowledge and wisdom, research and experimentation to more serious objectives like attaining spiritual growth, engaging institutes' quest for unknown, facilitating better lifestyle and developing scientific lifestyle'

With globalization education is becoming more open and multifaceted. Its scope requirements and functions are also enlarged. The responsibilities of higher education are greater than even before because, 'higher education is central to the creation of the intellectual capacity on which knowledge production and utilization depend and to the promotion of the lifelong learning practices necessary to update individual knowledge and skills' (Srivastav, Kumar, 2004,63) The role of higher education imbibing values, norms, ethics, attitude, knowledge in young generation for building knowledge society and promoting healthy practices is very crucial, particularly on the background of hedonism and materialism spread in the world. The major issues related to higher education are twofold- on one hand, facing the challenges posed by financial, infrastructural and material problems, on the other hand digesting the transition in the field of education from T resources to E resources. S. Jeyakumar (Kadam, Lalwani, Jadhav, 2010, 21) calling it a new paradigm in higher education says, 'In higher education older academics who are digital immigrants, are struggling to cope with the different mindset of students who are digital natives. The two groups come to e learning with different expectations.'

Expansion of higher education in the farthest corners of the world is the need of the hour. During post independence period, the strategies followed by Govt. of India for executing the right of education for all is resulted into growth of number of students. How to cater the educational requirements of larger number of students with varied grasping affected by regional, linguistic, cultural and financial problems is one of the challenges before higher education. More or less same challenge is also being faced by the World. To face the challenges the solution of OER seems more suitable. But before discussing the role of OER, conceptual understanding of Traditional resources and OER is must.

Traditional resources

Traditional resources of education are T resources. Teachers, textbooks are the traditional resources. These resources work according to traditional academic culture. They work within given structures where emphasis is on the system. Chickering and Gimson (Chickering and Gimson, 1987, 3-7) talk about a popular framework for evaluating teaching in traditional face to face courses. According to them student-faculty contact, cooperation among students, active learning, prompt feedback, time on task are some principals that rule traditional educational resources. So the most important idea that emerges from traditional resources is that it operates curb and spur on the process of learning.

Open Educational Resources - OER-

According to Yuan, McNeill and Kraan McNeill, Krann,(Yuan, MacNeill and Kraan McNeill, Krann2008,1),' the term open educational resources (OER) was first introduced at a conference hosted by UESCO in 2000 and was promoted in the context of providing free access to educational resources on a global scale'. The wide quoted definition of OER explains it as 'digitised materials offered freely and openly for educators, students and self learners to use and reuse for teaching, learning and research' (OECD, 2007) Out of the various areas of OER, we will focus on the content and mediums of the OER. The vision envisaged by The Cape Town Open Education declaration to promote OER states that, 'Educators worldwide are developing a vast pool of educational resources on the internet, open and free for all to use. These educators are creating a world where each and every person on earth can access and contribute to the sum of human knowledge-' (Yuan, McNeill, Krann, 2008, 4) This vision leads to the understanding that OER contains sea like reservoir of information on almost all topics, subjects, issues oldest and latest which is open to all for access and also promote the idea of self learning.

Opportunity or challenge

The conceptual interpretation of traditional resources and OER points out the scope and relevance of them. The interest lies in knowing whether TR and OER are opportunities for advancement or challenges to higher education and even to each other. Present generation of learners being tech savy, has easily developed the habit of using technology and through it self- learning. Since the syllabus are turned from text based to task based. TR are proving inadequate to keep in pace with and fulfil the requirements of contemporary higher education. In this sense OER prove itself an opportunity for a learner to be at global level even being local. Through OER, even a local learner can irrespective of academic diversity and multicultural framework of respective education systems, cope up with the global demands. While pointing out the features of higher education, N.V. Varghese (Varghese, UNESCO, 2011, 11) fingers at one challenge faced by higher education that, 'it is a sector that is expanding in all regions of the world. Between 1991 and 2006, the number of students enrolled in higher education institutions worldwide more than doubled from 68 to 143.9 million students (UNESCO-UIS-2008). The gross enrolment (GER) increased from 13.8 to 25% during this period. However this expansion of higher education was uneven between regions'. Along with large number of learners, paucity of infrastructure, finance, qualified faculty are some more challenges. On one hand higher education is needed to be spread to the farthest corners of the world, on the other hand number of diversities is needed to be coordinated. OER seems to be the best suitable solution to meet the above mentioned extreme ends. However TR and OER have their own plus points and drawbacks that need to be reconciled. The holistic purpose of education is best served by TR though it proved inadequate to fulfill the requirements of global education of global education and at the same time OER possibly adequate for the needs of global education, lacks the potential and strength of curb and spur for nurturing the learner as a virtuous human being. No doubt OER are beneficial for 'open learning communities' as in the words of Srivastav and Kumar (Srivastav, Kumar 2004, 15)who further say that '- to think of learning beyond the conventional school-teacher textbook modalities- to facilitate a shift from a culture of schooling to a culture of learning.' But this is not the only expectation from education. Its role is higher and broader. It is also granted that, 'The norms, values attitudes, ethics and knowledge that higher institutions can impart to students constitute the social capital necessary to construct healthy civil societies and socially cohesive cultures. (Srivastav and Kumar, 2004, 64). This responsibility could neither be fulfilled by TR or OER alone. It shows that TR and OER are both, opportunity as well as challenge.

Conclusion

It is essential to turn this challenge into opportunity. The schooling with the help of TR has many drawbacks like time bound learning dependant on teachers' ability as well as insufficient infrastructural facilities but has benefits like motivation, control on learners, value inculcation etc. OER also exercise some benefits like self learning, learning at individual pace and grasping, without time bondage, open learning etc. along with draw backs like no motivation, no control, more informative than holistic. Therefore it is must to integrate schooling with self learning through assimilation of TR and OER.

References

1. Chickering, A. and Gamson, Z.(1987) Seven Principles of Good Practice in Undergraduate Education, AAHE Bulletin, 39, 3-7

2. Nakrani Alpesh (2010)- Higher Education in India: Issues and Challenges. From 'Perspectives on Governance of Higher Education'(2010), Pune, Bharati Vidyapeeth, deemed University

3. Srivastav D. S. And Kumar Sarita(2004)Education and Information and Technology Challenges, New Delhi, Shree Publications

4. Varghese, N.V. (2011) Globalization and Cross- border Education: Challenges for development of higher education in Commonwealth Countries, France, International Institute For Educational Planning.

5. Yuan Li, MacNeill Sheila, Krann Wilbert (2008) Open Educational Resources- Opportunities and Challenges for Higher Education

32

Teaching Practice in Teacher Education

Introduction

Twentieth century Teacher Education in moving to the mode of digital teaching or virtual Teacher education programme. Whether it is personal or digital teaching concern about increasing the quality of education is the main thread running through the topics dealt in this education. It broadly throws light on computer assisted teaching methods, teaching-learning materials, imparting levels skills to rural students in different impact of Sarva Sikshaya Abhiyan, Role of village Education Committees, improving relations between teacher and the taught etc.

Definition

According to the Dictionary of education-C.V. GOOD (1973), teacher education is defined as "all formal and informal activities and experiences that help to qualify a person to assume the responsibility as a member of the educational profession or to discharge his responsibility most effectively.

According to the Encyclopedia Of Educational Research (1941), Walter.S.Monroe, defines teacher education as " The total education experiences which contribute to the preparation of a person but the term is completely employed to designate the program for the courses and other experiences offered by an educational institute for the announced purposes of preparing persons for teaching and other educational service and for contributing to their growth in competency for such service. Such teacher education programs are offered in teacher colleges, normal schools and colleges and universities.

The Educational Commission (1964-1966) said, "a sound program of professional education of teachers is essential for the qualitative improvement of education. Investment in teacher education can yield very rich dividends because the financial resources required are small when measured against the resulting improvement in the education of millions."

According to PASSI (1997)," Teacher education means programs of education, research or training of persons for equipping them to teach at primary, secondary, and senior secondary stages in schools and includes non-formal education, part time education, adult education and correspondence education.

Types of Teacher Education

1. In-service education
2. Pre-service education

Pre-Service Teacher Education

1. Training school for elementary teachers
2. Pre-primary schools or Nursing institutions
3. Secondary training schools
4. Training colleges or colleges of education
5. Institutes of advanced studies in education

6. Training colleges for special education. Example:- handicaps, deaf and dumb etc.
7. Training colleges for special subjects. Example:-preparing teachers in certain subjects like physical education, home science, craft etc.
8. Regional colleges of education
9. Comprehensive colleges
10. Summer schools -cum correspondence course.

Objectives

1. To develop in prospective teacher educators necessary skills and competencies needful for the preparation of the teacher
2. To impart the latest knowledge of the relevant disciplines
3. To upgrade their knowledge and develop a critical awareness.
4. To develop the capacity of elaboration, examination, interpretation and communication of ideas
5. To enable them to undertake meaningful educational research for improving the condition of education and society.

To develop among them the desire for lifelong learning for removing anachronism from them.

Knowledge-Base of Teacher Education

Teacher education needs a map of professional knowledge for four reasons,

1. To correct the over simplified notion about teacher education that are in circulation.
2. To illuminate the debate about theory -practice links and the role of experiential learning.
3. To highlight aspects of knowledge that have been somewhat neglected in teacher education program.

4. To shed light on the growing debate about competency -based approaches to professional standards and qualifications.

Knowledge must be seen as a means of teacher empowerment rather than of gaining power .Hammond(1997) puts it 'empowerment must occur through knowledge rather than through new controls that would enfranchise teacher at the cost of others ,especially parents ,who have a deep interest in children learning and success.

Practice in Teaching

Practice teaching requires knowledge, authority, skills, commitment, competency, mission, ability to provide the exclusive expert service and adherence to a professional ethical code. In the present curricula, a large number of activities - theoretical and practical, have to be carried out and assiduously practiced by prospective teachers for enhancing their professional competencies and commitments. Teacher education associations need to prescribe a professional code, the violation of which may debar a teacher from serving in school. It need not be emphasized that without increasing the duration of teacher education programmes, these targets cannot be achieved. Academic and professional skills are not independent of each other. Teacher education curricula have to integrate and blend them into a composite whole. The revamping of teacher education curricula has, thus, become a pressing need of the hour. The slant has to be towards a visible shift from information-based to experience- based and from the traditional instruction.

Teacher Education for Secondary Stage

For teaching at secondary stage, the qualification most sought after is one year B.Ed. which is in fact B.Ed. for secondary stage. However, at present, there are several variations for first degree level qualification which are also available. These include B.Ed. (Elementary); B.Ed. (Special Education); which too are programmes of one year duration; B.Ed. through correspondence or distance education mode which is now of two years duration. There are certain other variations in the form of vacation courses or part-time courses which were available before NCTE norms came into force. In addition, there are four-year integrated courses for elementary stage and also for secondary stage.

Teacher education programme at this stage, like at all other stages, will include the theory, practice teaching in schools, and practical work in the light of contexts, concerns, profile of teachers and general and specific objectives.

Practice teaching is essentially a joint responsibility of teacher training institution and the school involving teacher educators, prospective teachers and school teachers. Teacher educators will help in facilitating and guiding the activities as implied by the pre-instructional, instructional and post-instructional phases through which a student teacher has to progress. The role of a school teacher in this joint effort lies in extending cooperation to the teacher educator and the intending teacher. Various aspects as referred to above will have to be suitably adapted to varying structures and designs at different stages of teacher education.

The new curriculum frame not only transforms the nature and content of the traditional foundation courses but also includes several additional components. Emerging Indian Society will deal with factors and forces operating in the Indian society leading to the emergence of a new social order. The psychology of teaching and learning has been given a new thrust. It will also include findings of researches in life sciences, medicine, neurology, genetics and communication technology having their relevance for teaching and learning. A new course on Secondary Education has been included to provide deeper understanding of issues related to secondary education. Likewise, Guidance and Counselling has been incorporated to make teachers more functional in their jobs.

The practice teaching is now not merely confined to the teaching of certain subjects. Pedagogical analysis of the subjects offered for practice teaching has been made compulsory. The prospective teacher will analyse the subject before going to class and evolve a need-based pedagogy and transactional strategy. The teacher educators will now deliver model lessons of different types in actual classroom situation and the prospective teachers will not only learn the techniques but make its critical appraisal and evaluation to be subsequently discussed with the teachers. Teacher educators supervising the classroom performance, pupil teachers will discuss their observations with them for providing proper feedback to improve their performance. The practice teaching will, thus, require thorough preparation, detailed supervision and adequate time. Its gain would be acquisition of higher level of teaching competencies.

Practice Teaching and Practical Work

Pedagogical analysis should precede the actual teaching. The notes of lesson may be only indicative. Its centrality should be focused on the realisation of objectives. Supervision shall be the joint responsibility of the school and training colleges. At least three fourth of the lessons will be supervised by the expert in detail. Its nature should be formative. The projects shall be completed under the guidance of an expert and session/practical work shall be properly planned. The organisation of the student and physical education activities and services will be supervised by teacher educators.

Conclusion

The education of teachers has to be considered as an integral part of the system of education. It has to focus its attention on the new role of teacher educator. Hence education is a potent instrumentation for bridging about the desired changes in the society and teacher are to play a crucial role in this noble venture, human rights can be achieved and sustained mostly through education and training .

33

Innovative Instructional Method & Technique for Quality Teacher Education

"The status of teacher reflects the socio-cultural ethos of the society and no people can rise above the level of its teacher. Good teacher concerned it can be produced only when we have good and effective teacher education Programme" NPE 1986. Teaching is a noblest profession in the society, because its contribution for building a strong nation is remain unquestionable. All these centuries' teachers' community served has a unique agent for reforming society and reflecting what kind of educational experience needed for the societal development. Hence always education should be implemented according to the need and requirement of society. That is why school is called as miniature form of society. In this way Education is preparation for healthy, happy and wholesome living. In this context teaching community need to organize purposeful and socialize activities for students to create problematic act to carry out to completion in its natural settings. Among many innovative practices, project method/technique stands first. Project is modern contribution to educational theory and practice. It aims at providing community life experience in a small-scale in the school.

Project is an activity oriented method; it is revolt against traditional, bookish and passive atmosphere of the school. It ignores practicing disconnected subjects and water tight compartments and gives importance to real life experience to students. John Dewey of the opinion that “There should be integration between child’s life, his activities and the subjects he studied. The entire subjects to be taught to the child should be arranged around his activities in such a manner that he acquires knowledge in the process of doing activities to which he is accustomed”. Thus students are given opportunity to learn the information in the form of “Learning by Doing” & “Learning by Living”. As an end result it helps to impart real experience and develop strong societal attributes. Success of project fully depends up on quality teachers. A teacher who trained in project can import such activity in daily school education. Therefore there is need for developing this stuff during teacher education programme. To equip the same, prospective teachers are requiring to exposé for various projects, finally they implement in future profession. Hence the teacher training institution should adopt Project as an innovative method and technique for training. Though this method trainees expose to experience based activity and learn how to organize similar kinds of activity for various purposes.

Brief History of Project Method

The project Method is the outcome of the pragmatic educational philosophy of John Dewey; noted American Philosopher-cum educationist, who stressed the child centered education. He says that “Education should only be for life, but through life” and “Education is the process involving continuous reconstruction and reorganization of experience”. He pointed out that how gap is formed between life in school and life in society. He put the students in the real life situation of learning to bridge that gap. He treated School education is miniature form of society meant for providing societal experience. Hence he gave importance to experience centered education.

Further William Head Kilpatrick of University of Columbia propounded this method, who published a paper on “Project Method’ in 1918 A.D. in which he emphasized natural, whole hearted, problem solving and purposeful activity oriented education. He defined "Project is a whole heated purposeful activity proceeding in a social environment". As a perfect method of teaching it was presented by Dr. J.A. Stevenson.

Project is not a new method of teaching, but it was advocated for the adolescent's period by Rousseau in Emil (BK-III). This is a modified from old method called "Concentration of Studies". The main feature of concentration of studies is that some subject is taken as the core or centre and the other subject as they arise are studied in connection with it.

Meaning of Project Method

Project is a life like situation which provides actual and meaningful experience in co-operative situation. It adopt investigation, discovery and finding out something which was not known to the student before. Therefore many educationists highlighted that Project is an extension of Problem solving method. Thomas and Ling define project as "A voluntary undertaking which involves constructive effort or thought and eventuate into subjective results". Parker "A project is a unit of activity in which pupils are made responsible for planning and purposing". Prof. Ballard "A project is a bit of real life that has been imparted into the school".

Project Based Learning

Project based learning is the method of learning in which students learn the curriculum information through rigorous extended process of inquiry in response to a complex question, problem, or challenge learning activities. It is systematically built around authentic content & activity to engage the students in learning knowledge, life enhancing skills. According to Thomas "Project Based learning utilizes complex task based on challenging questions or problems that involves students in design, problem solving, design making, or investigative activities, give students the opportunity to work relatively autonomously over extended period of time, and culminate in realistic products or presentations".

Types of Project

Broadly projects can be divided into two categories 1. Individual Projects and 2. Social Projects. Individual Projects are purely academic in nature and carried out by individual. It may be assigned for the individual need of the students and suitable for all. Whereas Social projects are carried out in group. They are helpful to fulfill develop the social qualities among the students. W.H. Kilpatrick listed four types of project. They are as follows.

The Producer Type

It proceeds in the form of production or creation of materials or objective or material by the students.

The Consumer Type

It creates environment where in students involves in various activities such as reading, learning stories, listening musical delectations etc. It develops aesthetic or other type of experience though seeing others work.

The Problem Type

It utilizes the intellect of the students and kept them in problem solving environment. Ex: Students tries to find out the solution for various problems like caste system, population explosion etc.

The Drill Type

Here students acquire some knowledge, skill or experience in order to educate himself in a specific manner. Where the objective is to attain a certain degree of skill in a reaction – as learning a vocabulary.

Possible Project Areas for Teacher Education

Teacher Education institution may organize many projects. Visit/ Excursion to Important Places; Playing Historical Drama;

Establishment of subject Laboratory; Preparation of TLM KIT; Setting up of Aquarium; Botanical Ground; Studying Ecology of a Pond; Collection & Preservation of Insects; Civic sense oriented Survey; Model Parliament; Quiz Organization etc are the popular and useful projects for teacher training programme.

Creation of situation

The first step of this method is to creating a situation, where teacher educator discover the interest and need of the teacher trainees. An interest and resourceful teacher educator should provide different situation or occasions by conducting activity like informal discussion or story or question and answer technique or exhibitions or interactions or by showing pictures of places or personality. As result, many project float in the mind of students and arose out of the need of them.

Selection of Project

In this stage Teacher Educator gives direction and helps the trainees to select relevant and value oriented project. It must be selected according to the capacity, felt need, expense of the student. Here self-choice and self-impassion will enable the trainees to feel their project own & work wholeheartedly and energetically.

Planning of Project

After selection of project teacher trainees need prepare the plan of the project under the directions of teacher educator. It should be plan in such a manner that learner must learn information as a result of byproduct of purposeful activity. Kilpatrick opinions that "Chosen project should imply a purposeful activity pursued whole heartedly admits some relevant social surrounding, which are necessary for working it out. Though the project child is stimulated to apply himself wholeheartedly. The child is left on his own to pursue his purpose as best as he can".

For successful planning, Teacher Educator held the discussion with trainees to collect the opinions and suggestions. He forms opinion in friendly environment and where in directs the students ideas. He point out the difficulties and limitations; nature; schedule of the project; resources required; division of labour for its successful execution of project. In this stage both together plans the project for successful execution. At the end students assign with certain responsibilities. Students are expected written down the same.

Execution of Project

Execution is real experience stage; here the whole class put the project in practice under the directions of teacher educator. Class can be divided into group and each assigned with the various duties. Students are implementing the plan under different group in cooperation. The entire execution will be coordinated to get real life experience. Students record their direct experience in the form of note taking and other activity.

Project Evaluation

Evaluation meant to know the success and experience of the project. Self-criticism and self-evaluation is best method to know the success of project. After successful completion of project, students review their own work. They discuss and note their merits and demerits of the project. It serves as eye-openers for future. Finally students should write their improvised report based on the evaluation under the co-ordination of teacher Educator.

Report

At the end, the student records their detail experience in project report. It includes complete information of all activities connected to each step and gives comprehensive picture about whole project. They present and preserve in the form of project book for future reference. Well prepared project books may be awarded prizes to encourage the pupils.

Significance of Project is Teacher Education Programme

Projects are integral part of teacher education programme. The main aim of the programme is to produce quality teachers for future. Being teacher trainees they should trine about how to impart quality life experience to meet the requirement of society. They need to know how various activity help to improve the quality of learner and entire education field. That is why project oriented activity are included in teacher education programme. In USA, UK and Canada and most of the countries the teacher trainees try to cover unique content of the syllabus through this method. Case Study, Survey, Drama, Quiz Organization, excursion, visits etc are few such project oriented programme. These activities develop cognitive and affective objectives through practice.

Teacher educator should create democratic environment though project. He must help and co-ordinate the work like radical empiricist, essentially an experimentalist, a trial and error man. Entire planning and doing should go under the guidance of Teacher Educator.

Advantages of Project

Following are the advantages of project.

1. It provides community life activities on a small-scale.
2. It arouses the Individual interest and skills.
3. It is based on learning by doing and learning by living.
4. It adopts laws of learning such as law of readiness, law of exercise and law of effect.
5. It develops social discipline and adjustment ability though joint activity.
6. Develops social abilities such as leadership qualities, co-operation, sharing responsibility, team spirit, toleration, self-dependence etc among teacher trainees.
7. It upholds the dignity of labour.
8. It trains the democratic way of life.
9. It fulfills the curiosity and achieves the unique objectives of Teacher education programme.

10. It increases the efficiency in student participation.

11. It constructs the thoughts and actions of the students.

12. It makes curriculum real and interesting.

13. It widens the mental horizon of the student.

Totally project is a useful method and technique for teacher trainees to learn the subject matter in activity manner and same will to professional development of teacher trainees.

References

1. Prof. Chaube S.P. & Dr. Chaube Akhilesh (2002). Ideals of the Great Western Educators. Hyderabad; Neelkamal Publications Pvt Ltd. Pp-314-318.

2. Sharma Ram Nath (2003). Textbook of Educational Philosophy. New Delhi: Kanishka Publishers. Pp-506.

3. Aggarwal J.C. (2004). Principles Methods & Techniques of Teaching. Bangalore: Vikas Publishing House Limited. Pp-236.

4. Yadav K (2005). Teaching of Life Sciences. New Delhi: Anmol Publications Pvt Ltd. Pp-75.

5. Dash B.N. & Dr. Radhakrishna Murthy I.V. (2005). Methods of 'Teaching Social Studies. Hyderabad: Neelkamal Publications Pvt Ltd.

6. Shaida B.D. & Singh Sahab (1998). Teaching of History. New Delhi: Dhanapat Rai Publishing Co. Pvt Ltd.

7. Peter Westwood (2008). What Teacher Need to Know About-Teaching Methods. Victoria: ACER Press. PP-33.

34

Quality Concern in Teacher Education Threats, Opportunities and Suggestions

Teacher Education in India is passing through a period of transition. It is expanding very fast and adding to the quantity, but at the same time faces lot of crises, unless the quality of the teacher education programme is improved, it will be having its own impact on the quality of school education. In the present context of urbanization, privatization and globalization, teacher education programme is facing a great threat though the opportunities are very favorable.

The world conference in Higher Education organized by UNSECO in October 1998 while highlighting the importance of higher education states that higher education is being challenged by new opportunities relating to technologies that are improving the ways in which knowledge can be produced, managed, disseminated, accused and controlled. Same thing holds good for teacher education.

The rate at which the pre-service teacher education is expanding continuously is a good sign, provided it takes care of the quality. During 1947- 49 there were 184 elementary teacher education institution and 51 secondary teacher education institutions, but during 2001-02 it was increased to 1283 and 834 respectively. The quantitative expansion is not scientifically based on the relation between demand and supply of trained teachers. All these are due to improper manpower planning. Unless the quality is maintained, it is difficult to compete with other international institutions in future.

Quality concern in teacher education

The word quality refers to the degree or grade of excellence possessed by a thing. According to British Standard Institutions (1991) Quality refers to the totality of features and characteristics of a product or service that bear upon its ability to satisfy the stated or implied needs. Whereas the term Quality in education is understood and defined slightly in different way. For Heandrixk (1992) Quality refers to intrinsic validity of the product of education with regard to fulfilling its academic mission. Quality of education can also be judged by the perception and benefits received by the stake holders of education, namely students, parents and employers. Consumers are also right people to judge the quality of education. Teacher education being an important link in higher education should maintain quality

Threats in Teacher Education

1. Difficulty in bringing uniformity by overcoming the Regional disparities
2. Scarcity in getting candidates who have passed SLET/NET
3. Lack of co-operation from the practicing schools. The problem of maintaining quality in internship programmes.
4. The problem of maintaining balance between Arts and Science graduates.
5. Variation in the system of pre-service education, some of them are having annual and some of them are having semester scheme.
6. The difficulty in establishing correlation between theory papers and practicals. Those who do not have any formal experience are trying to experiment on running the professional courses.

7. Lack of teachers commitment to the profession.
8. The problem of competing with the foreign universities in future
9. Matching the training skills with the skills needed to teach at the school level.
10. The problem of providing link between different levels of education.
11. Majority of teachers have not changed their ways and style of teaching in the colleges by integrating technology.
12. Lack of commitment on the part of staff and students.
13. Not utilizing the research fund for projects.
14. Unable to upgrade the curriculum in pace with the growing changes.
15. Poor management of institutional resources.
16. Value area has been neglected.
17. Poor link between school and college education.
18. Rare opportunities to attend the standard capacity building programme.
19. Lot of demand and expectation exists from the students' side.

After the 1986 National policy on education, lot of opportunities were available to restructure the existing teacher education programme both in the pre-service and in-service education. Many centrally sponsored programmes are helping to improve the quality of teacher education.

Opportunities

1. Many avenues to meet the financial crisis and to develop the infrastructure facilities – NCERT & DSERT.
2. To go for autonomous status and to give quality education

3. More facilities to take the help of quality controlling / assurance and accreditation agencies like, NAAC, NCTE., etc.
4. Training facilities for the teachers through academic staff college.
5. Many leading organizations and software companies are very much interested to associate in the development activities of the in-service training-integrating technology, scholarship facilities etc.
6. To have collaboration and programmes with the other universities.
7. Lot of avenues for research activities

Suggestions

Establishment of Quality circle

It is a group of factory workers from the same Dept. who usually meet for an hour each week to discuss their quality problems, investigate causes, recommend solutions and take corrective actions, when authority is in their purview". "A small group to perform quality control activities voluntarily within the same work shop"

Objectives of Quality Circle

The objectives of quality circle are; Self Development, Mutual Development, Improvement in Quality, Improvement in communication and attitude, Waste Reduction, Job satisfaction, Cost reduction, Improvement in productivity, improvement in satisfy, Problem solving opportunities, Team building, Getting people involved, Improve participation.

The above objectives are specially designed and applicable to the commercially professional organizations, were quality service, product and profit is the main objective but in education though it is regarded as industry, profit is not only the objective in fact excellent knowledge, quality education and making the final product (i.e., student) well accepted by the society is the main aim of higher education. In order to achieve this aim quality circle can be a very useful technique. In education environment, quality circle should be established with certain specific objectives. These objectives are as fallows;

(1) To develop a sense of unity and equality through co-operation, cutting caste and communal barriers.

(2) To inculcate basic virtues like sincerity, self-control, courtesy and simplicity.

(3) To inculcate the sense of non-violence.

(4) To make the student of sound character and a healthy personality

(5) To develop the habit of personal cleanliness and cleanliness of surroundings.

(6) To develop proper respect for public and private property.

By taking into account all these objectives, if quality circles are implemented in their real sense in the education field then it will definitely lead to achievement of objectives of higher education.

Establishment of IQAC

The aim of Internal Quality Assurance Cell (IQAC) is to develop a system for conscious, consistent and catalytic action to improve the academic and administrative performance of the institution. IQAC is an instrument to ensure effectiveness, efficiency and accountability. It plays a significant role in initiating and establishing the quality assurance efforts.

The basic objectives of the IQAC

1. To ensure continuous improvement in the entire operations of the institution, and

2. To assure stakeholders connected with higher education-namely, students, parents, teachers, staff, would-be-employers, funding agencies and society in general of the accountability of the institution for its own quality.

The IQAC will evolve mechanisms and procedures for ensuring the following

1. Timely, efficient and progressive performance of academic administrative and financial tasks.
2. The relevance and quality of academic and research programmes.
3. Equitable access to and affordability of academic programmes for various sections of society.
4. Optimization and integration of modern methods of teaching learning.
5. Credibility of evaluation procedure
6. The adequacy, maintenance and proper allocation of support structure and services.
7. Research sharing and Networking with others

Seeking for autonomous status

Encouraging some of the teacher educational institutions to go for autonomous status, so that they can use their creative potential to give quality education.

1. Recruitment of teacher educators should be based on competency and professional responsibility. Professional responsibility falls mainly into five areas; to their subjects, to their students, to their institutions, to their profession and to their community.
2. Curriculum should be updated based on researched views and international norms and standards.
3. Teacher educators must be exposed to the training programmes, conferences to upgrade their professional knowledge and remain competent.
4. Making teachers to commit themselves for teaching profession.

References

1. Mukhopadhyaya M. (2001),Total quality management in education. National Institute of Education planning and Administration, New Delhi..
2. National Policy on Education (1986), Government of India MHRD publication- New Delhi.
3. Nigavekar, A. S. (1996), Quest for Quality, NAAC, Bangalore
4. Sunil Behari Mohanty(2003), Quality Improvement in higher education University News, vol.4,No. 94.

35

Rediscovering Peer Teaching in Teacher Education

Abstract

A wise person once said, *"If students do not learn the way we teach, then let us teach the way they learn."* From the past 3 decades peer teaching is gaining momentum. Peer teaching is a technique in helping students' perform better in understanding the different concepts, developing computational skills and their moral, social and emotional values most especially their ability to express their ideas. Teacher education is a course that is designed to equip prospective teachers with the knowledge, attitudes, behaviours and skills. The curriculum ranges from foundational knowledge of philosophy of education, educational psychology, and to skills in assessing student learning, using technology to improve teaching and learning etc. In this technological world it is most essential that all teacher trainees to have at least some working knowledge of computers and Internet. This study was conducted with a sample of 92 student teachers; peer teaching technique was adopted to teach the working knowledge of Microsoft office, email, internet browsing and moodles software. There were 20 Peer teaching sessions conducted in a span of three months. A 'paired samples T-test' was used to analyse the differences in the pre and post test scores. The effectiveness of peer teaching was seen in the results that showed a significant difference in all areas of working knowledge of computers and internet. This study highlights some interesting points within the field of teacher education. It provides evidence that student teachers can successfully and effectively design, develop, and co-ordinate a program to a large number of students. Learning can be generated in dialogues that take place between peer leaders and participants who are seeking to learn by a different route.

Introduction

There has been a shift from traditional teacher-centered teaching towards student-centered teaching approaches in all disciplines in higher education which increasingly focuses on professional standards. A student's colleagues often represent the least recognised, least used and possibly the most important of all resources available to him (Mackenzie et al., 1970). The quote suggests that students themselves have long been neglected as a potential instructional resource in higher education. In reality, much of what each of us learns is learned from peers. Hyman (1973) clearly expressed, when student works in groups on common projects, each pupil learns from his classmates in a significant way. From the past three decades the concept of peer teaching has gained momentum in college and university education.

Peer Teaching

To keep those brain cells alert and vital, however, one needs to always be striving for higher degrees of learning. And that's what peers teaching is really all about, learning more deeply and teaching your classmates or juniors. The Student Peer Teaching Strategy is student-centered and emphasizes on active teaching and learning approaches. Teachers and students both play active roles to induce hands-on, heads-on and hearts-on learning in the students (Tee Hwa, 2009). The students work in teams to prepare instructional materials under the mentorship of the teachers. The student teams then teach their personalized lessons to their peers in the same grade or in junior classes, and sometimes in demonstration classes to interested teachers and educators. They divide the various tasks like introducing the lesson, explaining and demonstrating the hands-on activities, supervising and assisting the student learner's in the laboratory. Division of teaching is done according to their talent and personality. Peer teaching promotes critical thinking and social skills among the student teams. It create a lot of interest and enthusiasm among the students, and provide many opportunities for hands on learning experiences. The mentor teachers need to supervise and guide the student teams as they research, prepare the teaching materials and practice the delivery of their lessons.

Teacher Education

Teacher education is a course that is designed to equip prospective teachers with the knowledge, attitudes, behaviours and skills. In this study teacher education relates to the Bachelor of Education course. The curriculum ranges from foundational knowledge of philosophy of education, educational psychology, skills in assessing student learning, using technology to improve teaching and learning, ICT etc. Generally the students' comprise of varied age levels and educational backgrounds. In this technological world it is most essential that all teacher trainees to have at least some working knowledge of computers and Internet. Some institutions offer training in computer and internet usage.

Areas of Computer training

In this study the areas in computer training are working knowledge of emailing, MS-Word, MS-Power point, MS-Excel, Moodles and Internet browsing.

Review of Related Studies

A review of related studies was done to construct, refine, and evaluate the present study. Mustafa S R, Oluwaseun S and Gore D (March, 2011) - Their aim was to deliver a structured teaching program to final year medical students, evaluate the efficacy of teaching given by junior doctors and review the pertinent literature.

The study showed that recent medical graduates are able to create and deliver a structured, formal revision program and provide a unique perspective to exam preparation that was very well received by our student cohort.

VasayE. T. (2010) researched on the effects of peer teaching in the performance of the students in College Algebra. The finding indicated that the experimental group had a significantly greater gain in their performance with the use of peer teaching while the control group did not.

LongarettiL, GodinhoS, ParrG & Wilson J (2005), investigated the perceptions of first year Bachelor of Teaching students and Diploma of Education students about their peer teaching experiences in the subject, Curriculum and Assessment at the University of Melbourne. Key findings were that students see the benefits of peer teaching as predominantly developing the skills and background knowledge to work in professional learning teams.

Goldschmid B &Goldschmid M.L. (1976) concluded that peer teaching, best used in conjunction with other teaching and learning methods, has great potentials for both student "teacher" and student "learner", especially if one seeks to enhance active participation and develop skills in cooperation and social interaction.

De Leon (1973) worked on the effect of grouping on achievement, classroom participation and interaction of students in Modern Geometry. The findings revealed that there was a significant difference in the achievement of the students in the specific ability group from that of the general ability group.

Methodology

This study comprises of 92 student teacher peer teaching technique was used to teach the working knowledge of computers at the B.Ed course. On the first day of the B.Ed course a self-rated questionnaire was administered to all the students. The items of the questionnaire covering the knowledge of computers in the areas mentioned above. The questionnaires was thoroughly analysed by the computer teacher and a group of 12 students were identified as peer tutors based on their rating on the knowledge of computers.

The tutors were assigned the task to design, plan and execute the training for their peers in the prescribed areas for 20 sessions in a span of three months. The instructional materials provided by the peer tutors and the methodology and validated by the computer teacher. For every session 4 tutors were the main trainers and the other 8 were assisting the students who needed extra help. The computer teacher was present in all sessions acting as a guide and keeping a tab on the objectives for the sessions. At the end of the semester a self-rated questionnaire was administered to all students. The scores from the questionnaires before and after peer teaching were tabulated and analysed. Paired sample T-test was used to analyse the difference in the mean scores of the pre-test and post-test.

Results and Analysis

Table-1: Indicating the number, mean, standard deviation, degrees of freedom, t-value and significance regarding the Pre-test and Post-test of email, MS-Word, MS-Power Point, MS-Excel, Moodles, and Internet browsing.

Pre-Test and Post-Test	N	Mean	S.D	df Value	t NS	Sig/
Pair 1 Pre-test – email	92	2.73	1.070	91	4.841	.000**
Post-test – email		3.40	0.680			
Pair 2 Pre-test – MS-Word	92	2.50	1.054	91	6.070	.000**
Post-test - MS-Word		3.29	0.672			
Pair 3 Pre-test – MS-Power Point	92	1.87	1.206	91	8.816	.000**
Post-test - MS-Power Point		3.13	0.750			
Pair 4 Pre-test – MS-Excel	92	1.57	1.009	91	8.454	.000**
Post-test –MS-Excel		2.60	0.696			
Pair 5 Pre-test – Moodles	92	0.22	0.591	91	37.542	.000**
Post-test – Moodles		3.42	0.667			
Pair 6 Pre-test – Internet browsing	92	2.48	1.322	91	6.054	.000**
Post-test - Internet browsing		3.41	0.744			

* Significant at the 0.05 level. ** Significant at the 0.01 level.

From the above table it is evident that there is a significant difference between the means of pre-test and Post-Test scores with respect to email, MS-Word, MS-Power Point, MS-Excel, Moodles and Internet browsing at 0.01 level. This indicates that peer teaching has affected the working knowledge of computers of all the students. Also, indicating that the computer training given by peer tutors was well accepted and working knowledge of computers in the prescribed areas was enhanced in all student teachers.

Benefits of Peer teaching

1. A harmonious environment is maintained in the teaching learning process.
2. Adult learners who take on the role of peer teachers derive psychological dividends by helping other people and in so doing; they help themselves at the same time.
3. Peer tutors as role models; they can sometimes in-still more enthusiasm for learning in the participants than perhaps a traditional teacher.
4. This creates a special bond or synergy that results in a very cooperative relationship.
5. The peer environment also creates active not passive learners; learners who are willing to engage in plenty of give and take.
6. Students learn to talk reflectively with each other and share their experiences.
7. Studies say that adult learners respond better to discussion formats rather than lecture formats; they want to be actively engaged in their learning. Therefore, since the peer tutor is not a professional in the subject, there is ease in learning.
8. The feeling of increased association translates into more active volunteers willing to take on the myriad of different tasks
9. Peer teaching helps the fast learners to have mastery on the different concepts.

10. Peers can develop their ability to express their ideas. They also develop values such as sharing, sense of responsibility, self-confidence, self-discipline, time management, etc.

11. A key principle and benefit of peer teaching is that peers can help other peers learn, consolidate and improve their knowledge in the process

Conclusion

This work has highlighted some interesting points within the field of Teacher Education. The findings are in line with the current research that teaching delivered by peer tutors are very well received by students in higher education. Furthermore this study provides evidence that student teachers can successfully and effectively design, develop, and co-ordinate a computer training program to their peers. As part of deeper learning, the experience of peer teaching may also in-still motivation in the leader to explore other topics and subjects, furthering a desire to continue teaching. The more a peer-teacher teaches, the more his/her self-confidence increases. Aristotle said it best. “We are what we repeatedly do. Excellence then is not an act but a habit.” Increased self-confidence also brings self-acceptance. That increased self-acceptance then leads to more awareness and tolerance of others, helping to create a harmonious environment. Peer teaching, just like other forms of teaching, must be subjected to continuous evaluation. Students must evaluate their own progress. In addition, students can check the performance of their peers as well as provide constant feedback to their teachers with respect to the instructional materials and learning environment. We therefore support the use of peer teaching as an effective teaching technique.

References

1. Depaz, I., &Moni , I. W. (5, 2008). Using peer teaching to support co-operative learning in undergraduate pharmacology. *Bioscience education journal*, Australia

2. Goldschmid, B.,& Goldschmid, M.L. (1976). Peer teaching in higher education: A Review, Higher Education. *Elsevier Scientific Publishing company,5,* 9-33. Amsterdam.
3. Hyman, R. (1973). Individualization: The Hidden Agenda. *The Education Digest.*
4. Lehr, F. (3, 1984). The reading teacher. *JSTOR, 37*(7), 636-639.
5. Longaretti, L. Godinho, S. Parr, G. &Wilson, J. (2005). Rethinking Peer Teaching.*http://www.aare.edu.au/02pap/lon02122.htm*
6. Mackenzie, N., Evans, M. & Jones, A.C. (1970).Teaching and Learning-An Introduction to New Methods and Resources in Higher Education. Paris: *UNESCO.* IAU
7. Mustafa, S. R., Oluwaseun, S. and Gore, D, (March, 2011). A near-peer teaching program designed, developed and delivered exclusively by recent medical graduates for final year medical students sitting the final objective structured clinical examination (OSCE). *bmc medical education journal. http://www.biomedcentral.com/1472-6920/11/11*
8. Tee, Hwa, T.(2009).Student peer teaching strategy, Malaysia. *UNESCO.* Bangkok
9. Vasay, E. T. (2, 2010). The Effects of Peer Teaching in the performance of Students in Mathematics. *E-International Scientific Research Journal, 2,* ISSN: 2094-1749

36

Role of Organisation and Working of Distance Education Council

Introduction

Distance Education Council (DEC) is a statutory body created for coordination, promotion and maintenance of standards of Distance Education System in India. Indira Gandhi National Open University (IGNOU) which was founded on September 20, 1985 by an Act of Parliament is responsible for the promotion, maintenance of standards and coordination of open and distance education in India in addition to functioning as university for open learning and distance programmes. It was too early to create such a council because as a part of UGC there were many inherent advantages to distance education system. The Dec is a statutory authority consisting of 14 members. The Vice Chancellor of IGNOU is its ex-officio chairman. The members of the Council include the Union Education Secretary, Secretary UGC, a member of UGC, two members of the Board of Management, two Vice-Chancellors of State Open Universities, two Directors of Correspondence Institutes, three nominees of the visitor and a teacher from the Distance education system. The Director, Distance Education Council is the Secretary of the Council. The Secretariat of the DEC consists of Director, Deputy Director, two Assistant Directors and a complement of supporting staff.

Functions of Distance Education Council

It Shall be the general duty of the Distance Education Council to take all such steps as are consistent with the provisos of this Act, the Statutes and the Ordinances for the promotion of the open universities/distance education system, its coordinated development and the determination of its standards and in particular.

1. To develop a network of open universities/distance education institutions in the country in consultation with the State Governments, universities and other concerned agencies.
2. To identify priority areas in which distance education programmes should be organized and to provide such support as may be considered necessary for organizing such programmes.
3. To identify the specific groups and types of programmes to be organized for them and to promote and encourage the organization of such progrmmes through the network of open universities/distance education institutions.
4. To promote the organization of progrmmes of human resource development for the open university/distance education system.
5. To advise State Government, universities and other concerned agencies on their proposals to set-up open universities or to introduce programmes of distance education.
6. Appoint Committees shall assess, in consultation with the concerned open university/distance education institutions, the development grants required by them for a five-year period and make recommendations to the Board of Management for sanctioning such grants.

7. Sanction grants to open universities/distance education institutions for specific projects on the basis of reports by duly appointed committees and in accordance with guidelines prescribed for the purpose and report such approvals to the Board of management.

In the Ninth Plan the following additional functions were discharged by Distance Educational Council:

1. Support in the project formulation of all new state open universities.
2. Consolidation of the development plans of all open universities, to prepare a national plan for Open University Network.
3. Support and development to distance education institutions of dual mode universities.
4. Design and development of the operation of the network.
5. Development and management of delivery networks.
6. Development and management of the common pool of programmes.
7. Development and maintenances of database and information dissemination.

All these additional functions are very crucial. The success of the OPENET will depend essentially upon the efficiency and effectiveness of the DEC especially in managing the network and its operations. As the guidelines indicate, DEC will no longer be a dispenser of grants alone, it will, on the other hand, create facilities and systems which the open university can access and use in delivering their programmes.

Working of DEC

Since its establishment, DEC has been promoting the growth, diversification and guidance to Distance Education System. Therefore had been a difficulty with DEC that Distance Education Institute which commands a substantial aspect of Distance Education system is under the control of the University system. Since its inception DEC has done some pioneering work within all limitations. Let us discuss some of the important achievements.

Maintenance of Standards

Distance Education Council has developed guidelines for design, development and delivery of programmes/courses through distance mode and published these in 1997. It's important contents are Planning of Academic Programme, Programme Development Strategy, Student support service, Student evaluation, Networking and sharing of resources, Monitoring and performance review, Quality assurance, HRD, Bench-mark for self-assessment and the explanation of standardization of terms attached as an appendix.

Establishment of Networking

The DEC has developed a common pool of programmes and courses prepared by different open universities. Guidelines have been prepared to make use of these programmes through adoption, adaptation and translation.

Directory of experts in Distance Education

DEC has published a directory of eminent persons in the field of distance education in most of the areas. This would provide a ready reference and would promote transparency in putting experts in different committees.

Collaborations

The different collaborations of the DEC on national and international level are as follows:

1. DEC collaboration is continuing since its inception on a number of fronts like exchange of information, data on distance education and quality concepts.

2. AICTE-DEC collaboration for recognition of MBA programmes offered through distance mode.

3. NCTE-DEC collaboration for devising norms for recognition of B.Ed. programmes offered through distance mode.

4. NAAC-DEC is in the process of evolving strategies for self assessment of the Open University system.

Development of Detailed Standards for Running Professional Programmes through Distance Education System

Distance education council has brought out some publications wherein detailed standards are mentioned for running professional programmes through distance education mode to ensure quality. Some of these are as follows:

1. Norms and standards for computer education (MCA, MBA).

2. Norms and standards for management education.

3. Norms and standards for library and information science programmes (BLIS and MLIS).

Distance Education Council discussed in July 1997 the additional activities to be undertaken by DEC during IXth Plan to promote excellence in distance education.

Future Plans

The scope of activities of the DEC is being broadened to enable it to perform the functions of an apex body for tertiary level open and distance education more effectively. There are proposals to extend the jurisdiction of DEC to Correspondence Course Institutes of Conventional Universities. The private initiatives in tertiary level of open and distance education will also be a concern of the DEC as far as maintenance of standards is concerned. Some of the thrust areas of the projected activities are:

1. Development of open education network.

2. Technical assistance for establishment of State Open Universities.
3. Development of promotional material (Print, Audio-Video) on distance education.
4. Encouragement to Research in distance education by instituting Research Fellowships and other awards.
5. Development of norms and guidelines for maintenance of standards of programmes offered through distance mode and other quality assurance measures.
6. Strengthening of database on open and distance education system.
7. Conversation of correspondence programmes into distance education programmes.

The emerging role of the DEC demands that its organizational structure is so designed that it can respond to all these demands. Broadly, the DEC will require additional competence in the following fields:

1. Educational Technology.
2. Information Technology.
3. Education Management.

Conclusion

At present the Distance Education Council (DEC) under IGNOU arbitrates standards and disburses funds for ODE institutions across the country. A new regulatory mechanism must be established by appointing a Standing Committee on Open and Distance Education under the Independent Regulatory Authority for Higher Education (IRAHE) proposed by NKC. This statutory body would be responsible for developing broad criteria for quality of accreditation as well as laying down standards for quality assurance. It would be accountable to stakeholders at all levels and to IRAHE and have representation from public, private and social institutions involved in the education and development sectors. These universities, conventional education institutes as well as chairpersons of the specialized bodies to set-up to look into infrastructural requirement of ODE. In addition, two specialized bodies should be established under the aegis of the Standing Committee.

Reference

1. Arun Goel & S.L. Goel "Distance Education", Deep & Deep Publications Pvt. Ltd., New Delhi.
2. John Vaizey, "Education in the Modern World", World University Library, Berlin.
3. NCRTE (1996), "Education and National Development"(Report of the education commission 1964-66), Published by NCRTE, New Delhi.
4. Panneer Selvam S.K. (2009), "Encyclopedia of distance education" (Vol.-I), A.P.H. Publishing Corporation, New Delhi.
5. Panneer Selvam S.K. (2009), "Encyclopedia of distance education" (Vol.-II), A.P.H. Publishing Corporation, New Delhi.
6. Venugopal Reddy V. & Manjulika S. (2000), "The World of Open and Distance Learning", Viva Books Pvt. Ltd., New Delhi.

37

Tablet Personal Computer: an Innovative Approach in Higher Education

Introduction

A technological evolution has considerable impact on Higher Education in the 21st century. In the last decades have been extremely fruitful for the Indian technological scene, One of its biggest impacts has been in the consumer electronics and appliances industry. Technology especially, computers, have grown tremendously in all areas of our lives.

Today's classroom technology should be changing to support the learning needs of the students who have grown up using technology every day. One opportunity is to engage students by allowing them to work from a mobile device in the classroom. Today, 75% of children between the ages of 13-17 have a cell phone. Many of those devices, specifically smart phones, have more computing power than PC's just a few years ago. So why not take advantage of cell phones and use them a centre piece for learning in the classroom? Here's a quote from a teacher, "*At least from the Special Education side - schools have the requirement to provide FAPE - Free and Appropriate Education*

- if schools begin to allow cell phone use for some, they would be required to provide equal access to phones for all students. it has wi-fi, runs android so has access to android/ google apps, can be used as an e-reader, internet searches etc. - These would provide many of the same functions that we're looking for in cell phone use, without some of the drawbacks."

The Tablet PC represents the computer industry's latest attempt at pen-based computing. Since their release in 2002, Tablet PC's have slowly gained attention as a useful tool for educators. The machines are currently in their second to third generation and now contain enough computing power to put them on par with relatively powerful desktop machines. An "official" Tablet PC, as designated by Microsoft, is essentially an x86-based notebook with an active screen digitizer running Windows XP Tablet Edition. This is a variant of Windows XP with add-ons to support pen-based input. Digital ink that is input by pen can be stored directly as ink or recognized as text.

As a Windows XP machine, the Tablet PC has the benefit that it can directly execute any program that runs on a standard Windows machine (e.g. PowerPoint, Word) without needing a translation step as required on many PDA's. Models are available today in "slate" and "convertible" form. The slate is a form factor that looks like a large PDA with a separate detachable keyboard. The convertible looks like a traditional laptop except the screen may also be swiveled 360 degrees and turn to lie flat on the keyboard to become a slate.

The Tablet PC is typically used in the classroom as a presentation device that takes the place of the blackboard. Video is output to a screen using a data projector. With products such as Microsoft OneNote, PowerPoint, or Journal, an instructor has the ability to prepare lecture material in advance or write "on the fly" during class as one would write on a blackboard. The latter is particularly useful for material that requires interaction – e.g. illustrating how to solve equations or illustrate dynamic processes that may be difficult to prepare in advance through a medium such as PowerPoint. It is also easy to switch between other computer applications – e.g. a web browser, telnet, or an integrated developer environment.

A number of universities have adopted pilot projects to study the efficacy of Tablet PC's. For example, Notre Dame and Seton Hall University have put Tablet PC's into the hands of faculty to examine their impact as a teaching tool.

Bentley College distributed Tablet PC's to students. MIT students used Tablet PC's to creatively and collaboratively design robots for the International Design Contest. Individual faculty at numerous institutions has also used Tablet PC's to deliver their courses.

Faculty at the University of Washington has developed the "Classroom Presenter" system based upon Tablet PC's. The system allows an instructor to lecture from a Tablet PC that communicates wirelessly with a server connected to a data projector. This allows the instructor to roam freely about the room and even into the audience, like a TV talk show host, and allows students to write comments that are visible to everyone in the class. Surveys indicated that students paid more attention, understood material better, and encouraged other faculty to also use Tablet PC's. The Classroom Presenter system was extended by Simon, et. al., to put Tablet PC's into the hands of all students in the class so that they can submit ink-based material to the instructor and the instructor may choose submissions to display on the projector. This allows greater collaboration and active learning within the classroom. Tablet PC demonstrates the important educational benefits in integrating innovative IT in the field of Higher Education.

Tablet Personal Computer replaced textbook as a learning tool and created a complete revolution in the field of Education. Teachers develop their skill by searching updated information from this device to reach their students. Tablet PC along with internet connectivity helped universities in reaching more students in a very short time. Visual learning is extremely effective in learning. More over online learning has helped in interacting students with teachers in different parts of the whole world.

Description of the Tablet PC

Tablet PC is a lightweight version of a PC in the shape of a flat panel with a LCD screen. User interacts with it's by tapping the screen and hand-writing with a pen like device. Tablet PCs will also let users wirelessly connect to the internet and other PCs. In a word, a Tablet PC combines the mobility of a handheld computer with the computing power of a notebook.

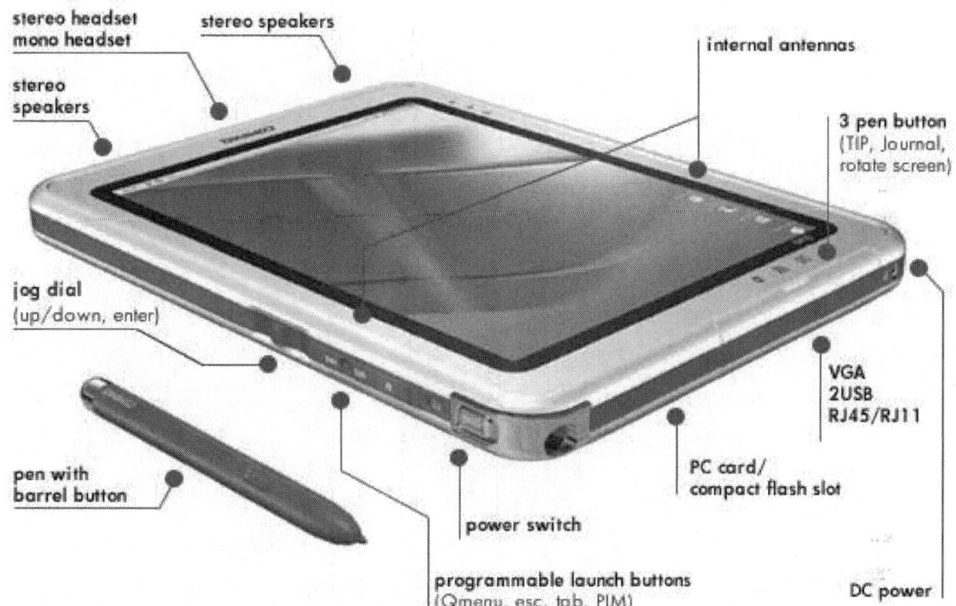

Tablet PC Differs From Laptop

The Tablet PC has all the benefits of a laptop as well as the added ability to become like a notepad tablet. The Tablet PC can be oriented either horizontally like a laptop or vertically like a notepad. The primary advantage of the Tablet PC is that it is lighter than most laptops and its touch screen. Unlike the laptop the normal way of entering data in a Tablet PC is with a stylus or pen rather than a keyboard. This product has a SIM plt, put an external SIM card and also can be use as a cell phone. It is supporting wireless hands-free calling, GPS, Bluetooth and built in 3G Tablet PC becomes more personal to the user than a laptop. Since everyone has a different style of holding and using pens, the Tablet PC will become unique to the user, and even the user will become unique to the pen. In fact, there are handwriting recognition applications that will train the tablet PC to understand your handwriting and convert it into text up to 99 percent accuracy. Students can be more organized using tablet PC since they do not have multiple binders and loose papers. Students are also able to E-mail their homework to the teacher.

Use of Tablet PC in Education

The Tablet PC represents the computer industry's latest attempt at pen-based computing. Since their release in 2002, Tablet PC's have slowly gained attention as a useful tool for educators. This technology bridges the gap between students and teacher and helps them to connect with the bigger world, beyond the boundaries of their classroom.

Tablet technology provides a much higher level of connectivity, which allows students and staff to collaborate and handle assignments. Tablets allow teachers to offer feedback instantaneously, going as far as leaving handwritten feedback directly on the tablet. Overall, the education sector, has quickly adapted to this new technology, using it at both the collegiate and elementary levels. This can take place both, in the smart use o technology in education helps to 'enhance the experience' of learning and thereby, leads to a 'higher degree' of literacy and better quality of higher education.

Implications for the Classroom

The Tablet PC offers most of the advantages of the PCs commonly used in the classroom Note-taking, Accessibility, Portability, Horizontal Orientation, Digital Art. The application of Tablet PC in the classroom as well as outside the classroom has its essential key uses such as replace the blackboard, focusing student attention, effective presentation material using e-projection, digital ink helps to take class notes in your own handwriting using digital pen and save them as digital files.

Conclusion

It's reasonable innovative approach in Higher Education that Tablet PCs will become real however, its usability gains come through integration. In India, Tablet PC is known for Superpower, its benefits have not yet satisfactorily reached in all areas. But there are several companies came forward with low cost tablet PC designed for students especially. As announced by Ministry of Human Resource Development and presently it has been ordered in Lakhs by the students and faculties. This device would be made available to students at least by 2012. Hope the device will empower the students as well as teachers to create a better learning environment.

References

1. Anderson, R., et. al. (2004). Experiences with a Tablet PC Based Lecture Presentation System in Computer Science Courses. In Proceedings of SIGCSE '04, Norfolk, Virginia March 2004. ACM Press.

2. Clark, C. (January, 2004). Notre Dame Tablet PC Initiative. Retrieved 3/10/2004 from http://www.nd.edu/~learning/tabletpc/

3. Hursh, T, Tablet PCs for classroom Use: Technology and Application, Department of Educational Psychology, University of Illinois at Urbana-Champaign. Retrieved from www.ed.uiuc.edu/courses/edpsy317/sp03/challenge-reports/hursh-tabletpc.html

4. www.ed.uiuc.edu/courses/edpsy317/sp03/challenge-reports/hursh-tabletpc.htmlLowe, P. (March, 2004). Bentley College students evaluate Tablet PCs. Retrieved 3/10/2004 from http://www.hp.com/hpinfo/newsroom/feature_stories/2004/04bentley.html

5. Microsoft Corp. (April, 2004). Future Professor Puts Note Taking to the Test Retrieved 5/25/2004 from http://www.microsoft.com/Education/StefanucciFeature.aspx

6. Mock, K. (2003). The Development of a CS0 Course for Distance Delivery. The Journal of Computing Sciences in Colleges, 19 (2), p. 30-38

7. Simon, B., et. al. (2004). Preliminary Experiences with a Tablet PC Based System to Support Active Learning in Computer Science Courses. In Proceedings of SIGCSE '04, Norfolk, Virginia March 2004. ACM Press.

38

Simulated Social Skill Training

A number of techniques are being used currently in India as well as in other countries for the modification of teacher-behavior. The simulated social skill training is one of them. Cruick Shank (1968) has developed a teacher training system. This system of training is being denoted by several terms such as: Role playing, artificial teaching, Pilot training, Laboratory method. Clinical method and Inductive scientific method. The current teaching practices of our teacher education programmes have the following limitations.

a. The pupil-teacher are sent to actual classroom teaching during teaching practices programme without inductive the role of teacher. Some training institutions have the provision for demonstration lesson.

b. There is no provision for providing reinforcement for the pupil-teacher behavior. The supervisors give remarks for their reaching task in general, may be as criticism of lesson. There is no scope to follow the suggestions given by the supervisor.

c. The teaching practices involve risk and humiliation for pupil-teachers because they do not know even the classroom manners.

The simulated social skill training (SSST) has the direct improvement over these limitations of traditional teaching practices.

Meaning and Definition

The simulation technique is to induce certain behavior and artificial situation. A pupil-teacher has to play several roles as a teacher as a student and as a supervisor. Simulation gives us greater control over the teaching variables. It is based upon socio-drama. The socio-drama is very much related to the practice. The most important aspect of simulation is the introduction of the student to teaching is non-stressful conditions.

The simulated social skill training can be defined as mechanism or feedback devices to induce certain desirable behavior among pupil-teachers by playing the role of teacher in their own group as an artificial situation of classroom teaching. Cruick Shank considers that much more work needs to be done in developing the technique of simulation.

Assumptions Regarding Simulation Technique

The SSST is based upon the following assumptions.

1. The teacher-behavior is modifiable by the use of feedback devices.
2. The basic assumption is that there are certain patterns of teacher behavior, which are essential in effective teaching. These behavior can be described and practiced like any other skill the observe identifies those behavior and teacher practice those pattern of teaching behavior.
3. The teacher-behavior has its taxonomy Karl Openshaw has developed the taxonomy of teacher-behavior by the use of simulated technique.
4. Another assumption is that social skills are developed by practice and imitation in a group. All members of the group have an opportunity to practice in controlling and improving their own behavior for teaching purposes.

The Procedure of SSST

This technique is used for developing the social skill of teaching in classroom situation. This is generally employed for the pupil-teachers before sending them in real classroom in their teaching practices. Certain steps have been outlined merely as suggestions. The teacher educators can develop their own procedure of SSST. Generally the following six steps are used in SSST technique.

1. The pupil-teachers are assigned the roles, which they have to play in SSST. Each individual has a chance to be as teacher, student, and an observer.
2. After assigning the role, certain social skills are discussed which are to be practiced. The skills are discussed for a topic. Each candidate has to select a topic of his interest.
3. A schedule of organizing SSST is prepared who will start? Who will stop? When should it be stopped? And who will intervene the conversation?
4. The procedure and technique of observation is also decided. What kind of data of observation is to be recorded? How can the data be best interpreted?
5. The scheduled is followed for the first practice session. The teaching is organized and observations are taken for evaluating the teaching task of an actor. The teaching is followed by discussion and demonstration to provide the feedback to the pupil-teacher by giving the awareness of his social skill of teaching and suggestions for the improvement. Changing topic, teacher, pupils, observer and social skills now changes.
6. In this procedure every pupil teacher should have the interest as high as possible in playing the every role, which is assigned to him. The topic and social skills should not be too easy or too difficult.

The Elements of Simulated Training

The procedure consists of three rotes teacher, pupil and observer.

Cruick Shank considers that this teaching paradigm also includes three elements:

1. Diagnosis
2. Prescription, and
3. Evaluation

Taxonomy of teacher-Behaviour

Under this teaching the student teachers simulate a particular activity or role and they try to develop an identity with the actual classroom situation. The whole simulated teaching programme becomes training in role perception and role-playing the handling of behavioral problems of classroom are better mastered through simulated teaching sessions:

Karl Openshaw and others of Ohio State University have tried to develop taxonomy of teacher-behaviour where they feel that a comprehensive view of teacher behavior includes four major dimensions:

1. A Source Dimension,
2. A Direction Dimension,
3. A Function Dimensions, and
4. A Sign Dimension.

Each of these dimensions of teaching according to Karl Openshaw are observable and quantifiable, analysis of which provides empirical evidence about what does a teacher do, how does he behave while teaching.

1. The source dimension of teaching provides interaction between the relationship of students and teacher at a basic level. Teaching is an interaction between projector entity called teacher and receptor entities within a classroom situation.

2. The identification and classification of the nature of receptor entities provides the director dimension to teaching in the study conducted by K. Openshaw and others.

3. The teacher has to perform certain task. This task (Presentation of subject-matter) should be dealt with beliefs, attitudes, skills and process of instruction. The second task is to establish and to maintain interpersonal relationship among students in classroom. The third task is to facilitate the learning process. These three tasks constitute the function dimension of teaching.

4. In order to observe behavior it should be communicated in some way. The communication may require more than one mode of expression in fulfilling a given function. The mode of behavior makes the sign dimension. The following diagram illustrates the taxonomy of teacher behavior:

This diagram indicates that the source of behavior controls other dimensions of teacher-behaviour but it may be determined though the observer's recognition of the target of focus, the direction dimension. The mode of interaction together with the purpose of behavior gives meaning while other purposes may limit the modes behavior available to the teacher. A given behavior may be classified in more than one category of the function direction. Each encounter may have a number of shifts within sign dimension. Any change in the source and direction dimension indicates new encounter.

Advantages of Simulated Training

Cruick Shank has suggested a number of advantages of simulated technique:

1. The major advantage if that in using the technique, we are forging close links between theory and practice.

2. The student teachers are given an opportunity to study and analyze critical teaching problems.

3. The students can acquire classroom manners through the technique of simulation.

4. The student can understand behavioral problems of classroom and develop insight to encounter them.

5. The technique provides reinforcement to students to develop teaching skills and avoid the risk of actual classroom encounter.

Use of Simulated Social Skill Training

The technique may be used in the following problems of teaching.

1. The appropriateness of open or closed question skills is ascertained in teaching situations.
2. The ability to ask questions is developed in which pupils have expressed the concepts and logical sequence previously.
3. The confidence in teaching is developed to encounter the face-to-face situation in pupil-teachers.
4. The SST technique provides a situation to expose the pupil-teacher to play the role of teacher and observer prior going to actual classroom teaching. It helps in developing social skill of teaching.
5. It is a best replacement of demonstration lesson because every teacher-educator is not an effective teacher. It eliminates an opportunity of imitation of certain skills; of teaching.
6. The ability to demonstrate and explain the rules of logic in classroom teaching helps in maintaining consistency in the meaning of words.
7. The Microteaching can be best used for developing certain teaching skills but it is difficult to use in our teacher-education programme during teaching practices. It can combine with SSST to be employed in our situations to develop teaching skills.
8. It provides the feedback to each pupil-teacher and also helps them to act as teacher, pupil. And observer to perceive the role in each situation. This may provide insight to take a decision about his own teaching activities. It helps in predicting consequences of teaching and may change the flow of actions of teaching.

39

Modern Teaching Techniques for Open and Distance Education

Introduction

Alteration is the key constituent for the twenty first century that poses many challenges and huge force on our daily life, work and society. Political, economical, social, and technological environments are changing considerably and rapidly. Information and communication technologies (ICT) transform all aspects of education and distance education (DE), which is a rapidly growing segment. The advent of the Internet as a means of information access and distribution and the explosive growth of the World Wide Web (Web) have transformed distance teaching from a broadcast mode to an interactive one. Faculty and librarians are all at the crossroads and being pressured to increase their productivity and to change instructional strategies to accommodate changes and educational reforms.

What is Distance Education?

Distance education or distance learning is a field of education that focuses on teaching methods and technology with the aim of delivering teaching, often on an individual basis, to students who are not physically present in a to learning when the source of information and the learners are separated by time and distance, or both traditional educational setting such as a classroom. It has been described as "a process to create and provide access

History

Distance education dates to at least as early as 1728, when "an advertisement in the Boston Gazette...[named] 'Caleb Phillips, Teacher of the new method of Short Hand" was seeking students for lessons to be sent weekly.

Modern distance education initially relied on the development of postal services in the 19th century and has been practised at least since Isaac Pitman taught shorthand in Great Britain via correspondence in the 1840s.The University of London claims to be the first university to offer distance learning degrees, establishing its External Programme in 1858. This program is now known as the University of London International Programmes and includes Postgraduate, Undergraduate and Diploma degrees created by colleges such as the London School of Economics, Royal Holloway and Goldsmiths.In the United States William Rainey Harper, first president of the University of Chicago developed the concept of extended education, whereby the research university had satellite colleges of education in the wider community, and in 1892 he also encouraged the concept of correspondence school courses to further promote education, an idea that was put into practice by Columbia University. In Australia, the University of Queensland established its Department of Correspondence Studies in 1911.

More recently, Charles Wedemeyer of the University of Wisconsin–Madison is considered significant in promoting methods other than the postal service to deliver distance education in America. From 1964 to 1968, the Carnegie Foundation funded Wedemeyer's Articulated Instructional Media Project (AIM) which brought in a variety of communications technologies aimed at providing learning to an off-campus population. According to Moore's recounting, AIM impressed the UK which imported these ideas when establishing in 1969 The Open University, which initially relied on radio and television broadcasts for much of its delivery. Athabasca University, Canada's Open University was created in 1970 and followed a similar, though independently developed, pattern. Germany's Fern University in Hagen followed in 1974 and there are now many similar institutions around the world, often with the name Open University (in English or in the local language). All "open universities" use distance education technologies as delivery methodologies and some have grown to become 'mega-universities' a term coined to denote institutions with more than 100,000 students.

The development of computers and the internet have made distance learning distribution easier and faster and have given rise to the 'virtual university, the entire educational offerings of which are conducted online. In 1996 Jones International University was launched and claims to be the first fully online university accredited by a regional accrediting association in the US.

In 2006, the Sloan Consortium, a body which arguably has a conflict of interest in the matter, reported that: More than 96 percent of the very largest institutions (more than 15,000 total enrolments) have some online offerings, which is more than double the rate observed for the smallest institutions and that almost 3.2 million US students were taking at least one online course during the fall term of 2005. A study published in 2011 by the U.S. Department of Education found that "From 2000 to 2008, the percentage of undergraduates enrolled in at least one distance education class expanded from 8 percent to 20 percent, and the percentage enrolled in a distance education degree program increased from 2 percent to 4 percent."

Today, there are many private and public, non-profit and for-profit institutions worldwide offering distance education courses from the most basic instruction through to the highest levels of degree and doctoral programs. Levels of accreditation vary: some of the institutions receive little outside oversight, and some may be fraudulent diploma mills, although in many jurisdictions, an institution may not use terms such as "university" without accreditation and authorisation, often overseen by the national government - for example, the Quality Assurance Agencyin the UK. In the US, the Distance Education and Training Council (DETC) specializes in the accreditation of distance education institutions.

What Problem Does Distance Education Solve?

Although most institutions have become involved in some form of distance learning, their rationales for doing so are not always clear. Often presidents, trustees, faculty and students feel that they are being swept along by a tidal wave of public expectations for distance learning, and none of them wants to be left behind. Among those institutions with more well-defined reasons for embracing distance education, the rationales vary, but they often fall into one of four broad categories:

1. **Expanding access.** Most states need to expand access to education in order to meet the education and training needs of state residents and companies and to educate under-served populations. For many people in the past, academic program calendars have not matched work and family responsibilities, and program offerings may not have met learner needs.

2. **Alleviating capacity constraints.** Many states are expecting more college students over the next decade than their facilities can accommodate. Some are hoping to leverage the scalability of distance education to avoid overwhelming their bricks-and-mortar capacities.

3. **Capitalizing on emerging market opportunities.** The public's growing acceptance of the value of lifelong learning has fueled an increased demand for higher education services among people outside the traditional 18-24 age range. Emerging student segments, such as executives seeking further education and working adults, may be more lucrative than traditional markets. By capitalizing on emerging market opportunities, many educational institutions hope to generate significant revenue.

4. **Serving as a catalyst for institutional transformation.** Higher education institutions are being challenged to adapt rapidly to an increasingly competitive environment. Distance education can catalyze institutional transformation.

At the University of North Carolina, we believe that each of these rationales has its merit, but in exploring them it became obvious that we could not meet all four goals with a single model of distance education. Each rationale determines the organizational structure, governance and financial model required to serve it. For example, if we chose to enhance access to education for the state's citizens, we would likely choose a different technology, different courses, and different delivery systems from those we would choose if we were trying to capitalize on emerging market opportunities. Enhancing educational access might cause us to focus on general education courses, whereas capitalizing on emerging market opportunities would lead us to offer courses in the state's high-growth fields such as financial services, genomic sciences, or marine sciences.

Whom Should Distance Education Serve?

Almost everyone recognizes the rapid expansion in the market for distance education. The desire for lifelong learning and educational flexibility and the growth in student populations are among the trends fuelling this growth. The distance education "market," however, is not homogeneous. Learners range from traditional students seeking additional scheduling flexibility to "recreational learners" engaged in expanding their personal knowledge.

Once a school chooses its rationale for distance education, it is important to identify the type of learner it intends to serve (i.e., to define learner segments). Segment definitions depend upon several factors, including the goals and maturity level of the learner as well as who makes the purchasing decision. Different segments also signal the need for alternative educational approaches. The kind of program designed to serve those interested primarily in personal fulfillment will be quite different from one designed for corporate learners. In working to develop a system-wide instructional technology strategy, the University of North Carolina and PricewaterhouseCoopers defined these learner segments:

1. **Life fulfillment learners** are interested in education for its own sake. They enjoy learning and the academic environment, and they view additional education as a hobby or a source of personal development. They make their own decisions whether or not to purchase education.
2. **Corporate learners** are seeking education to advance their careers with their corporate employers. The purchase decision is made by the corporation, not by the individual. Corporate learners demand a broad range of services, from instructional technology end-user training to advance scientific training.
3. **Professional enhancement learners** are seeking to advance their careers or shift careers. They work for companies but are making the purchase decision themselves.
4. **Degree completion adult learners** are seeking to complete a degree later in life than usual. They are frequently working adults who must balance work and family responsibilities with their educational goals.
5. **"College experience" learners** (a.k.a. the "traditional student") are preparing for life. This segment includes many 18-to-24-year-old residential college students for whom the "coming of age" process is as important as academic learning. They may make the purchase decision themselves, or it may be made by their parents.
6. **Pre-college (K-12) learners** are interested in taking baccalaureate-level work prior to the completion of high school. This segment may be interested in getting a "jump start" on college. Their purchase decision is most often made by their parents.
7. **Remediation and test prep learners** are interested in learning as a prerequisite for an examination or enrolment in another program. The decision to purchase distance education in this case often depends upon the age of the learner.

Is Distance Education About Education or Technology?

Complicating the issues of goals and learner segments even further is the tendency to see distance education as a technology issue. Certainly the advent of new technologies has enabled institutions to think quite differently about distance education. However, distance education should be an educational issue rather than a technology one. Some strongly believe that new distance education possibilities have the potential to alter (and perhaps transform) our traditional institutions of higher education; others argue that this technology may lead to a reduction in educational quality.

Innovative Teaching Techniques (ITT)

Internet: The Internet as a medium of learning is explored to the maximum for the creative use and positive impact of such knowledge on the learning process. Topics from recent advances in the subject are allocated to them. Through Internet search, the students acquire the latest know how on the assigned topics and compile the projects in the form of a brochure.

Web-based Instruction (WBI) is defined broadly as any form of innovative approach for delivering instruction to a remote audience in which the Web is included as a tool (Relan & Gillani, 1997). Presently, several Web sites have been developed to provide learners with access to instructional resources from a distance. However, Hill (1996) noted that, most course-based or learning sites simply post course materials. In such instances, use of the Web falls far short of the potential this medium affords. According to Casey (1998), currently used Web models of learning can be identified as one of the followings:

1. The Web as Source of Information: This is the simplest use of the Web. It is used as a convenient place to store supporting information for traditionally offered courses.

2. The Web as Electronic Book: Many institutions have moved to use the Web to present information in a more structured way for teaching process. Students use the screen to read materials, activate multimedia demonstrations, and take self-correcting quizzes or other activities. The course material is mostly factual information, which is to be learned from the Web page and any accompanying media. There is no interaction between teacher and the students through the Web.

3. The Web as Teacher: Some Web-based courses include some form of personal communication between students and other students via the use of email and perhaps chat rooms.

4. The Web as a Communication Medium between Teacher and Students: In this model, students learn from the teacher but "through" the Web and not "from" the Web. Thus, the Web acts as the communication medium for the necessary interaction. A model such as these aims to mirror a face-to-face learning Innovative Teaching Techniques for Distance Education environment, within which the students will be able to establish some form of human relationship with the teacher. (Ruksasuk, 1999).

According to Reeves (1997), the WBI has a rich mix of media features and the pedagogical dimensions to deliver. The aim of Web-based education must surely be to develop a model, which will enable a relatively large proportion of the student population to learn relatively easily and successfully **(Casey, 1998).** Computer-assisted learning (learning through CD-ROM) - The opportunities associated with the development of computer-based technology in contributing to effective science education have grown exponentially within the past decade. The multimedia software available on CD-ROM plays a powerful role with applications in labs and lectures, tutorials and project work.

Seminars –To have interaction, weekly seminars are held and all the students are required to participate actively. The best speaker of the seminar from the entire batch is given an award. The awards are given to inculcate a competitive spirit among the students and bring the best out of the students.

Virtual laboratories - Virtual laboratories detail the preparation, essential equipment, and method relevant to the practical and students then actively perform experiments themselves with simulated responses. Virtual laboratory presents a range of equipment on-screen and may offer a very high degree of interactivity. Training through audiovisual aids can play an important role in medical education.

Students as project coordinators - The department inculcates leadership qualities in students. The students actively participate as coordinators of the on-going departmental research projects, by which they are encouraged.

Teleconferencing – It is a new mixed model approach for DE combining satellite teleconferencing with hands-on activity session. It was developed to adjust for many of the disadvantages associated with DE and traditional in person training. The mixed model used live teleconference speakers, video clips, interactive call-in sessions and local sessions.

Telemetric Education – Enables students to access teaching programmes and learning materials at a more flexible time, place and pace, and results in many flexible learning opportunities.

Quiz - After all the above techniques, the most encouraging one could be the conducting quiz for the students at various rounds (six). The first round, consisting of question-answers, is based on simple recall of factual information. Rounds II and III, consisting of Jumbled Words, Multiple Choice Questions (MCQs) and Graphs and Flow Diagrams to indicate missing links are based on interpretation of information from charts, graphs, or flow diagrams or interpretation from two concepts that have a relationship. Rounds IV, V and VI, having Match the Following, Ascending Order, Trace the Path and Rapid-Fire Questions are based on testing primarily the application of knowledge to the solution of a specific problem and the fitting together of a variety of elements into a meaningful whole. The quiz conducted for students inculcates in them team spirit, leadership, better organizing abilities and interest and better comprehension of the subject. The Quizzes help in improving memory power, scientific nomenclature, and vocabulary and active learning through integrative reasoning, which helps in improving intellectual power.

Conclusion

The field of education all over the world is swept by a paradigm shift that is the result of a new awakening in the teaching-learning process. The onus is now on the learner and the teacher is now looked upon as a facilitator. Understanding that the traditional chalk and talk method can no longer enthuse the students, the college continuously strives to innovate methods that will sustain their interest and make the learning process more productive and interesting. Innovative teaching can take many forms. Educators must learn to change with the times and the methods offered for instructing students. These changes will ultimately benefit the students and the education system. The ability to adapt to these changes may be one of the most important attributes for today's educators. Academic librarians perform an in dispensable function in the educational process. DE librarians have much more critical roles to play in supporting the DE system in the new learning environment. The question remains as to whether they will remain merely information providers as in the past or whether librarians as facilitators of other's people learning should take a proactive roles in the changing context as instructors of the information literacy skill or partners in the teaching /learning process to create information literate distance students. As a result professional public awareness of librarians as educators and faculty status of librarians as equal to teaching faculty will be enhanced.

References

1. Jerusalem, Israel, 13 – 18 Aug, 2000. Innovative Teaching Techniques for Distance Education.
2. Brine, Alan and Feather, John. (2002). Supporting skills development – LTSN-ICS. In 68th IFLA Council and General Conference Bangkok, Thailand, 18 – 24 Aug, 2002.
3. Casey, D. (1998). Learning "From" or "Through" the Web: Models of Web Based Education.
4. Sacchanand, Chutima. (2002). Information literacy instruction to distance students in higher education: Librarians' key role.

In 68th IFLA Council and General Conference, Glasgow, 18 – 24 Aug, 2002. Thomas, G.M. (1995). Education-past, present, future. In D.R. Walling, ed. At the threshold of the millennium, Bloomington, Indiana: Phi Delta Kappa.

40

Globalization: Effects and Opportunities for Igher Education

The Historical Role of English

As a mode of communication, Latin transcended other communication venues as the formal language of the Roman Republic and Roman Empire. Later on, Latin was adopted by medieval scholars. For centuries, Latin served as the scholars' language. High schools and postsecondary schools around the world offered classes in Latin. Globally, this served as the common language between professors and students. Subsequently, German surpassed Latin and gained the language lead. French speakers attempted to dominate the language world, as then the English. With such diversification, Latin became relegated to philosophers and theologians. Schools, on a general scale, ceased teaching Latin. This historical leading language was limited to specialized schools. Journals published scientific articles in German, French and English. Because of an increased number of English-speaking universities in the United States, United Kingdom and other parts of the world, coupled with the United State's openness to international markets, the English language became essential. In order to communicate knowledge, English evolved as the common language not only for scholars, but for everyone participating in the international market. This language dynamic provided an advantage to American professors who published journals in their native tongue, under rules established by their peers, and with peer review from academicians from the same country. In a second instance, advantages were realized in world class universities located in some parts of the world, such as South Korea, India and Japan. To compete internationally, many countries decided to teach English as a second language. This was (and remains)the choice without exception. The English language subsequently opened doors of new opportunities for students to study in foreign countries. Some government actions in regards to mandated instruction in English provided many country advantages in the long run. For example, China's governmental requirements for English language proficiency enabled the possibility for many students to obtain their tertiary education in the US while they worked as Teaching Assistants (TAs).

Teaching Assistants Language Capabilities and the Diverse Professor Population

Historically in the universities of the United States, the English proficiency requirements to obtain a TA position consisted of a written English exam. In written form, the Chinese students where quite well prepared. Chinese students studied the English dictionary with fervour. A custom of eating the pages of the dictionary once the written English competency exams were successfully completed was widely practiced by Chinese youth. Many American institutions of higher education were loosing government financial support and found that foreigners were willing to pay international tuition fees to attend school in the States. This helped increase revenues of the universities. A paradigm change resulted in western universities as a result of students' complaints: they were not able to understand Asian professors due to under developed oral communication skills. The criteria changed, and an additional oral exam is generally now required for aspiring TAs. In the meantime, Chinese students were awarded many TA placements that American students did not secure. Naturally, there are additional factors that influence whether American or international students would secure the limited resource of TA positions at a university. One other significant variable seems to be the American students' sense of expediency: to work immediately following completion of the bachelor's degree. Another is the US graduate student "TA applicant pool". When the US economy becomes sluggish, as was the case status post September 11th, American students seem more interested or willing to pursue advanced degrees. A slow job market naturally translates to fewer career opportunities. This same phenomenon was illustrated during the double-digit unemployment era of the early 1980's: More Americans decided to pursue a higher education degree while waiting for an improvement in the employment market. Thus, in the past few years, more Americans seemed to be in the TA positions that previously were held by Chinese and other international students. What transpired, then, with the large number of foreign graduate students after they completed their degrees? Many international students, especially the ones that did not have the obligation to return to their home countries, found jobs in US. If one looks at the number of professors holding a laureate Nobel Prize from the most recognized universities in US, the data shows that most recipients originated in other countries. These outstanding achievers came to study in US, found employment in the States and established their lives accordingly. A most interesting facet related to foreign professors is that at one time, their native countries referred to them as "lost brains". Their home country held a paradigm that this knowledge base and the associated intellectual talents were lost forever. Although this seems to be supported by high- profile cases such as the Nobel Prize recipients, many academicians that have migrated to the US have actually retained close contact with colleagues and original institutions of higher education "at home". Some even returned to their home country after establishing careers abroad too. Some are conducting research in their native countries. What then, was the result for higher education on an international basis? With fewer options available in the United States, "India, China and other countries are making strong investments to bring their research universities to world-class status". In general, foreign professors maintain a deep relationship with their country of origin and frequently return home for lectures or collaborative research during sabbaticals. New technologies for communication facilitate foreign professors and even Americans to conduct research and to author collaborative documents for publication (in English, of course). For now, English remains the "Latin" of the 21st century. The English language is the mechanism for knowledge communication and for instruction, even in countries where English is not the language of higher education. English also facilitates cross-border degree arrangements and other programs. China, for example, now attracts a multitude of students from other Asian countries and is no longer sending as many students to study abroad as before. Korea University has determined that it will be teaching two-thirds of its classes in English by the year 2010 (they are currently at30%).To understand the future, perhaps one can consider the past. India, as a country, although deeply rooted in its own traditions and culture, has accepted the challenge of English language assimilation. Indians have adopted new language paradigms markedly sooner than many other countries have considered doing so.

English and India

In India, 100 million people know the English language. According to NationMaster.com [5], India is second in the world (only to the United States) in the number of English speakers by country. Hindi is the national language and primary tongue of 30% of India's people; yet there are 14other official languages: Bengali, Telugu, Marathi, Tamil, Urdu, Gujarati, Malayalam, Kannada, Oriya, Punjabi, Assamese, Kashmiri, Sindhi, and Sanskrit. Hindustani is a popular variant of Hindi/Urdu spoken widely throughout northern India but is not an official language. English enjoys associate status in most areas, yet continues to be the most important language for national, political, and commercial communication. Evolution of the English language in India began when the British recruited local people to work in kitchens and in clerical jobs. Thus, the Indians learned English. In India, their independence struggle was first led by the 'babus'(English-educated Indians). A commonality of English language helped people network for their cause. English also supported establishment of a national spirit through a common mode of communication. Language trended toward native dialect usage under Mahatma Gandhi. For nearly 40 years, the emphasis was on education in mother tongues. In modern India, this has changed. The contemporary choice is, once again, English. This paradigm shift did not evolve as a result of government policies, but as a result of the perceptions of the Indian people. Especially for those who belong to high or medium classes, but also for working parents, Indians prefer that their children attend English schools. A scope of the possibility of studying English in India and an illustration of contemporary language offerings can be found in the 1992 Fifth All-India Education Survey. English in India is offered as a second language (six years of study) in51 percent of rural primary schools, 55 percent of urban primary schools, 57 percent of rural high schools, and 51 percent of urban high schools. As a third language (three years of study), English is offered in 5 percent of rural primary schools, 21 percent of urban primary schools, 44 percent of rural high schools, and 41 percent of urban high schools. These statistics show a considerable desire to study English among people receiving a mostly vernacular education, even in the country side. In higher education, English continues to be the premier, prestige language. Careers in business and commerce, government positions of high rank (regardless of stated policy), along with science and technology (attracting many of the brightest) continue to require fluency in English. Fluency is also necessary for the many students who contemplate study overseas. The advent of computers encouraged English literacy as it became a common machine language. Jobs in information technology-oriented careers (computer software, hardware, and data entry) suddenly enhanced the necessity of knowledge of the English language. English as a prestige language and the tongue of first choice continues to serve as the medium of instruction in elite schools at every level without apology. All large cities and many smaller cities have private, English-language middle schools and high schools. Even government schools that are run for the benefit of senior civil service officers are conducted in English because only that language is an acceptable medium of communication throughout the nation. Working-class parents, themselves rural-urban migrants and perhaps bilingual in their village dialect and the regional standard language, perceive English as the tool their children need in order to advance. Schools in which English is the mode of instruction are a "growth industry". Facility in English enhances a young woman's chances in the marriage market. This is not merely a small advantage in the often protracted marriage negotiations between families. The English speaker in India also encounters more courteous situational responses than does a speaker of an indigenous language.

Higher Education in the Student-Student Interface

In Kerala, India, the Student-Student Interface [9] was designed primarily to involve senior students by imparting knowledge to juniors. The basis emanated from the famous quote "To learn more, you should teach more". That is, through the act of teaching others, senior students were themselves required to learn more than what they would have learned from listening to traditional class lectures. Students in these relationships were not, however, leading free-handed. Before a Student-Student Interface was organized, the students of senior status were provided training on how to conduct a class, what to teach and what to emphasize. For field interns, students were provided additional training on the management of students in groups. All Student-Student Interface classes/field interns were conducted in the presence of the teacher. This offered confidence to the senior students that they would not be troubled with enigmatic (dubious) doubts. Students of senior classes were asked to conduct classes or field internships for the juniors. Here, the professor's role as a teacher remains omnipotent and the interface turns purely into a student-student one. In this new interface, the professor is more of a planner than a deliverer. The professor could then evaluate the actions of the students. The senior and junior students alike experienced a quality, value-added educational experience. Once students began to engage in classes, the students realized many facts. The enlightening included the students' personal lack of knowledge and their own absurdities in the classroom. The students seemed to develop a sense of responsibility towards their own education by attending classes regularly, by visiting libraries and by keeping regular notes. They developed a cordial behavior in the classroom, which otherwise was difficult to develop professorially. Altogether, their field classes and tutorials had provided them productive results for themselves. These students performed extremely well in examinations and their answers were often graded as remarkable. The Student-Student Interface also improved students' quality of communication and evaluative ability in understanding facts. This dimension was proven in the students' oral tests. As for students in junior classes, the Student-Student Interface process brought about a transitional and comfortable interface with their teacher. Students could ask as many questions as they desired to the seniors, without age and position acting as hindrance. Many times it was noted that a junior student showed much enthusiasm when questioning the senior's views. Productive discussions that evolved from this interface filliped the spirit of student reasoning. In fact, the' art of questioning' was indeed nurtured through these processes. The experiment of creating a Student-Student Interface in teaching is therefore productive and advantageous for students in adding value and quality to their education. What can educators do, however, when teaching diverse people, from different cultures? Perhaps experimentation with various techniques would enhance pedagogy.

Diversity and Pedagogy

When teaching in a diverse student environment, the following techniques can enhance delivery and transfer of training:

Include Visual Aids with Lecture When teaching in diverse classrooms, visual aids become a tool of utmost importance. PowerPoint handouts are helpful: the visual learning capabilities of students are enhanced, but also, students are provided with a written copy of main lecture points via the handout format. Students of diverse backgrounds often utilize these aids to further read, study, or translate materials for assigned coursework. If teaching abroad, ensure you will have projector capability. Sometimes finding even a slide projector can become a challenge.

Show Photos

In many countries, passing around photo albums to guests visiting people's homes is a popular custom. Students may expect their instructors to show photos off as well! Photos of various locations around a professor's hometown (supermarket, bank, bookstore, shopping mall) may be well received. Also important in various cultures are pictures of special occasions or family get-togethers.

Incorporate Pictures

Engage students' desires to write or speak about topics via pictures. Save and incorporate subject-oriented pictures from calendars, advertisements, or trade journals. Pictures should be action-oriented, interesting, and chosen to elicit student response.

Consider Humor

Although humor varies widely with country differences, comic strips or other picture sequences may help students follow a thought process in an interesting manner.

Offer a Participative Activity

Board games with pieces, dice, playing cards, or including" Monopoly money" in an activity or session review encourages all students to participate.

Include Movies

American Academy-Award winning films are usually popular choices. If teaching abroad, check as to which VCR system is offered (the US is NTSC, while China, for example is PAL-D). Some schools offer a dual system VCR. DVD compatibility is an issue when teaching abroad as well.

Vary Handouts

Depending upon the subject matter, consider including maps, posters, brochures, programs or schedules.

Use Fill-in-the-Blank Notes

Popularized in the US in youth populations by the "Mad Lib" series, fill-in-the blank notes offer many advantages when teaching diverse students. Students must listen attentively tithe professor, however, they only need to scribe a word every so often in order to complete a quality set of class notes. The positive affect for the instructor is that the lecturer does not need to slow the pace of delivery for foreign students. Simultaneously, students are provided with a written synopsis of the lecture in a manageable format. Those who need further study or translation leave each class with the text needed for additional review in hand.

A Call to Action

Many people, especially in the United States, believe that because English is the language today for communication and scientific publication, it is not necessary to learn another mode of communication. The same English-only speaking population is the one who truly have a short-sighted view of the necessary qualities that will be needed to succeed in the global market world. Truly, not seeing the possibilities for preparing for global success contributes to the problem. This narrow thinking has resulted in the US falling behind in many industries in which they used to dominate. Decades ago, many cultures realized that communicating in at least two languages provide marked advantages for managers, professors, and people that lead organizations in other parts of the world. Today, people will perhaps need three languages, if they truly desire to succeed in global markets. Professors, thus, need to adopt new paradigms. Educators need to inspire students to consider multilingual education and to develop a familiarity of working with global cultures. This is how higher education may empower and prepare students to succeed. As a global population, and especially in higher education, instructors need to begin changing the way they think and act. Those who believe that the others are the ones that need another language to communicate with those who already speak English, may just be wrong. Perhaps, in a short time, English-speakers will need to learn another language in order for others to understand them. As professors, we should show our students new ways to interact in the world and encourage an awareness of international cultures.

References

1. Altback, P.G. Globalization and the University: Myths and Realities in anunequal world. Tertiary Education and Management No. 1, 2004.
2. Fulbright Group Suggests Ways to Ensure Global Equity in Higher Education. Section: International Volume 53, Issue 11, pageA49.
3. Lloyd Armstrong, Jr. Does the future of higher education belong to the for-profit sector? As seen on Januaryhttp://changinghighereducation.com/2006/12/i_commented_rec.html
4. NationMaster.com, Language Language Statistics, English Speakers by County, http://www.nationmaster.com/graph/lan_eng_spe-language-english-speakers, accessed March 17, 2007.
5. Luan, Shanglin, "Wen: China to Increase Education Spending", GOV.cnWednesday, November 22, 2006.
6. Semana Magazín. Ala, mi chino! Sección Vida Moderna. December 29,2006.
7. Vest, C.M. "Openness and globalization in higher education: The age of the internet, terrorism, and opportunity. June-2006. Research & Occasional paper series:CSHE.7.06 University of California, Berkeley.

41

Base of Teacher Education Through the Ncte, Ncert, Ciet, Scert

Introduction

According to Sri *Sarvepalli Radha Krishnan*, Teacher is a national builder. Education is a powerful instrument of national development. Education is a solution of all types of problems in the society. Through education we get knowledge, good habits, character, morals and values. We have thousands of years of tradition and culture. In Vedas the teacher was called 'Guru'. According to Indians teacher is third god. We give more respect to teacher after mother and father in the society.

Teacher is a national builder. It is necessary to give importance to teacher education. Today's children are tomorrow's citizens. By taking good steps in the framing of teacher education curriculum, we can give good quality and value based education to the teachers. National Council for Teacher Education, National Council of Educational Research and Training, Central Institute of Educational Technology, State Council of Educational Research and Training etc.

are the institutions for the strengthening the teacher education in India.

National Council for Teacher Education (NCTE)

The National Council for Teacher Education, in its previous status since 1973, was an advisory body for the Central and State Governments on all matters pertaining to teacher education, with its Secretariat in the Department of Teacher Education of the National Council of Educational Research and Training (NCERT). Despite its commendable work in the academic fields, it could not perform essential regulatory functions, to ensure maintenance of standards in teacher education and preventing proliferation of substandard teacher education institutions. The National Policy on Education (NPE), 1986 and the Programme of Action there under, envisaged a National Council for Teacher Education with statutory status and necessary resources as a first step for overhauling the system of teacher education. The National Council for Teacher Education as a statutory body came into existence in pursuance of the National Council for Teacher Education Act, 1993 (No. 73 of 1993) on the 17th August,1995.

Objective of NCTE

The main objective of the NCTE is to achieve planned and coordinated development of the teacher education system throughout the country, the regulation and proper maintenance of Norms and Standards in the teacher education system and for matters connected therewith. The mandate given to the NCTE is very broad and covers the whole gamut of teacher education programmes including research and training of persons for equipping them to teach at pre-primary, primary, secondary and senior secondary stages in schools, and non-formal education, part-time education, adult education and distance (correspondence) education courses.

Organizational Structure of NCTE

NCTE has its head quarter at New Delhi and four Regional

Committees at Banglore, Bhopal, Bhubaneshwar and Jaipur to look after its statutory responsibilities. In order to enable the NCTE to perform the assigned functions including planned and co-ordinated development and initiating innovations in teacher education, the NCTE in Delhi as well as its four Reginal Committees have administrative and academic wings to deal respectively with finance, establishment and legal matters and with research, policy planning, monitoring, curriculum, innovations, co-ordination, library and documentation, in-service programmes. The NCTE Headquarters is headed by the Chairperson, while each Regional Committee is headed by a Regional Director.

The Parliament appreciated the role of quality teacher education in providing quality teachers for quality school education and passed an Act in 1993 for setting up of the National Council for Teacher Education (NCTE) as a statutory body. The broad mandate given to the NCTE is to achieve planned and co-ordinated development of the teacher education system throughout the country, the regulation and proper maintenance of norms and standards in the teacher education system and for matters connected therewith.

The NCTE has been conducting orientation programmes on education in human values for teacher educators and repackaging electronically the contributions of the experts and those of the participants. The outcomes of its programmes are distributed to each of its recognized institutions on multimedia CD-ROMs and through the World Wide Web of the Internet. Full texts of publications on value education in easily downloadable form have been made available on the NCTE web site (http://www.ncte-in.org). Titles related to value education available from the NCTE web site are: Education for Character Development; Education for Tomorrow; Report of the Working Group to Review Teachers' Training Programme; Role and Responsibility of Teachers in Building up Modern India; Gandhi on Education; Sri Aurobindo on Education; and Tilak on Education. The titles of the NCTE CD-ROMs on value education are New Education for New India - Integral Education of Sri Aurobindo, Jeevan Vigyan and Teachers as Transformers. A CD-ROM based on the workshop that was organised by the NCTE jointly with the Chinmaya World Centre will be released shortly. Recently, in December 2001 two workshops on value orientation in teacher education for teacher educators of the Southern States were organised by the RIMSE (Ramakrishna Institute for Moral and Spiritual Education). It may be appreciated that the role of the NCTE in bringing any curricular change in teacher education programme, even providing facilitation in integration of education in human values in it, at best, is that of a catalytic agent. What NCTE is trying is to make available a basketful of resource materials on education in human values to teacher education institutions.

National Counsel of Educational Research and Training (NCERT)

The National Council of Educational Research and Training (NCERT) is an apex resource organisation set up by the Government of India, with headquarters at New Delhi, to assist and advise the Central and State Governments on academic matters related to school education. NCERT doing so many researches to improve the quality of teacher education. The objective of NCERT is to assist and advise the Ministry of Education and Social Welfare in the implementation of its policies and major programmes in the field of education, particularly school education. The NCERT provides academic and technical support for improvement of school education through its various constituents, which are:

1. National Institute of Education, New Delhi
2. Central Institute of Education Technology, New Delhi
3. Pandit Sunderlal Sharma Central Institute of Vocational Education, Bhopal
4. Regional Institute of Education, Ajmer
5. Regional Institute of Education, Bhopal
6. Regional Institute of Education, Bhubaneswar
7. Regional Institute of Education, Mysore.
8. North Eastern-Regional Institute of Education, Shillong

Priorities

Among the top priorities of NCERT are:

1. Implementation of National Curriculum framework
2. Universalization of Elementary Education (UEE)
3. Vocational education
4. Education of groups with special needs
5. Early childhood education
6. Evaluation and examination reform information technology (IT) education
7. Value Education
8. Educational Technology
9. Development of exemplary textbooks/workbooks/teacher's guide/supplementary reading materials
10. Production of the girl child
11. Identification and nurturing of talent
12. Guidance and counselling
13. Improvement in teacher education
14. International relations

By conducting national seminars, workshops and conferences NCERT gives valuable recommendations to teacher education. Now we are living in the technological world.

Research

Being an apex national body for research in school education, the NCERT performs the important functions of conducting and supporting research and offering training in educational research methodology. The different Departments of the National Institute of Education (NIE), Regional Institutes of Education (RIEs), Central

Institute of Educational Technology (CIET) and Pandit Sunderlal Sharma Central Institute of Vocational Education (PSSCIVE) undertake programmes of research related to different aspects of school education, including teacher education.

Besides conducting in-house research, the NCERT supports research programmes of other institutions/organizations by providing financial assistance and academic guidance. Assistance is given to scholars for publication of their Ph.D. theses. Research fellowships are offered to encourage studies in school education to create a research base for developmental, training and extension programmes and to create a pool of competent research workers. It also organizes courses for educational research workers. The NCERT also organizes educational research in the country. It has computer facilities for storing, processing and retrieval of data. It collaborates with international agencies in inter-country research projects.

Development

Developmental activities in school education constitute an important function of the NCERT. The major developmental activities include development and renewal of curricula and instructional materials for various levels of school education and making them relevant to changing needs of children and society. The innovative developmental activities include development of curricula and instructional materials in school education in the area of pre-school education, formal and non-formal education, vocationalisation of education and teacher education. Developmental activities are also undertaken in the domains of educational technology, population education, and education of the disabled and other special groups.

Training

Another important dimension of NCERT's activities is the pre-service and in-service training of teachers at various levels; pre-primary, elementary, secondary and higher secondary, and also in such areas as vocational education, educational technology, guidance and counseling, and special education. The pre-service teacher education programmes at the Regional Institutes of Education (RIEs) incorporate innovative features such as integration of content and methodology of teaching, long-term internship of teacher trainees in the actual classroom setting, and participation of students in community work. The RIEs also undertake the training of key personnel of the states and of state level institutions and training of teacher educators and in-service teachers.

Extension

The NCERT has comprehensive extension programmes in which various Departments of the NIE, RIEs, CIET, PSSCIVE and the offices of the Field Advisers in the states are engaged in various ways. It works in close collaboration with various agencies and institutions in the states and also works extensively with Extension Service Departments and Centres in teacher training colleges and schools with the purpose of providing assistance to various categories of personnel, including teachers, teacher educators, educational administrators, question-paper setters, textbook writers, etc. Conferences, seminars, workshops and competitions are organized *as* regular on-going programmes as a part of the extension activities. Several programmes are organized in rural and backward areas in order to reach out to the functionaries in these areas where special problems exist and where special efforts are needed. Special programmes are organized for the education of the disadvantaged sections of the society. The extension programmes cover all States and Union Territories of the country.

Publication and Dissemination

The NCERT publishes textbooks for different school subjects for Classes I to XII. It also brings out workbooks, teachers guides, supplementary readers, research reports, etc. In addition, it publishes instructional materials for the use of teacher educators, teacher trainees and in-service teachers. These instructional materials, produced through research and developmental work, serve as models to various agencies in States and Union Territories. These are made available to state level agencies for adoption and/or adaptation. The textbooks are published in English, Hindi and Urdu.

For dissemination of educational information, or the NCERT publishes six journals: *The Primary Teacher* is published both in English and Hindi and aims at giving meaningful and relevant educational inputs to primary school teachers for direct use in the classroom; *School Science* serves as an open forum for discussion on various aspects of science education; *Journal of Indian Education* provides a forum for encouraging original and critical thinking in education through discussion on current educational issues; *Indian Educational Review* contains research articles and provides a forum for researchers in education; and *Bharatiya Adhunik Shiksha,* published in Hindi, provides a forum for encouraging critical thinking in education on contemporary issues and for dissemination of educational problems and practices. Besides these, a house journal called *NCERT Newsletter* is also published in English and Hindi. The title of the Hindi version of the newsletter is *Shaikshik Darpan.*

Exchange Programmes

The NCERT interacts with international organisations such as UNESCO, UNICEF, UNDP (United Nations Development Progammes), NFPA (National Federation of Paralegal Associations) and the World Bank to study specific educational problems and to arrange training programmes for personnel from developing countries. It is one of the Associated Centres of APEID (Asia-Pacific Programme of Educational Innovation for Development). It also acts as the Secretariat of the National Development Group (NDG) for Educational Innovations. The NCERT has been offering training facilities, usually through attachment programmes and participation in workshops, to educational workers of other countries. The NCERT also acts as a major agency for implementing the Bilateral Cultural Exchange Programmes entered into by the Government of India with the governments of other countries in the fields of school education and teacher education by sending delegations to study specific educational problems relevant to Indian requirements and by arranging training and study visits for scholars from other countries.

Educational materials are exchanged with other countries. On request, the faculty members are deputed to participate in international conferences, seminars, workshops, symposia, etc.

Central Institute of Educational Technology (CIET) – India

Central Institute of Educational Technology (CIET) is a constituent unit of the National Council of Educational Research and Training (NCERT), an autonomous organisation under the Ministry of Human Resources Development, Government of India. Established in 1984 with the merger of the Centre of Educational Technology and Department of Teaching Aids. Its chief aim is to promote Educational Technology especially mass media singly or in combinations (multimedia packages) to extend educational opportunities and improve quality of educational processes at the school level. As a premier institute of Educational Technology at the apex level, major functions of the CIET are:

0. To design, develop, try out and disseminate alternative learning systems to achieve the national goal of universalisation of primary education and

1. To address various educational problems at micro and macro levels. The broad areas of activities of the CIET are as given below:

2. To design and produce media software materials viz., television/ radio (for both broadcast as well as non-broadcast use) film, graphics and other programmes for strengthening the transaction of curricular and co-curricular activities at the school level.

3. To create competencies in development and use of educational software materials mentioned above through training in areas such as script development, media production, media communication, media research, technical operations, setting up studios, repair and maintenance of equipment.

4. To train the faculty of Institutes of Advanced Study in Education/Colleges of Teacher Education and District

Institutes of Education and Training in the use of Educational Technology in their teacher education programmes.

5. To undertake research evaluation and monitoring of the systems, programmes and materials with a view to improving the materials and increasing their effectiveness.
6. To document and disseminate information, materials and media programmes for better utilization and to function as a clearing house / agency in the field of Educational Technology.
7. To advise and coordinate the academic and technical programmes and activities of the SIET set up by the MHRD in six states of India.
8. To ensure a continuous progress in the quality of production, various evaluation studies are carried out on a regular basis. Some of the important research programmes undertaken during the year 1997-98 are:
   i. Monitoring and evaluation of Training
   ii. Analysis of viewer's mail
   iii. Field-testing of media programmes
   iv. Review of research with implications for media production
   v. A need assessment for media programmes for the middle schools.

Sate Counsel of Educational Research and Training

The State Council of Educational Research and Training (SCERT) Andhra Pradesh was established on 27-07-1967, amalgamating the following institutions:

The State Institute of Education.

The State Bureau of Education and Vocational Guidance.

The State Science Education Unit and

The State Evaluation Unit

Objectives

1. To organize in – service training for teacher educators and to teachers of Primary, Upper Primary and Secondary Schools.

2. To Act as a clearing house for ideas and information to keep the teacher educators and teachers abreast of the latest developments in the field of Education
3. To provide academic guidance to the schools through extension services.
4. To undertake studies, investigations and surveys relating to educational matters on the appraisal of educational programmes.
5. To Undertake and co – ordinate action research projects on instructional practices, Educational problems etc.
6. To undertake publication of books, periodicals and other literature necessary for furtherance of knowledge for teachers.
7. To undertake evaluation and research studies to find out the impact of educational programmes in the state.

Functions

Based on its objectives as the academic wing of the Department of School Education.

The following are the functions of SCERT.

1. Preparation of curricula, syllabi, instructional material for Primary, Upper Primary, Secondary and alternative systems of education.
2. Department of evaluation procedures and material which are helpful to the practicing teachers.
3. Bridging gaps between the methods and techniques advocated in training and the actual classroom practices.
4. Dissemination of knowledge to improved methods and techniques to be followed by educational institutions.
5. Co-ordination with national and international organizations in academic programmes.

6. Organization of orientation programmes for the professional growth of teachers, teacher – education, supervisor's etc.
7. Publication of journals, periodicals, books etc. ,
8. Resource support to implement the academic policies lay down by the Government.

Services

Constituent Units

SCERT has some constituent units spread over the entire state. They are:

1. Institutes or Advances Study in Education (IASEs) Colleges of Teacher Education. (CTEs)
2. District institutes of Education and Training (DIETs) / Teacher Training institutes (T. T. I. s)
3. Extension Service Departments.
4. Science Teacher's Centres.

Professional Growth

For the professional growth of teachers, SCERT takes up in-service training courses for Primary, Upper – Primary, Secondary teachers and teacher–educators, besides providing sources material like hand books, manuals and other publications. SCERT also organizes seminars. Workshops, conferences involving teachers, teacher - educators, supervisors and administrators.

Research and Evaluation

SCERT undertakes action research, studies, experimental research and evaluation of the programmes implemented by it. It also promotes research and evaluation studies by teacher educators and action research by the practicing teachers.

Co–ordinate Efforts

SCERT co-ordinates various academic programmes of IASE's CTE's. DIETs. TTIs and the Extention Services Departments functioning in IASE, CTEs and DIETs.

Future Vision of the Department

National Policy of Education 1986 and Programme of action lay a lot of stress on the qualitative improvement of education. The Govt. of India has made the State Councils of Education Research and Training as nodal agencies to look into the task of qualitative improvement of Elementary Education at Elementary and Secondary Education levels. Teacher Education Institution like DIETs, IASEs, CTEs etc., co-ordinate and implement UNICEF projects like UGC, EFA (Education For All) and other projects like MLL (Minimum Level of Learning), Distance Education. The institution's major responsibility is to ensure quality in teacher education. SCERT organizes seminars, workshops, conferences with the help of NCERT, NCTE AND NIEPA to give quality education for teachers.

Conclusion

We know teacher is a national builder. He has a power to change the world. It is necessary to take care about teacher education. NCTE, NCERT, CIET and SCERT have to play prominent role in the development of quality in teacher education. NCTE has major role in framing of teacher education curriculum and establishment of teacher education institutions. We are living in the modern world. It is necessary to use technology. It is necessary to provide computer and technology labs and other type of labs.

42

Literacy and Employment in India

Literacy in India is key for socio-economic progress, and the Indian literacy rate grew to 66% in 2007 from 12% at the end of British rule in 1947. Although this was a greater than fivefold improvement, the level is well below the world average literacy rate of 84%, and India currently has the largest illiterate population of any nation on earth. Despite government programs, India's literacy rate increased only "sluggishly," and a 1990 study estimated that it would take until 2060 for India to achieve universal literacy at then-current rate of progress. The 2001 census, however, indicated a 1991-2001 decadal literacy growth of 12.63%, which is the fastest-ever on record.

There is a wide gender disparity in the literacy rate in India: adult (15+ years) literacy rates in 2009 were 76.9% for men and 54.5% for women. The low female literacy rate has had a dramatically negative impact on family planning and population stabilization efforts in India. Studies have indicated that female literacy is a strong predictor of the use of contraception among married Indian couples, even when women do not otherwise have economic independence. The 2001 census provided a positive indication that growth in female literacy rates (14.38%) was substantially faster than in male literacy rates (11.13%) in the 1991-2001 decadal period, which means the gender gap appears to be narrowing.

Comparative Literacy Statistics

About 35% of world's illiterate population is Indian and, based on historic patterns of literacy growth across the world, India may account for a majority of the world's illiterates by 2020.The table below shows the adult and youth literacy rates for India and some neighboring countries in 2002. Adult literacy rate is based on the 15+ year's age group; while Youth literacy rate is for the 15–24 years age group (i.e. youth is a subset of adults).

Country	Adult Literacy Rate	Youth Literacy Rate
China	93.3% (2007)	98.9% (2004)
Sri Lanka	90.8 (2007)	98.0
Burma	89.9% (2007)	94.4% (2004)
Iran	82.4% (2007)	95% (2002)
World Average	84% (1998)	88% (2001)
India	66.0% (2007)	82% (2001)
Nepal	56.5 (2007)	62.7
Pakistan	54.2 (2007)	53.9
Bangladesh	53.5 (2007)	49.7

Growth of literacy

Literacy in India grew very slowly until independence in 1947. An acceleration in the rate of literacy growth occurred in the 1991-2001 period. During the British period, progress of education was rather tardy. Between 1881-82 and 1946-47, the number of primary schools grew from 82,916 to 134,866 and the number of students grew from 2,061,541 to 10,525,943. Literacy rates in British India rose from 3.2 per cent in 1881 to 7.2 per cent in 1931 and 12.2 per cent in 1947. In 2000-01, there were 60,840 pre-primary and pre-basic schools, and 664,041 primary and junior basic schools. Total enrollment at the primary level has increased from 19,200,000 in 1950-51 to 109,800,000 in 2001-02. The number of high schools in 2000-01 was higher than the number of primary schools at the time of independence.

In 1944, the Government of British India presented a plan, called the Sergeant Scheme for the educational reconstruction of India, with a goal of producing 100% literacy in the country within 40 years, i.e. by 1984. Although the 40 year time-frame was derided at the time by leaders of the Indian independence movement as being too long a period to achieve universal literacy, India had only just crossed the 64% level by the 2001 census.

Post Independence

The provision of universal and compulsory education for all children in the age group of 6-14 was a cherished national ideal and had been given overriding priority by incorporation as a Directive Policy in Article 45 of the Constitution, but it is still to be achieved more than half a century since the Constitution was adopted in 1949. Parliament has passed the Constitution 86th Amendment Act, 2002, to make elementary education a Fundamental Right for children in the age group of 6–14 years. In order to provide more funds for education, an education cess of 2 per cent has been imposed on all direct and indirect central taxes through the Finance (No.2) Act, 2004.

Since independence, the literacy rate grew from 18.33 per cent in 1951, to 28.30 per cent in 1961, 34.45 per cent in 1971, 43.57 per cent in 1981, 52.21 per cent in 1991, and 64.84per cent in 2001. During the same period, the population grew from 361 million to 1,028 million.

Literacy rate variations between states

Kerala is the most literate state in India, with 90.92% literacy,followed closely by Mizoram at 88.80%. Bihar is the least literate state in India with 47% literacy. Several other social indicators of the two states are correlated with these rates, such as life expectancy at birth (71.61 for males and 75 for females in Kerala, 65.66 for males and 64.79 for females in Bihar), infant mortality per 1,000 live births (10 in Kerala, 61 in Bihar), birth rate per 1,000 people (16.9 in Kerala, 30.9 in Bihar) and death rate per 1,000 people (6.4 in Kerala, 7.9 in Bihar). Ernakulam district in Kerala was the first district to reach the 100% literacy level in India.

Every census since 1881 had indicated rising literacy in the country, but the population growth rate had been high enough that the absolute number of illiterates rose with every decade. The 1991-2001 decade is the first census period when the absolute number of Indian illiterates declined (by 32 million), indicating that the literacy growth rate is now outstripping the population growth rate. Bihar, Nagaland and Manipur were the only states in the 1991-2001 period where the absolute number of illiterates rose, although even there the percentage of illiterates fell.

Bihar was the only remaining Indian state in the 2001 census where the majority of the population (53%) was illiterate. It was also the only state where less than 60% of the male population was literate. Six Indian states account for about 70% of all illiterates in India: Uttar Pradesh, Bihar, Madhya Pradesh, Rajasthan, Andhra Pradesh and West Bengal. Slightly less than half of all Indian illiterates (48.12%) are in the six Hindi-speaking states of Uttar Pradesh, Bihar, Rajasthan, Madhya Pradesh, Jharkhand and Chhattisgarh. Large variations in literacy exist even between contiguous states. While there are a few states at the top and bottom, most states are just above or below the national average.

Learnings from state literacy efforts in India

Several states in India have executed successful programs to boost literacy rates. Over time, a set of factors have emerged as being key to success: official will to succeed, deliberate steps to engage the community in administering the program, adequate funding for infrastructure and teachers, and provisioning additional services which are considered valuable by the community (such as free school lunches).

Bihar literacy challenges

Bihar has the lowest literacy rate in India and, in the 2001 census, was the only Indian state where the majority of the population (53%) was illiterate. Even in Bihar, however, the literacy rate is rising: from 39% in 1991 to 47% in 2001. The Government of Bihar has launched several programs to boost literacy, and its Department of Adult Education even won a UNESCO award in 1981.

Extensive impoverishment, entrenched hierarchical social divisions and the lack of correlation between educational attainment and job opportunities are often cited in studies of the hurdles literacy programs face in Bihar. Children from "lower castes" are frequently denied school attendance and harassed when they do attend. In areas where there is no discrimination, poor funding and impoverished families means that children often cannot afford textbooks and stationery. When children do get educated, the general lack of economic progress in the state means that government jobs are the only alternative to farm labor, yet these jobs, in practise, require bribes to secure - which poorer families cannot afford. This leads to educated youths working on the farms, much as uneducated ones do, and leads parents to question the investment of sending children to school in the first place. Bihar's government schools have also faced teacher absenteeism, leading the state government to threaten withholding of salaries of teachers who failed to conduct classes on a regular basis. To incentivize students to attend, the government announced a Rupee 1 per schooldays grant to poor children who show-up to school.

Kerala literacy successes

Kerala undertook a "*campaign for total literacy* in Ernakulam district in the late 1980s," with a "*fusion between the district administration headed by its Collector on one side and, on the other side, voluntary groups, social activists and others.*" On February 4, 1990, Ernakulam was certified as being 100% literate. The Government of Kerala then replicated the initiative on a statewide level, launching the Kerala State Literacy Campaign. First, households were surveyed with door-to-door, multistage survey visits to form an accurate picture of the literacy landscape and areas that needed special focus. Then, *Kala Jathas* (cultural troupes) and *Saksharta Pad Yatras* (Literacy Foot Marches) were organized to generate awareness of the campaign and create a receptive social atmosphere for the program. An integrated management system was created involving state officials, prominent social figures, local officials and senior voluntary workers to oversee the execution of the campaign.

Himachal Pradesh literacy successes

Strong government action and community support made Himachal Pradesh one of India's most literate states by 2001 Himachal Pradesh underwent a "Schooling Revolution" in the 1961-2001 period that has been called "*even more impressive than Kerala's*." Kerala has led the nation in literacy rates since the 19th century and seen sustained initiatives for over 150 years, whereas Himachal Pradesh's literacy rates in 1961 were below the national average in every age group. In the three decadal 1961-1991 period, female literacy in the 15–19 years age group went from 11% to 86%. School attendance for both boys and girls in the 6-14 year age group stood at over 97% each when measured in the 1998-99 school year. A key factor that has been credited for these advances is Himachal's cultural background. Himachal Pradesh is a Himalayan state with lower social stratification than many other states, which enables social programs to be carried out more smoothly. Once the Government of Himachal Pradesh was able to establish a social norm that "*schooling is an essential part of every child's upbringing*," literacy as a normal attribute of life was adopted very rapidly. Government efforts in expanding schools and providing teachers were sustained after the 1960s and communities often responded very collaboratively, including with constructing school rooms and providing firewood essential during the Himalayan winters.

Mizoram literacy successes

Mizoram's literacy rate rose rapidly after independence: from 31.14% in 1951 to 88.80% in 2001. As in Himachal Pradesh, Mizoram has a social structure that is relatively free of hierarchy and strong official intent to produce total literacy. The government identified illiterates and organized an administrative structure that engaged officials and community leaders, and manned by "animators" who were responsible for teaching five illiterates each. Mizoram established 360 continuing education centers to handle continued education beyond the initial literacy teaching and to provide an educational safety net for school dropouts.

Tamil Nadu literacy successes

Tamil Nadu is the most literate state of India according to the HRD ministry of India's 2003 statistics. Starting in 1982, Tamil Nadu took an approach to promoting literacy based on free lunches for schoolchildren, "*ignoring cynics who said it was an electoral gimmick and economists who said it made little fiscal sense.*" The then chief minister of Tamil Nadu, M G Ramachandran launched the program, which resembled a similar initiative in 19th century Japan, because "*he had experienced as a child what it was like to go hungry to school with the family having no money to buy food*". Eventually, the program covered all children under the age of 15, as well as pregnant women for the first four months of their pregnancy. Tamil Nadu's literacy rate rose from 54.4% in 1981 to 73.4% in 2001. In 2001, the Supreme Court of India instructed all state governments to implement free school lunches in all government-funded schools, but implementation has been patchy due to corruption and social issues. Despite these hurdles, 120 million receive free lunches in Indian schools every day, making it the largest school meal program in the world.

Rajasthan literacy successes

Rajasthan had the biggest percentage decadal (1991-2001) increase in literacy of all Indian states, from about 38% to about 61%, a leapfrog that has been termed "spectacular" by some observers. Aggressive state government action, in the form of the District Primary Education Programme, the Shiksha Karmi initiative and the Lok Jumbish programme, are credited with the rapid improvement. Virtually every village in Rajasthan now has primary school coverage. When statehood was granted to Rajasthan in 1956, it was the least literate state in India with a literacy rate of 18%.

Social commentary

In his essay on *Social Infrastructure As Important As Physical Infrastructure* published in *India Development Report 2002,* Kirit S. Parikh had pointed out, "With a literacy rate of 65, we have 296 million illiterates, age seven years and above, as per the 2001 census. The number of illiterates today exceeds the population of the country of around 270 million at Independence, age seven and above."

In his book *The Argumentative Indian*, Amartya Sen notes, on the basis of investigations by Pratichi Trust, set up with the proceeds of his Nobel award, carried out in West Bengal and Jharkhand, that absenteeism of comparatively well-paid teachers, particularly where bulk of the students come from scheduled castes and tribes, poses a major problem. Students are circumstantially forced to go in for private tuitions. He concludes, "Sometimes the very institutions that were created to overcome disparities and barriers have tended to act as reactionary influences in reinforcing inequality... The teachers' unions, which have a very positive role to play in protecting the interests of teachers and have played that part well in the past, are often are turning into an influence that reinforces the neglect of the interests of children from desperately underprivileged families. There is evidence of hardening of class barriers that separate the newly affluent teachers from the impoverished rural poor."

Literacy efforts

The right to education is a fundamental human right, and UNESCO aims at education for all by 2015. India, along with the Arab states and sub-Saharan Africa, has a literacy level below the threshold level of 75%, but efforts are on to achieve that level. The campaign to achieve at least the threshold literacy level represents the largest ever civil and military mobilization in the country. *International Literacy Day* is celebrated each year on 8 September with the aim to highlight the importance of literacy to individuals, communities and societies.

National Literacy Mission

The *National Literacy Mission*, launched in 1988, aimed at attaining a literacy rate of 75 per cent by 2007. It imparts functional literacy to non-literates in the age group of 15–35 years. The *Total Literacy Campaign* is the principal strategy of the NLM for eradication of illiteracy. The *Continuing Education Scheme* provides a learning continuum to the efforts of the Total Literacy and Post literacy programmes.

Sarva Siksha Abhiyan

The *Sarva Siksha Abhiyan* (Hindi for *Total Literacy Campaign*) was launched in 2001 to ensure that all children in the 6–14 year age-group attend school and complete eight years of schooling by 2010. An important component of the scheme is the *Education Guarantee Scheme and Alternative and Innovative Education*, meant primarily for children in areas with no formal school within a one kilometre radius. The centrally sponsored *District Primary Education Programme*, launched in 1994, had opened more than 160,000 new schools by 2005, including almost 84,000 alternative schools.

Mid-day Meal Scheme

Of the estimated 205 million child population in the age group 6–14 years on March 1, 2002, nearly 82.5% were enrolled in schools. However, the drop-out rate in 2002-03 was 34.9% at the primary level and 52.8% at the upper primary level. The high drop-out rate has been a matter of major concern. One of the most popular schemes adopted to attract children to schools is the *Mid-day Meal Scheme*, launched in 1995. Several other special programmes have also been launched with varying degrees of success.

Non-governmental efforts

The bulk of Indian illiterates live in the country's rural areas, where social and economic barriers play an important role in keeping the lowest strata of society illiterate. Government programmes alone, however well intentioned, may not be able to dismantle barriers built over centuries. Major social reformation efforts are sometimes required to bring about a change in the rural scenario.

Asha for Education

Sandeep Pandey won a Ramon Magsaysay Award in 2002 in recognition of "*the empowering example of his commitment to the transformation of India's marginalized poor.*" While pursuing a Ph.D. at the University of California, Berkeley, he co-founded *Asha for Education* to support education for poor children in India by tapping the resources of Overseas Indians, raising ten thousand dollars in the first year. The organization has since expanded to 36 North-American chapters and disbursed nearly one million dollars for programs in India.

Pandey has returned to India and works full-time towards Asha's stated mission of bringing about socio-economic change in India through education. Asha's teachers are unpaid volunteers and support themselves with side-occupations, such as making candles and greeting cards from handmade paper. While working with impoverished low caste families and dalits in Ballia district of Uttar Pradesh, Pandey discovered that few children went to school and those that did remained unemployed. With local volunteers, Pandey established schools in the villages of Reoti and Bhainsaha focused on instilling self-reliance and the value of social justice among students. He has also established an *Asha Ashram* in the predominantly Dalit village of Lalpur, outside Lucknow, where students live and study among traditional artisans, and learn the crafts of bee-keeping, vegetable gardening and cottage industries.

Mamidipudi Venkatarangaiya Foundation

Shantha Sinha won a Magsaysay Award in 2003 in recognition of "*her guiding the people of Andhra Pradesh to end the scourge of child labour and send all of their children to school.*" As head of an extension program at the University of Hyderabad in 1987, she organized a three-month-long camp to prepare children rescued from bonded labour to attend school. Later, in 1991, she guided her family's *Mamidipudi Venkatarangaiya Foundation* to take up this idea as part of its overriding mission in Andhra Pradesh. Her original transition camps grew into full-fledged residential "bridge schools." The foundation's aim is to create a social climate hostile to child labour, child marriage and other practices that deny children the right to a normal childhood. Today the MV Foundation's bridge schools and programs extend to 4,300 villages.

Definition of literacy

The United Nations Educational, Scientific and Cultural Organization

(UNESCO) has drafted a definition of literacy as the "ability to identify, understand, interpret, create, communicate, compute and use printed and written materials associated with varying contexts. Literacy involves a continuum of learning in enabling individuals to achieve their goals, to develop their knowledge and potential, and to participate fully in their community and wider society."

The National Literacy Mission defines literacy as acquiring the skills of reading, writing and arithmetic and the ability to apply them to one's day-to-day life. The achievement of functional literacy implies (i) self-reliance in 3 R's, (ii) awareness of the causes of deprivation and the ability to move towards amelioration of their condition by participating in the process of development, (iii) acquiring skills to improve economic status and general well being, and (iv) imbibing values such as national integration, conservation of environment, women's equality, observance of small family norms. The working definition of literacy in the Indian census since 1991 is as follows:

1. *Literacy rate*: The total percentage of the population of an area at a particular time aged seven years or above who can read and write with understanding. Here the denominator is the population aged seven years or more.
2. *Crude literacy rate*: The total percentage of the people of an area at a particular time aged seven years or above who can read and write with understanding, taking the total population of the area (including below seven years of age) as the denominator.

The History of HIV/AIDS in India

At the beginning of 1986, despite over 20,000 reported AIDS cases worldwide, India had no reported cases of HIV or AIDS. There was recognition, though, that this would not be the case for long, and concerns were raised about how India would cope once HIV and AIDS cases started to emerge. One report, published in a medical journal in January 1986, stated: "Unlike developed countries, India lacks the scientific laboratories, research facilities, equipment, and medical personnel to deal with an AIDS epidemic. In addition, factors such as cultural taboos against discussion of sexual practices, poor coordination between local health authorities and their communities, widespread poverty and malnutrition, and a lack of capacity to test and store blood would severely hinder the ability of the Government to control AIDS if the disease did become widespread."

Later in the year, India's first cases of HIV were diagnosed among sex workers in Chennai, Tamil Nadu. It was noted that contact with foreign visitors had played a role in initial infections among sex workers, and as HIV screening centres were set up across the country there were calls for visitors to be screened for HIV. Gradually, these calls subsided as more attention was paid to ensuring that HIV screening was carried out in blood banks.

In 1987 a National AIDS Control Programme was launched to co-ordinate national responses. Its activities covered surveillance, blood screening, and health education. By the end of 1987, out of 52,907 who had been tested, around 135 people were found to be HIV positive and 14 had AIDS. Most of these initial cases had occurred through heterosexual sex, but at the end of the 1980s a rapid spread of HIV was observed among injecting drug users (IDUs) in Manipur, Mizoram and Nagaland - three north-eastern states of India bordering Myanmar (Burma).

At the beginning of the 1990s, as infection rates continued to rise, responses were strengthened. In 1992 the government set up NACO (the National AIDS Control Organisation), to oversee the formulation of policies, prevention work and control programmes relating to HIV and AIDS. In the same year, the government launched a Strategic Plan for HIV prevention. This plan established the administrative and technical basis for programme management and also set up State AIDS bodies in 25 states and 7 union territories. It was able to make a number of important improvements in HIV prevention such as improving blood safety.

By this stage, cases of HIV infection had been reported in every state of the country. Throughout the 1990s, it was clear that although individual states and cities had separate epidemics, HIV had spread to the general population. Increasingly, cases of infection were observed among people that had previously been seen as *'low-risk'*, such as housewives and richer members of society. In 1998, one author wrote: "HIV infection is now common in India; exactly what the prevalence is, is not really known, but it can be stated without any fear of being wrong that infection is widespread... it is spreading rapidly into those segments that society in India does not recognise as being at risk. AIDS is coming out of the closet."

In 2001, the government adopted the National AIDS Prevention and Control Policy. During that year, former Prime Minister Atal Bihari Vajpayee addressed parliament and referred to HIV/AIDS as one of the most serious health challenges facing the country. Vajpayee also met the chief ministers of the six high-prevalence states to plan the implementation of strategies for HIV/AIDS prevention.HIV had now spread extensively throughout the country. In 1990 there had been tens of thousands of people living with HIV in India; by 2000 this had risen to millions.

Current estimates

In 2006 UNAIDS estimated that there were 5.6 million people living with HIV in India, which indicated that there were more people with HIV in India than in any other country in the world. In 2007, following the first survey of HIV among the general population, UNAIDS and NACO agreed on a new estimate – between 2 million and 3.1 million people living with HIV.

In 2008 the figure was confirmed to be 2.31 million,[19] which equates to a prevalence of 0.3%. While this may seem a low rate, because India's population is so large, it is third in the world in terms of greatest number of people living with HIV. With a population of around a billion, a mere 0.1% increase in HIV prevalence would increase the estimated number of people living with HIV by over half a million.

The national HIV prevalence rose dramatically in the early years of the epidemic, but a study released at the beginning of 2006 suggests that the HIV infection rate has recently fallen in southern India, the region that has been hit hardest by AIDS. In addition, NACO released figures in 2008 suggesting that the number of people living with HIV has declined from 2.73 million in 2002 to 2.31 million 2007.

Some AIDS activists are doubtful that the situation is improving:

"It is the reverse. All the NGOs I know have recorded increases in the number of people accepting help because of HIV. I am really worried that we are just burying our head in the sand over this." *Anjali Gopalan, the Naz Foundation, Delhi* "the statement that India has the AIDS problem under control is not true. There is a decline in prevalence in some of the Southern states... In the rest of the county, there are no arguments to demonstrate that AIDS is under control"

The HIV/AIDS situation in different states

Map of India showing the worst affected states.

The vast size of India makes it difficult to examine the effects of HIV on the country as a whole. The majority of states within India have a higher population than most African countries, so a more detailed picture of the crisis can be gained by looking at each state individually.

The HIV prevalence data for most states is established through testing pregnant women at antenatal clinics. While this means that the data are only directly relevant to sexually active women, they still provide a reasonable indication as to the overall HIV prevalence of each area. The following states have recorded the highest levels of HIV prevalence at antenatal and sexually transmitted disease (STD) clinics over recent years.

Andhra Pradesh

Andhra Pradesh in the southeast of the country has a total population of around 76 million, of whom 6 million live in or around the city of Hyderabad. The HIV prevalence at antenatal clinics was 1% in 2007. This figure is smaller than the reported 1.26% in 2006, but is still highest out of all states. HIV prevalence at STD clinics was very high at 17% in 2007. Among high-risk groups, HIV prevalence was highest among men who have sex with men (MSM) (17%), followed by female sex workers (9.7%) and IDUs (3.7%).

Goa

Goa, a popular tourist destination, is a very small state in the southwest of India (population 1.4 million). In 2007 HIV prevalence among antenatal and STD clinic attendees was 0.18% and 5.6% respectively. The Goa State AIDS Control Society reported that in 2008, a record number of 26,737 people were tested for HIV, of which 1018 (3.81%) tested positive.

Karnataka

Karnataka, a diverse state in the southwest of India, has a population of around 53 million. HIV prevalence among antenatal clinic attendees exceeded 1% from 2003 to 2006, and dropped to 0.5% in 2007. Districts with the highest prevalence tend to be located in and around Bangalore in the southern part of the state, or in northern Karnataka's "devadasi belt". Devadasi women are a group of women who have historically been dedicated to the service of gods. These days, this has evolved into sanctioned prostitution, and as a result many women from this part of the country are supplied to the sex trade in big cities such as Mumbai. The average HIV prevalence among female sex workers in Karnataka was just over 5% in 2007, and 17.6% of men who have sex with men were found to be infected.

Maharashtra

Maharashtra is a very large state of three hundred thousand square kilometres, with a total population of around 97 million. The capital city of Maharashtra - Mumbai (Bombay) - is the most populous city in India, with around 14 million inhabitants. The HIV prevalence at antenatal clinics in Maharashtra was 0.5% in 2007. At 18%, the state has the highest reported rates of HIV prevalence among female sex workers. Similarly high rates were found among injecting drug users (24%) and men who have sex with men (12%).

Tamil Nadu

With a population of over 66 million, Tamil Nadu is the seventh most populous state in India. Between 1995 and 1997 HIV prevalence among pregnant women tripled to around 1.25%. The State Government subsequently set up an AIDS society, which aimed to focus on HIV prevention initiatives. A safe-sex campaign was launched, encouraging condom use and attacking the stigma and ignorance associated with HIV. Between 1996 and 1998 a survey showed that the number of men reporting high-risk sexual behaviour had decreased.

In 2007 HIV prevalence among antenatal clinic attendees was 0.25%. HIV prevalence among injecting drug users was 16.8%, third highest out of all reporting states. HIV prevalence among men who have sex with men and female sex workers was 6.6% and 4.68% respectively.

Manipur

Manipur is a small state of some 2.4 million people in northeast India. Manipur borders Myanmar (Burma), one of the world's largest producers of illicit opium. In the early 1980s drug use became popular in northeast India and it wasn't long before HIV was reported among injecting drug users in the region. Although NACO report a state-wise HIV prevalence of 17.9% among IDUs, studies from different areas of the state find prevalence to be as high as 32%. HIV is no longer confined to IDUs, but has spread further to the general population. HIV prevalence at antenatal clinics in Manipur exceeded 1% in recent years, but then declined to 0.75% in 2007. Estimated adult HIV prevalence is the highest out of all states, at 1.57%.

Mizoram

The small northeastern state of Mizoram has fewer than a million inhabitants. In 1998, an HIV epidemic took off quickly among the state's male injecting drug users, with some drug clinics registering HIV rates of more than 70% among their patients. In recent years the average prevalence among this group has been much lower, at around 3-7%. HIV prevalence at antenatal clinics was 0.75% in 2007.

Nagaland

Nagaland is another small northeastern state where injecting drug use has again been the driving force behind the spread of HIV. In 2003 HIV prevalence among IDUs was 8.43%, but has since declined to 1.91%

in 2007. HIV prevalence at antenatal clinics and STD clinics was 0.60% and 3.42% respectively in 2007.

The Punjab

The Punjab, a state in northern mainland India, has shown an increase in prevalence among injecting drug users (13.8% in 2007) in recent years. One of the richest cities in the Punjab, Ludhiana, has an HIV prevalence of 21% among IDUs. Denis Broun, head of UNAIDS in India has stated..."the problem of IDUs has been underestimated in mainland India, as most of the problem was thought to be in the northeast."

Who is affected by HIV and AIDS in India?

People living with HIV in India come from incredibly diverse cultures and backgrounds. The vast majority of infections occur through heterosexual sex (80%), and most of those who become infected would not fall into the category of 'high-risk groups' - although members of such groups, including sex workers, men who have sex with men, truck drivers and migrant workers, do face a disproportionately higher risk of infection. See our page on affected groups in India for more information.

HIV prevention

Educating people about HIV/AIDS and how it can be prevented is complicated in India, as a number of major languages and hundreds of different dialects are spoken within its population. This means that, although some HIV/AIDS prevention and education can be done at the national level, many of the efforts are best carried out at the state and local level.

Each state has its own AIDS Prevention and Control Society, which carries out local initiatives with guidance from NACO. Under the second stage of the government's National AIDS Control Programme (NACP-II), which finished in March 2006, state AIDS control societies were granted funding for youth campaigns, blood safety checks, and HIV testing, among other things. Various public platforms were used to raise awareness of the epidemic - concerts, radio dramas, a voluntary blood donation day and TV spots with a popular Indian film-star. Messages were also conveyed to young people through schools. Teachers and peer educators were trained to teach about the subject, and students were educated through active learning sessions, including debates and role-play.

The third stage of the National AIDS Control Programme (NACP-III), was launched in July 2007 and runs until 2012. The programme has a budget of around $2.6 billion, two thirds of which is for prevention and one sixth for treatment. Aside from the government, this money will come from non-governmental organisations, companies, and international agencies, such as the World Bank and the Bill and Melinda Gates Foundation.

The government has announced that this campaign will place a strong focus on condom promotion. It has already supported the installation of over 11,000 condom vending machines in colleges, road-side restaurants, stations, gas stations and hospitals. With support from the United States Agency for International Development (USAID), the government has also initiated a campaign called 'Condom Bindas Bol!' (Condom-Just say it!), which involves advertising, public events and celebrity endorsements. It aims to break the taboo that currently surrounds condom use in India, and to persuade people that they should not be embarrassed to buy them.

In one unique scheme, health activists in West Bengal are attempting to promote condom use through kite flying, which is popular before the state's biggest festival, Durga Puja: "The colourful kites carry the message that using a condom is a simple and instinctive act... they can fly high in the sky and land at distant places where we cannot reach."

This initiative is an example of how HIV prevention campaigns in India can be tailored to the situations of different states and areas. In doing so, they can make an important impact, particularly in rural areas where information is often lacking. Small-scale campaigns like this are often run or supported by non-governmental organisations, which play a vital role in preventing infections throughout India, particularly among high-risk groups. In some cases, members of these risk groups have formed their own organisations to respond to the epidemic.

The government has however funded a small number of national campaigns to spread awareness about HIV/AIDS to complement the local level initiatives. On World AIDS Day 2007 India flagged off its largest national campaign to date, in the form of a seven-coach train called the 'Red Ribbon Express.' A year later the train journey was completed, having travelled to 180 stations in 24 states and reaching around 6.2 million people with HIV/AIDS education and awareness.

Pmtct

In 2004 only 5% of pregnant women living with HIV received antiretroviral to prevent mother-to-child transmission. By 2007 this had risen to 14% but with such low coverage 21,000 children below the age of 15 are still infected every year through mother-to-child transmission in India.

Testing

The general consensus among those fighting AIDS worldwide is that HIV testing should be carried out voluntarily, with the consent of the individual concerned. This view has been supported by the Indian government and NACO, who have helped to establish hundreds of integrated counselling and testing centers (ICTCs) in India. By the end of 2008 there were 4817 ICTCs in India, compared to just 62 in 1997. In 2007 these centers tested 5.9 million people for HIV, an increase from 0.14 million in 2001.

Although voluntary testing is officially supported in India, some states have tried to implement policies that would force people to be tested for HIV against their will. In Goa and Andhra Pradesh the state governments proposed a bill in 2006 to make HIV tests compulsory before marriage, and in Punjab it has been proposed that all people wishing to obtain or retain a driver's license should be tested for HIV. Neither of these plans has come to pass, but they have concerned activists, who argue that HIV testing should never be imposed on people against their wishes. Unfortunately, cases of people being tested without their consent or knowledge are common in Indian hospitals. In one 2002 study, it was suggested that over 95% of patients listed for surgical procedures are tested against their will, often resulting in their surgery being cancelled. Hospital staff and health professionals, much like the rest of the Indian population, are often unaware of the facts about HIV. This leads to unnecessary fears and, in some cases, causes them to stigmatise HIV positive people and discriminate against them, including testing them without consent. India has certainly made progress in expanding HIV testing to its large population. However, considering only 50% of those currently infected with HIV are aware of their status there is still significant work to be done in this area.

Treatment for people living with HIV

Antiretroviral drugs (ARVs), which can significantly delay the progression from HIV to AIDS – have been available in developed countries since 1996. Unfortunately, as in many resource-poor areas, access to this treatment is limited in India; an estimated 285,000 people were receiving ARVs by November 2009 through government health centers and another 35,000 through private health facilities. This represents less than half of those estimated to be in need of antiretroviral treatment in India.

While the coverage of treatment remains unacceptably low, improvements are being made. The government has started to expand access to ARVs in a number of areas; by November 2009 there were 266 reported sites providing antiretroviral therapy. Increasing access to ARVs also means that an increasing number of people living with HIV in India are developing drug resistance. When HIV becomes resistant to the ARVs the treatment regimen needs to be changed to 'second-line' ARVs. As with many other parts of the world, second-line treatment in India is far more expensive than first-line treatment.

In 2008, NACO began to roll out government funded second-line antiretroviral treatment in two centers in Mumbai and Chennai. By 2009 second-line therapy was available in a total of eight states but treatment remains very limited. Of the 3,000 who need to be on second line treatment, about 750 were receiving it as of December 2009. One reason for this is expense; second line ARV drugs, unlike first line ARVs, are not produced on a large scale in India due to patent issues that control drug pricing and can be more than 10 times more expensive than first line ARVs. Another reason why coverage is so limited is the eligibility requirements imposed on second line ARVs; only those 'living below the poverty line, widows and children' and those who have received first-line ARVs from a government centre for at least two years are eligible.

Ironically, India is a major provider of cheap generic copies of ARVs to countries all over the world. However, the large scale of India's epidemic, the diversity of its spread, and the country's lack of finances and resources continue to present barriers to India's antitretroviral treatment programme. "It is a sad irony that India is one of the biggest producers of the drugs that have transformed the lives of people with AIDS in wealthy countries. But for millions of Indians, access to these medicines is a distant dream" *Joanne Csete, Director of the HIV/AIDS programme at Human Rights Watch.*

Stigma and discrimination in India

In India, as elsewhere, AIDS is often seen as *"someone else's problem"* – as something that affects people living on the margins of society, whose lifestyles are considered immoral. Even as it moves into the general population, the HIV epidemic is still misunderstood among the Indian public. People living with HIV have faced violent attacks, been rejected by families, spouses and communities, been refused medical treatment, and even, in some reported cases, denied the last rites before they die.

As well as adding to the suffering of people living with HIV, this discrimination is hindering efforts to prevent new infections. While such strong reactions to HIV and AIDS exist, it is difficult to educate people about how they can avoid infection. AIDS outreach workers and peer-educators have reported harassment, and in schools, teachers sometimes face negative reactions from the parents of children that they teach about AIDS: "When I discussed with my mother about having an AIDS education program, she said, 'you learn and come home and talk about it in the neighbourhood, they will kick you'. She feels that we should not talk about it."

Discrimination is also alarmingly common in the health care sector. Negative attitudes from health care staff have generated anxiety and fear among many people living with HIV and AIDS. As a result, many keep their status secret. It is not surprising that for many HIV positive people, AIDS-related fear and anxiety, and at times denial of their HIV status, can be traced to traumatic experiences in health care settings. "There is an almost hysterical kind of fear ... at all levels, starting from the humblest, the sweeper or the ward boy, up to the heads of departments, which make them pathologically scared of having to deal with an HIV positive patient. Wherever they have an HIV patient, the responses are shameful."

A 2006 study found that 25% of people living with HIV in India had been refused medical treatment on the basis of their HIV-positive status. It also found strong evidence of stigma in the workplace, with 74% of employees not disclosing their status to their employees for fear of discrimination. Of the 26% who did disclose their status, 10% reported having faced prejudice as a result. People in marginalized groups - female sex workers, hijras (transgender) and gay men - are often stigmatised not only because of their HIV status, but also because they belong to socially excluded groups.

Stigma is made worse by a lack of knowledge about AIDS. Although a high percentage of people have heard about HIV and AIDS in urban areas (94% of men and 83% of women) this is much lower in rural areas where only 77% of men and 50% of women have heard of HIV and AIDS. However, the real challenge lies with ignorance about how HIV is transmitted - for example the majority of men and women in rural areas believe that AIDS can be transmitted by mosquito bites. In 2009, NACO carried a population based survey in Nagaland, which showed that 72.8% of people believed HIV could be transmitted by sharing food with someone.

The future of HIV and AIDS in India

Various groups have made predictions about the effect that AIDS will have on India and the rest of Asia in the future, and there has been a lot of dispute about the accuracy of these estimates. For instance, a 2002 report by the CIA's National Intelligence Council predicted 20 million to 25 million AIDS cases in India by 2010 - more than any other country in the world. India's government responded by calling these figures completely inaccurate, and accused those who cited them of spreading panic. The government has also disputed predictions that India's epidemic is on an African trajectory, although it claims to acknowledge the seriousness of the crisis.

Indeed, recent surveys do suggest that national HIV prevalence has probably fallen slightly in recent years. This trend is mainly due to a drop in infections in southern states; in other areas there has been no significant decline. "In the north-east, the dual HIV epidemic driven by unsafe sex and injecting drug use is highly concerning. Moreover, there are many areas in the northern states where HIV is increasing, particularly among injecting drug users." *Sujatha Rao, Director General of NACO*

HIV spending has been steadily increasing in India in recent years. In 2006-2007 $171 million was spent to contain and prevent the growth of HIV, which represented an increase of 28% from the previous year. Currently, India spends about 5% of its health budget on HIV and AIDS. However, the World Bank has warned that India will have to scale up prevention efforts in order to avoid spending more of its health budget in the future. According to the World Bank's report, by 2020 India will have to spend 7% of its health budget on AIDS if the rising tide of the AIDS epidemic in New Delhi, Mumbai, the north and the north east is not halted. This would put further strain on a struggling health sector which, on top of HIV and AIDS, faces a growing multitude of health challenges including malaria, diabetes, heart disease and cancer.

Even if the country's epidemic does not match the severity of those in southern Africa, it is clear that HIV and AIDS will have a devastating effect on the lives of millions of Indians for many years to come. It is essential that effective action is taken to minimise this impact.

Specimen Data Tables: Demographics

Statewise Population in India (Census 2001)

State	Total	Male	%	Female	%
INDIA	1027015247	531277078	51.7	495738169	48.3
Jammu & Kashmir	10069917	5300574	52.6	4769343	47.4
Himachal Pradesh	6077248	3085256	50.8	2991992	49.2
Punjab	24289296	12963362	53.4	11325934	46.6
Chandigarh	900914	508224	56.4	392690	43.6
Uttaranchal	8479562	4316401	50.9	4163161	49.1
Haryana	21082989	11327658	53.7	9755331	46.3
Delhi	13782976	7570890	54.9	6212086	45.1
Rajasthan	56473122	29381657	52	27091465	48
Uttar Pradesh	166052859	87466301	52.7	78586558	47.3
Bihar	82878796	43153964	52.1	39724832	47.9
Sikkim	540493	288217	53.3	252276	46.7
Arunachal Pradesh	1091117	573951	52.6	517166	47.4
Nagaland	1988636	1041686	52.4	946950	47.6
Manipur	2388634	1207338	50.5	1181296	49.5
Mizoram	891058	459783	51.6	431275	48.4
Tripura	3191168	1636138	51.3	1555030	48.7
Meghalaya	2306069	1167840	50.6	1138229	49.4
Assam	26638407	13787799	51.8	12850608	48.2
West Bengal	80221171	41487694	51.7	38733477	48.3
Jharkhand	26909428	13861277	51.5	13048151	48.5
Orissa	36706920	18612340	50.7	18094580	49.3
Chhatisgarh	20795956	10452426	50.3	10343530	49.7
Madhya Pradesh	60385118	31456873	52.1	28928245	47.9
Gujarat	50596992	26344053	52.1	24252939	47.9
Daman & Diu	158059	92478	58.5	65581	41.5
Dadra & Nagar Haveli	220451	121731	55.2	98720	44.8
Maharashtra	96752247	50334270	52	46417977	48
Andhra Pradesh	75727541	38286811	50.6	37440730	49.4
Karnataka	52733958	26856343	50.9	25877615	49.1
Goa	1343998	685617	51	658381	49
Lakshadweep	60595	31118	51.4	29477	48.6
Kerala	31838619	15468664	48.6	16369955	51.4
Tamil Nadu	62110839	31268654	50.3	30842185	49.7
Pondicherry	973829	486705	50	487124	50
Andaman & Nicobar Islands	356265	192985	54.2	163280	45.8

Percent Distribution of Estimated Population by Age-Group, Sex and Residence in India (1999)

Age-Group	Total			Rural			Urban		
	Total	Male	Female	Total	Male	Female	Total	Male	Female
0-4	11.6	11.8	11.5	12.2	12.4	12.0	10.0	10.1	9.9
5-9	11.2	11.3	11.1	11.7	11.8	11.6	9.9	9.9	9.8
10-14	12.0	12.2	11.8	12.3	12.5	12.0	11.0	11.1	10.9
15-19	10.3	10.6	9.9	10.2	10.6	9.8	10.3	10.4	10.2
20-24	9.2	9.1	9.3	8.8	8.8	8.9	10.1	9.9	10.4
25-29	8.1	8.0	8.2	7.9	7.7	8.0	8.9	8.9	8.9
30-34	7.5	7.3	7.8	7.3	7.0	7.6	8.2	8.1	8.2
35-39	6.3	6.3	6.4	6.1	6.1	6.2	6.9	6.9	6.9
40-44	5.7	5.7	5.7	5.5	5.5	5.5	6.3	6.3	6.3
45-49	4.4	4.5	4.3	4.2	4.3	4.2	4.9	5.2	4.6
50-54	3.8	3.8	3.8	3.7	3.7	3.8	4.0	4.1	3.9
55-59	2.9	2.9	2.9	2.8	2.8	2.9	2.9	3.0	2.8
60-64	2.5	2.4	2.7	2.6	2.4	2.7	2.3	2.2	2.4
65-69	2.0	1.9	2.1	2.0	1.9	2.1	1.8	1.7	1.9
70-74	1.3	1.2	1.4	1.3	1.2	1.4	1.2	1.1	1.3
75-79	0.7	0.7	0.8	0.7	0.7	0.8	0.7	0.6	0.7
80-84	0.3	0.3	0.4	0.3	0.3	0.4	0.3	0.3	0.3
85+	0.2	0.2	0.2	0.2	0.2	0.2	0.2	0.2	0.2
Total	100.0	100.0	100.0	100.0	100.0	100.0	100.0	100.0	100.0

Growth of Indian Population by Sex (1901-11 to 1991-2001)

Year	**Average Growth rate Percent**	**Annual**	**Exponential**
	Female	**Male**	**Total**
1901-1911	0.53	0.61	0.56
1911-1921	-0.08	0.01	-0.03
1921-1931	1.01	1.06	1.04
1931-1941	1.30	1.36	1.33
1941-1951	1.27	1.25	1.25
1951-1961	1.93	1.99	1.96
1961-1971	2.15	2.27	2.22
1971-1981*	2.23	2.18	2.20
1981-1991**	2.10	2.17	2.14
1991-2001	1.97	1.90	1.94

Note : * : The 1981 Census could not be held in Assam. The Populationfigures for 1981 for Assam worked out by interpolation have been included. ** : The 1991 Census was not held in Jammu & Kashmir. The population figures include projected population of Jammu

& Kashmir as projected by the Standing Committee of Experts on population projections (Oct 1989).

Summary-Training and Employment Opportunities

Several organizations in three countries, including NYC in the Philippines, DoVE and DSD in Thailand, and MARD in Viet Nam, have undertaken measures to provide training for the rural youth. However, there was limited access to formal training in all the survey sites. This was either because such training programmes did not exist, or the respondents were unaware of them. While a few respondents in each surveyed sites had informal training from their parents, almost all respondents expressed an interest in receiving formal training.

In terms of employment, an evident trend is the influx of rural youth into the urban areas in search of employment. This is against the backdrop of the concentration of employment opportunities in urban areas, especially those created due to trade and technology advancements in the anufacturing and service sectors. Meanwhile, the field studies suggested potential for community-based employment opportunities. The areas of employment common to the three countries are tourism, handicraft making (such as bamboo, rattan crafts and embroidery), and service related work (such as motorcycle delivery, security guard and domestic work), in addition to fishing (in the case of the Philippines), and agribusiness and construction (in the case of Thailand), and brick making and infrastructure projects, and public sector works, including teaching and commune office work (in the case of Viet Nam).

Recommendations

Policy coordination

The findings from the country studies demonstrated that there are four, interrelated areas of major challenges with regard to employment and training of the rural youth. These areas are education, training, employment and income generation, and labour market information. While the governments of the Philippines, Thailand and Viet Nam have all sought to address concerns in these areas, local level impacts have been limited. This is due to the limited human (both in number and quality) and financial resources particularly in terms of reaching the local and community levels. Recommendation 1: There is a need for better policy coordination, both among national level government agencies and between the national and local level government agencies, as a means to address the challenges relating to resource limitations including their use and effective policy implementation. In addition, decentralization of implementation may also be pursued, on the condition that appropriate monitoring and evaluation are provided by the respective central and/or decentralized governments. It is also essential to ensure broad-based ownership in improving the employment and training prospects of the rural youth, through capacity building of the staff involved, as well as collaboration with other stakeholders, such as labour market institutions (i.e. employers' and workers' organizations, and representatives of interest groups, such as youth associations).

This section summarizes the opportunities and challenges concerning the promotion of training and employment among the rural youth, and presents recommendations.

Employment and Income Generation

Rather than a lack of employment opportunities per se, a major issue is a lack of decent work opportunities. While large numbers of rural youth migrate to urban areas, they are often disappointed by a lack of such opportunities. The youth may prefer to stay in rural areas provided that employment and income generation opportunities are improved. Recommendation 2 a): Given the important role of agriculture in rural communities, priority must be directed towards improving productivity in the agricultural sector, which can contribute to economic development and poverty reduction in rural areas. Livelihood diversification, along with the application of improved agri-business and technology application, can be explored. Recommendation 2 b): It is critical to create options for the rural youth to seek employment in rural areas through creating and improving the quality of employment in the on, off and non-farm sectors. In this undertaking, it is important to take local contexts into account to ensure that knowledge and skills attained are in line with rural labour markets and employment needs.

Recommendation 2 c): There is a need to promote an entrepreneurial culture and enabling environment for youth in wage- and/or self-employment sectors. Entrepreneurship provides greater opportunities for employment, skills development, as well as innovation in products and services. Consideration needs to be taken that entrepreneurship does not come at the expense of education. Recommendation 2 d): It is important to place greater emphasis on improving access to micro-credit schemes, financial/business training, business development services and market information, as a means to encourage youth entrepreneurial activity/self employment.

Training

In addition to the availability and affordability of training, a major issue facing the rural youth is the lack of information and resultant awareness among the youth, their families and communities on the available training, particularly the ones meeting labour market demands. In addition, the youth or their families do not deem the time spent in training as a desirable trade-off to earning immediate income which may come from a low-paying and low-productivity job.

1. Recommendation 3 a): In order to ensure the quality and relevance of training, efforts must be made to first assess the labour market needs in the given local context, and then to create opportunities for skills training to meet these needs, as well as the preferences of the rural youth.
2. Recommendation 3 b): It is important to encourage families and the rural youth to recognize the benefits of training, while disseminating information on available training opportunities, scholarships, youth programmes, and job fairs through the use of appropriate media, such as newspapers, television and radio. The promotion of training should not come at the expense of higher level education, but can be promoted in such a way as to supplement formal education.
3. Recommendation 3 c): It is important to secure funding for training programmes to benefit the current and future youth, and make training affordable and accessible to women and disadvantaged groups.

Formal Education

The main barriers to formal education identified from the case studies are access, affordability, quality and relevance, particularly in rural areas where physical access to secondary schools is difficult and the incidence of poverty is high. An added problem is a lack of teachers, appropriate learning equipment and infrastructure.

1. Recommendation 4 a): Countries should continue to strive for free, quality education and training up until the minimum working age. For those countries still striving to achieve free basic education, lowering the direct (e.g. school fees) and indirect costs (e.g. text books, uniforms, transport) of education can help prevent early school drop-out among poor families and ensure that young people have a smooth transition from school to work in the rural and remote areas.
2. Recommendation 4 b): There is a need for continuous efforts to ensure gender parity and raise overall equality in education for migrant, minority, working children, and otherwise marginalized, disadvantaged groups in order for inclusive and easily accessible education.
3. Recommendation 4 c): In order to improve the quality of education available for rural youth, greater investment is needed to ensure adequate classroom materials, safe and well-maintained school environments, quality of teachers through training, along with better remuneration. Labour Market Information There is a scarcity of labour market information in general, particularly in rural areas. This is an obstacle for governments to devise informed policies and also for the youth to make informed decisions on employment and training. It is also a challenge in matching the supply and needs of rural youth with the demands of the labour market.
4. Recommendation 5 a): It is essential to strengthen the promotion and dissemination of information on the opportunities and services that are available to rural youth, as well as the risks and benefits associated with migration to urban areas or abroad. Appropriate media needs to be used,

such as radio, newspapers, television, internet and leaflets, in addition to schools and training institutions, as well as call centres and private companies. Recommendation 5 b): It is important to enhance employment assistance and career guidance for rural youths by creating and improving facilities in rural areas with trained professionals and access to technologies such as Internet-based information databases.

Country specific observations and recommendations

The following country specific observations are highlighted as possible areas for country specific recommendations and follow up action:

Philippines

1. "Ladderized education", (i.e. the breaking-up of the four-year curricular programme into several associate programmes that can be completed in one or two years) can be explored. Upon the completion of one associate programme, students can either seek employment or pursue the next level associate programme until a Baccalaureate degree is obtained.

2. Emphasis should be placed on creating jobs in the areas of business and entrepreneurship, ICTs, tourism related services and environment and sustainable development related occupations. There is also the need to focus more on ICT employment opportunities in rural areas, such as call centres, business procurement outsourcing, and internet cafes. The youth are generally knowledgeable about ICT, and are well placed to take advantage of such job opportunities. ICTs are also a source for labour market information.

3. Institutions such as the National Youth Commission and the Technical Education and Skills Development Authority, as well as local NGOs are well placed to disseminate information regarding grants, and scholarships available to youth, and the labour market.

Thailand

1. His Majesty the King's philosophy of a "sufficiency economy", which stresses balanced development and highlights the importance of development of each a region relevant to their resource conditions, is considered essential to the development and integration of the principles of the sufficiency economy into the school curriculum. This concept should be further encouraged and strengthened. The principles and farm-level diversification should be further explored to reduce unemployment among the rural poor. Educational opportunities for youth in remote and poor areas should be broader, more diverse and more flexible to meet diver se backgrounds, needs and abilities. In addition, strategies should be developed to promote cooperative enterprises and social services, as well as an entrepreneurial culture. These initiatives are an important means of enhancing job opportunities for the rural youth.

Viet Nam

2. It is particularly important in Viet Nam to create community-based employment opportunities, since the country study indicated that many youths would prefer to stay in rural areas provided that better training, employment and income generation opportunities are available. In this regard, areas of off-farm employment to be explored include bamboo and rattan product and handicraft making. These can supply marketable and environmentally friendly products while providing income generation opportunities for the youth.

3. The export of labour to other countries is a priority in Viet Nam's employment strategy. This may be pursued as a means to develop the technical skills of the rural youth who, upon returning to their country, could contribute to a raised human resource capacity. This programme needs to be balanced with appropriate and sustained investment in enhancing coordinated education, training and decent work opportunities in rural communities.

Reference

1. World Youth Reports 2003, 2005 and 2007
2. Guide to the Implementation of the World Programme of Action for Youth
3. Making commitments matter: a toolkit for young people to evaluate national youth policy
4. A brief guide to youth delegates to the United Nations General Assembly
5. Various Reports of the Secretary-General related to youth issues

43

Teaching-learning and Research Through WWW for the Global Outlook Class Room

Introduction

World wide web has created a sea change in providing information and as well as information transfer, Information scientists have undergone a perceptible change and have become IT centered, which is evinced from the publications pattern of articles, citations in journals, seminars, conferences act., The world wide web provides access to materials that were previously not available to the researchers, students and faculty now able to view, listen to, and read materials that just few years ago were difficult, if not impossible, to access. Images, texts, historical documents, video clips, sound files etc, are now available over the web to anyone that has internet access. Almost anyone can put almost anything online, and because that information is not filtered or mediated in any way. Academic, Research and development organizations are supported by well equipped library and information services unit to augment the objectives of the parent organizations. Proliferation of knowledge growth has resulted in information explosion, which has made the users so difficult to find the relevant information of research and development.

The modern libraries are able to provide information services to their patrons more efficiently with applications of information communication technology (ICT) in their environment, which satisfy the currency of information. In the recent years, the publishers and the professional societies are able to add value to their publications by means of providing the full text contents in electronic form. The networked environment of the organizations and the availability of internet connectivity give the users and easy access to the full text of the document.

Purpose

The purpose of present paper is to determine the awareness of electronic resources among library users and promote the usage of electronic resources by the students and members of faculty in engineering colleges in Tamil Nadu. Questionnaire was distributed to 210 randomly selected faculty and students in the various research institutions in Tamil Nadu. The researcher collected many articles i.e. print and online.

Nearly 54 articles have been received. Through this articles we identified the use of e-resources for various purpose i.e. teach, learn and research. Majority of the user using for research purpose. The 40% of user using for teaching purpose. The considerable percentage of users is using the e-resources for learning purpose. Through this articles reveals that the researcher and faculties are using e-resources through www, so the user's categories also increase day by day. Because the Government also to allot more fund innovative consortium for the user categories. In future e-resources are a pillar for servicing various information.

Retrieval Systems

The study is an attempt to determine the level of using various types of resources by the research scholar in various Universities, Scholars felt that about various issue surrounding the electronic resources and whether changing attitude depend upon subject. Further reports have been presented about the factors supporting the growth and academic work with the help of web. The world of academics enjoying the fruits of electronic resources by the way of resources retrieval is highly thankful to the person like Tim Bern Lee for their tremendous effort. The 50% web resources as noted by the respondents give the positive signs of the growth of IT world in the academic venture. Though the users of the web are having basic knowledge to handle the electronic resources, the institution involved in academic work should provide technical training to their students. The free internet access available in most of the universities may be retained and may be extended to other universities also. The mushrooming of new website development may lead to unreliable resources to the students at large and the research scholars in particular, hence, a board may be constituted to check the validity of resources before it is uploaded in to the web.

E-Resources

E-Publishing: Electronic publishing (e-publishing) is 16 years old and the first e-book was published in Germany in 1985. The products of e-publishing are mostly secondary sources, reference materials and the primary periodicals. The problems associated with e-publications are integration with traditional forms, cost of acquisition, collection development, non-availability of selection tools, etc. These challenges should be taken as opportunities and prepared to find out the standards. When the father of the printing press, John Gutenberg, looked towards the future, he could never have dreamed that one small invention could revolutionize the world. The gift of publishing benefited not only the authors who could now create new words, but also the readers who would be exposed to new ideas, and new concepts. The creation of the printing press sparked a new revolution-a literary revolution. Now, with the widespread availability of computers and the internet, technology, enables virtually anyone to self-publish their literary works. E-Publishing is primed to revolutionize the world, by giving every individual the ability to publish their ideas, stories, books, without the prohibitive costs associated with conventional publishing. E-publishing is a process for production of typeset-quality documents containing text, graphics, pictures, tables, equations etc. In general, it is used to mean any information source published in electronic

E-Books

Libraries form a vital part of the world's systems of education and information storage and retrieval. They make available – through books, films, recordings, and other media-knowledge that has been accumulated through the ages. People in all walks of life -including students, teachers, business executives, government officials, scholars and scientists – use library resources in their work. Large numbers of people also turn to libraries to satisfy a desire for knowledge or to obtain material for some kind of leisure-time activity. In addition, many people enjoy book discussions, film shows, lectures, and other activities that are provided by their local library. There are a considerable number of concepts being explored in future libraries research and development. The focus is in distributed and local collections of information objects – in the hybrid library including analogue as well as digital objects and on ways of identifying objects of interest to a user and arranging for the user to access them. The library of the future will be less a place where information is kept than a portal through which students and faculty will access the vast information resources of the world. The library of the future will be about access and knowledge management, not about ownership.

E-Journals

Advancement in science and technology has changed the knowledge communication in the form of e-media. Order of the day is e-publishing and tradition print sources are replaced by e-sources. An attempt has been made to study the utilization and satisfaction among the users of various institutions and research centers towards e-journals using survey. The modern society is dynamic and complex. The duty of the research scholar towards social change, scientific development and social uplift is undisputable. E-Journals will definitely make its own impact on the users in terms of scholarly communication of research.

The change in information technology and digital library has made us to move from print to electronic media in terms of acquiring information resources and to provide services. Libraries are undergoing rapid changes due to the developments in information communication technology paper based resources are giving way to electronic resources. The CD ROM and E-journals are providing information to the user from various research communities. An attempt has been made in this study to identify the usage of CD ROM s and E-resources among the various research communities in Tamil Nadu.

E-Government

The term "e-government" is used in this paper to denote the concept of using information communication Technology (ICT) as a means to organize and manage the administrative processes of the government, especially the interactive processes between the government and the public. Though ICT has been available widely for more than four decades and many governments around the world have indeed used ICT in certain aspect of government, the concept of e-government is relatively new in the sense mentioned above. Only a handful of governments have progressed to a high degree in harnessing the immense power of ICT in re-organizing their government infrastructure and in serving their citizenry, and have done so in an efficient and effective manner. E-government is not mere "technologising" of government. It is not just a matter of automating some manual processes nor is it a simple introduction of technology where none existed. E-government requires a fundamental re-thinking of governance itself and, as some have suggested, re-inventing of government. If bureaucracy is the invention of the 19th century, we might say e-government is the invention of the 21st century. E-government re-examines the organizing principles of bureaucracy and governance, re-defines the objectives and deliverables of government and re-deploys the resources available. In this process of re-invention, the basic intent is both refinement of the old and introduction of the new. E-government is not throwing the baby with the bathwater.

Consortiums for E-Resources

Consortium a strategic alliance of libraries with a common interest, not under the same institutional control, but usually restricted to a geographical area, number of libraries, types of materials, or subject of interest, which is established to develop and implement resource sharing among member. This paper discussed about the benefits and limitations of e-resources through consortium. Makes a comparative study of two major library consortium of India i.e. INDEST-AICTE & UGC- INFONET in terms of objectives, governance, members, access pattern, resources etc. Analysis the study and makes suitable suggestions for its improvement. Concludes with the remarks that these consortiums will bring remarkable change in the library scenario and also the educational system of India. In modern library environment, information technology is playing a pivotal role. Today's technology, interactivity, digital media, expanding network and communications capabilities compel the libraries to move from organizational self-sufficiency to a collaborative mode of acquisition of library materials. Library consortia are one of the emerging tool kits. The consortium should take a lead role in the development of a national strategy for information provision for research in higher education. Librarians should seriously rethink and reinitiate consortium movement like developed countries for maximum utilization of resources at a reduced cost, time and space. It is an encouraging sign that both INDEST-AICET and UGC INFONET consortia are functioning well. These will bring remarkable change in the library scenario as well as the educational system of India.

The UGC - INFONET programme will be a boon to higher education systems in several ways. It is a vehicle for distance learning to facilitate the quality education all over the country. It is a major source for research scholars for tapping the most up-to-date information. It is a medium for collaboration among research guide and research scholars. One of the major developments in libraries and information systems in the past 15 years is the advent and spread of electronic information resources, services and networks mainly as a result of developments in information and communication technologies. The change is basically of physical form where information content is increasingly being captured, processed, stored and disseminated in electronic form. The unique features of the information needs of users in electronic environments relate to the physical form in which information content is made available in electronic information environments. Users normally desire the content to be made available within the constraints of their skills and technological capabilities so that it is possible to access and use the required information content to resolve the felt gap in knowledge.

The E-Journal programme is corner stone of the UGC-Info net effort which aims at addressing the teaching, learning and research collectively and governance requirements of the universities and research centers. It would facilitate free access to scholarly journals and databases in all areas of learning to the research and academic community. This article discusses the need for sharing of electronic resources among Libraries and Information Centers in developing countries. Highlights the importance of 'Library consortia' in this digital era, stating its salient features, functions and responsibilities. Examines in detail the emergence of various resource sharing models in the developing countries with special reference to India.

Emergence of Library Networks in India

In India library networks actually started due to the initiatives by NISSAT in forming CALIBNET in 1986, DELNET in 1988 and another networks subsequently. The UGC (University Grants Commission, India) set up INFLIBNET in 1988, NIC (National Informatics Centre) also set up DELNET, which are the first operational library networks in India. CALIBENT and INFLIBNET have not been able to project their performance as they were planned but they are trying to achieve their goal. Functions, organizations, cooperation's, progress and creation of databases amongst libraries of BONET and CALIBNET as library networks are still dissatisfactory. Institute of Economic Growth (IEG) was founded in 1958 as a autonomous institution recognized by the University of Delhi. The IEG library has its networking with different libraries e.g. RatanTata Library, Delhi School of Economics, Delhi University library. NCAER library, IIPA Library, DELNET etc. for helping the readers in getting the desired books and journals which are not available in the IEG library on inter-library loan basis. There are other examples of networking and resource sharing of Astronomy libraries in India. They jointly established a networking for resource sharing amongst the libraries e.g. Indian Institute of Astrophysics (IIA) library, Inter- University Centre for Astronomy and Astrophysics (IUCAA) Library, National Centre for Astronomy and Astrophysics (NCRA) Library, Nizamiah Observatory (NO) Library, Physical Research Laboratory (PRL) Library, Raman Research Institute (RBI) Library, Tata Institute of

Fundamental Research (FIFR) Library, Uttar Pradesh State Observatory (UPSO) Library. The main purposes of this networking are for better resource sharing, to reduce costs, for speedy delivery of documents, to keep abreast of new developments etc. No efforts have been made in India to network public libraries though it is very much essential to cater networked information to the general public where more than 70% of the total people are residing in rural areas. However, much emphasis should be given at the national level in India for the development of documentary information resources because it is considered as one of the vital resources to promote the development of economy, science, technology and culture etc.

Resource Sharing Networking Models

The fundamental object of information resource sharing is to solve the problems faced by the libraries such as information explosion, several needs of users, increasing cost of subscribing periodicals, sharing library budgets, fluctuation of the exchange rates etc. Now-a-days, to solve the above problems different resource sharing networking models are observed at local, regional, national and international levels. Generally, there are three levels of national resource sharing networks exist:

(a) **Local:** Information is stored in local libraries in the form of Union Catalog for local collection available in local libraries:

(b **Regional:** Information is stored in regional libraries and services are provided on broad subject area basis; and

(c) **National:** Information is stored in national library in the form of national Union Catalog for normally national collection available in national library and services are rendered to users as national resources. There are four existing resource sharing networking models, which have been shown in tabular form in Table-1.Various Models to Resource Sharing:

UGC –Info net Electronic Journal Consortium is an innovative project launched by University Grant Commission (UGC) to promote the use of electronic data bases and full text access to journals by the research and academic community in the country. This project will bring about a qualitative change in the academic environment. The research and academic community can now have an access to resources at their finger tips.

Consortia Initiatives in India

The information revolution and proliferation have brought about drastic changes to the function and service in all types of libraries in India during last two decades. Many libraries in India till today are not in affording position to procure all documents and subscribe to core journals in major disciplines or CDROM databases, due to their financial crunch. At the national level, the UGC (University Grant Commission, India) setup INFLIBENT in 1988. It has taken imitation about a formidable change in developing adequate infrastructure in libraries, especially university libraries, to be a part in the networked environment. Since January 2004, University Grants Commission through its one point programme (UGC) / INFONET is providing access to e-subscription to all-important journals for the entire university community. The Ministry of Human Resource Development (MHRD) through its INDEST (Indian National Digital Library in Science and Technology) has launched consortia-based subscription to electronic resources for higher – technical education systems in India.

Besides, there are a few national and regional library consortia developed in the recent years. Council of Scientific & Industrial Research (CSIR) Tata Institute of Fundamental Research (TIFR),, Department of Atomic Energy (DAE), Indian Institute of Technology (IIT), and Indian Institute of Management (IIM) have already formed their sectoral consortia and have been subscribing to electronic sources like Science Direct, MathSciNet, and Blackwell, John Wiley, ABI/INFORM and Business Sources Premier. Also, both Institute of Mathematical Science (IMSc) and TIFR have been subscribing to MathSciNet database under their own consortia consisting group of libraries in their region. And many more are expected to come soon.

Increasing the Discovery and use of e-resources in University Libraries and Research Centres: There is a large quantity of subscribed e-resources in our libraries and they contain quality information, though expensive. In spite of advantages in terms of access and search capabilities, they are underused. Systematic plan has to be in place for their promotion of use. While a good ICT infrastructure is a prerequisite, it alone will not do. Proactive strategies are required and these need to be adopted imaginatively. Access to e-resources need to be made easier for both on campus and off campus users. As a priority, active users need to be identified and they need to be converted to heavy users of e resources.

Secondly, non users are converted to active users various methods have to be tried in order to grab the attention of the users towards the e-resources. User training will increase the confidence level of the users. Traditional awareness methods include: Personal visits, user training, brochures, posters and displays. Newer technologies from the Web 2.0 such as RSS alert service, Blogs, Wikis and Face-book make the interaction with the library not only interesting but also add more value. Finally, the effectiveness of various promotional strategies needs to be measured by monitoring the usage and user feed-back. This research sought to determine use of online resources and databases and to assess current user characteristics associated with use of online resources by the Faculty and researcher of various universities

Suggestions

1. The university library should make necessary arrangement for continuing subscription for the on line journals along with print journals.
2. The University library should conduct orientation, training programme regularly to assist the users of agricultural consortium programme.
3. The authorities of the university should take keen interest for providing better infrastructure facilities for the improvement of Internet speed, e-journals, e-books, e-directories, e-conference proceedings, e-thesis, e-dissertation and e-dictionaries. So that users can feel more comfortable in browsing on line information.

Conclusion

Remote access of e-resources has been a major boon to academic and research libraries. Online journals are considered the note chord of any library's collection and have become indispensable for research in any field. Many online journals available in the form of databases as well as they directly access through the Internet. The quantity of online journals is growing larger and has become a quite visible entity in serial publication. Today most of the online journals appear as parallel version of its print counterparts and more publishers are making their journals available in electronic format. Many academic institutions are currently building substantial collections of full - text journals and continue to increase access to various online databases. Because these resources come at a great cost, it becomes important to understand database and full-text journal use among university patrons and the characteristics accompanying today's remote and in-house library users. Increased access to computers, the Internet, online databases full text journals necessitates reassessing online use patterns and user characteristics.

Nowadays it is impossible for libraries to procure all the documents and subscribe to core journals that are in demand by the users. There are many online journals and databases are available open access. Subscription of online journals and databases through the consortium(s) are much economic for the libraries.

Reference

1. ISI Reseachsoft.2003a.EndNote-Product Information, 5 August 2002,

2. Asksamsystems.2003,cittion Bibliographic and Research Note Software, 15 Feb 2003,

3. Craztsqyurrek cinoekte siytuibs, 2003 Refas – The Reference Assistant, 2002,

4. Scholars aid inc.2003 is scholars aid right for you?, 27 aug 2002, http://scholarsid.com/ right4 you_research.html

5. Brown, C.M. 1999, "Information seeking Behaviour of Scientists in the Electronic Information Age: Astronomers, Chemists, Mathematicians, and Physicists: Journals of the American society for Information Science 50 (10): pp 929-943.

6. Green, R (2000) Locating sources in Humanities scholarship: The efficacy of following bibliog. graphic references, Library quarterly 70 (2) pp 201-229.

7. Bates, M J (2002) The cascade of interactions in the digital interface. Information processing & management, 38 (3), 381-400.

8. MathesA (2005) Preserving Public Domain Books.

9. Barrett A (2005) The information seeking habits of graduate student researchers in the humanities. The journal of Academic Librarianship, 31(4), pp.324-331.

10. Workloc, Kate (2002) Electronic Journals: User Realities – The Trusty about content usage among the STM community, learned publishing 15 (3): pp.223-226.

44

The Education System in India

In the Beginning

In ancient times, India had the Gurukula system of education in which anyone who wished to study went to a teacher's (Guru) house and requested to be taught. If accepted as a student by the guru, he would then stay at the guru's place and help in all activities at home. This not only created a strong tie between the teacher and the student, but also taught the student everything about running a house. The guru taught everything the child wanted to learn, from Sanskrit to the Holy Scriptures and from Mathematics to Metaphysics. The student stayed as long as she wished or until the guru felt that he had taught everything he could teach. All learning was closely linked to nature and to life, and not confined to memorizing some information.

The modern school system was brought to India, including the English language, originally by Lord Thomas Babington Macaulay in the 1830s. The curriculum was confined to "modern" subjects such as science and mathematics, and subjects like metaphysics and philosophy were considered unnecessary. Teaching was confined to classrooms and the link with nature was broken, as also the close relationship between the teacher and the student.

The Uttar Pradesh (a state in India) Board of High School and Intermediate Education was the first Board set up in India in the year 1921 with jurisdiction over Rajputana, Central India and Gwalior. In 1929, the Board of High School and Intermediate Education, Rajputana, was established. Later, boards were established in some of the states. But eventually, in 1952, the constitution of the board was amended and it was renamed Central Board of Secondary Education (CBSE). All schools in Delhi and some other regions came under the Board. It was the function of the Board to decide on things like curriculum, textbooks and examination system for all schools affiliated to it. Today there are thousands of schools affiliated to the Board, both within India and in many other countries from Afghanistan to Zimbabwe.

Universal and compulsory education for all children in the age group of 6-14 was a cherished dream of the new government of the Republic of India. This is evident from the fact that it is incorporated as a directive policy in article 45 of the constitution. But this objective remains far away even more than half a century later. However, in the recent past, the government appears to have taken a serious note of this lapse and has made primary education a Fundamental Right of every Indian citizen. The pressures of economic growth and the acute scarcity of skilled and trained manpower must certainly have played a role to make the government take such a step. The expenditure by the Government of India on school education in recent years comes to around 3% of the GDP, which is recognized to be very low.

"In recent times, several major announcements were made for developing the poor state of affairs in education sector in India, the most notable ones being the National Common Minimum Programme (NCMP) of the United Progressive Alliance (UPA) government. The announcements are; (a) To progressively increase expenditure on education to around 6 percent of GDP. (b) To support this increase in expenditure on education, and to increase the quality of education, there would be an imposition of an education cess over all central government taxes. (c) To ensure that no one is denied of education due to economic backwardness and poverty. (d) To make right to education a fundamental right for all children in the age group 6–14 years. (e) To universalize education through its flagship programmes such as Sarva Siksha Abhiyan and Mid Day Meal." Wikipedia: Education in India.

The School System

India is divided into 28 states and 7 so-called "Union Territories". The states have their own elected governments while the Union Territories are ruled directly by the Government of India, with the President of India appointing an administrator for each Union Territory. As per the constitution of India, school education was originally a state subject —that is, the states had complete authority on deciding policies and implementing them. The role of the Government of India (GoI) was limited to coordination and deciding on the standards of higher education. This was changed with a constitutional amendment in 1976 so that education now comes in the so-called *concurrent list*. That is, school education policies and programmes are suggested at the national level by the GoI though the state governments have a lot of freedom in implementing programmes. Policies are announced at the national level periodically. The Central Advisory Board of Education (CABE), set up in 1935, continues to play a lead role in the evolution and monitoring of educational policies and programmes.

There is a national organization that plays a key role in developing policies and programmes, called the National Council for Educational Research and Training (NCERT) that prepares a National Curriculum Framework. Each state has its counterpart called the State Council for Educational Research and Training (SCERT). These are the bodies that essentially propose educational strategies, curricula, pedagogical schemes and evaluation methodologies to the states' departments of education. The SCERTs generally follow guidelines established by the NCERT. But the states have considerable freedom in implementing the education system.

The National Policy on Education, 1986 and the Programme of Action (POA) 1992 envisaged free and compulsory education of satisfactory quality for all children below 14 years before the 21st Century. The government committed to earmark 6% of the Gross Domestic Product (GDP) for education, half of which would be spent on primary education. The expenditure on Education as a percentage of GDP also rose from 0.7 per cent in 1951-52 to about 3.6 per cent in 1997-98.

The school system in India has four levels: lower primary (age 6 to 10), upper primary (11 and 12), high (13 to 15) and higher secondary

(17 and 18). The lower primary school is divided into five "standards", upper primary school into two, high school into three and higher secondary into two. Students have to learn a common curriculum largely (except for regional changes in mother tongue) till the end of high school. There is some amount of specialization possible at the higher secondary level. Students throughout the country have to learn three languages (namely, English, Hindi and their mother tongue) except in regions where Hindi is the mother tongue and in some streams as discussed below.

There are mainly three streams in school education in India. Two of these are coordinated at the national level, of which one is under the Central Board of Secondary Education (CBSE) and was originally meant for children of central government employees who are periodically transferred and may have to move to any place in the country. A number of "central schools" (named Kendriya Vidyalayas) have been established for the purpose in all main urban areas in the country, and they follow a common schedule so that a student going from one school to another on a particular day will hardly see any difference in what is being taught. One subject (Social Studies, consisting of History, Geography and Civics) is always taught in Hindi, and other subjects in English, in these schools. Kendriya Vidyalayas admit other children also if seats are available. All of them follow textbooks written and published by the NCERT. In addition to these government-run schools, a number of private schools in the country follow the CBSE syllabus though they may use different text books and follow different teaching schedules. They have a certain amount of freedom in what they teach in lower classes. The CBSE also has 141 affiliated schools in 21 other countries mainly catering to the needs of the Indian population there.

The second central scheme is the Indian Certificate of Secondary Education (ICSE). It seems that this was started as a replacement for the Cambridge School Certificate. The idea was mooted in a conference held in 1952 under the Chairmanship of Maulana Abul Kalam Azad, the then Minister for Education. The main purpose of the conference was to consider the replacement of the overseas Cambridge School Certificate Examination by an All India Examination. In October 1956 at the meeting of the Inter-State Board for Anglo-Indian Education, a proposal was adopted for the setting up of an Indian Council to administer the University of Cambridge, Local Examinations Syndicate's Examination in India and to advise the Syndicate on the best way to adapt its examination to the needs of the country. The inaugural meeting of the Council was held on 3rd November, 1958. In December 1967, the Council was registered as a Society under the Societies Registration Act, 1860. The Council was listed in the Delhi School Education Act 1973, as a body conducting public examinations. Now a large number of schools across the country are affiliated to this Council. All these are private schools and generally cater to children from wealthy families.

Both the CBSE and the ICSE council conduct their own examinations in schools across the country that are affiliated to them at the end of 10 years of schooling (after high school) and again at the end of 12 years (after higher secondary). Admission to the 11th class is normally based on the performance in this all-India examination. Since this puts a lot of pressure on the child to perform well, there have been suggestions to remove the examination at the end of 10 years.

Exclusive Schools

In addition to the above, there are a relatively small number of schools that follow foreign curricula such as the so-called Senior Cambridge, though this was largely superseded by the ICSE stream elsewhere. Some of these schools also offer the students the opportunity to sit for the ICSE examinations. These are usually very expensive residential schools where some of the Indians working abroad send their children. They normally have fabulous infrastructure, low student-teacher ratio and very few students. Many of them have teachers from abroad. There are also other exclusive schools such as the Doon School in Dehradun that take in a small number of students and charge exorbitant fees.

Apart from all of these, there are a handful of schools around the country, such as the Rishi Valley School in Andhra Pradesh, that try to break away from the normal education system that promotes rote learning and implement innovative systems such as the Montessori Method. Most such schools are expensive, have high teacher-student ratios and provide a learning environment in which each child can learn at his/her own pace. It would be interesting and instructive to do a study on what impact the kind of school has had on the life of their alumni.

State Schools

Each state in the country has its own Department of Education that runs its own school system with its own textbooks and evaluation system. As mentioned earlier, the curriculum, pedagogy and evaluation method are largely decided by the SCERT in the state, following the national guidelines prescribed by the NCERT.

Each state has three kinds of schools that follow the state curriculum. The government runs its own schools in land and buildings owned by the government and paying the staff from its own resources. These are generally known as *government schools*. The fees are quite low in such schools. Then there are privately owned schools with their own land and buildings. Here the fees are high and the teachers are paid by the management. Such schools mostly cater to the urban middle class families. The third kind consists of schools that are provided grant-in-aid by the government, though the school was started by a private agency in their own land and buildings. The grant-in-aid is meant to help reduce the fees and make it possible for poor families to send their children. In some states like Kerala, these schools are very similar to government schools since the teachers are paid by the government and the fees are the same as in government schools.

The Case of Kerala

The state of Kerala, a small state in the South Western coast of India, has been different from the rest of the country in many ways for the last few decades. It has, for instance, the highest literacy rate among all states, and was declared the first fully literate state about a decade back. Life expectancy, both male and female, is very high, close to that of the developed world. Other parameters such as fertility rate, infant and child mortality are among the best in the country, if not the best. The total fertility rate has been below the replacement rate of 2.1 for the last two decades. Probably as a side-effect of economic and social development, suicide rates and alcoholism are also very high. Government policies also have been very different from the rest of the country, leading to the development model followed in Kerala, with high expenditure in education and welfare, coming to be known as the “Kerala Model” among economists.

Kerala has also always shown interest in trying out ways of improving its school education system. Every time the NCERT came up with new ideas, it was Kerala that tried it out first. The state experimented with the District Primary Education Programme (DPEP) with gusto, though there was opposition to it from various quarters, and even took it beyond primary classes. The state was the first in the country to move from the traditional behaviorist way of teaching to a social constructivist paradigm. It was mentioned in the National Curriculum Framework of NCERT in the year 2000, and Kerala started trying it out the next year. The transaction in the classroom and the evaluation methodology were changed. Instead of direct questions that could be answered only through memorizing the lessons, indirect questions and open ended questions were included so that the student needed to think before answering, and the answers could be subjective to some extent. This meant that the students had to digest what they studied and had to be able to use their knowledge in a specific situation to answer the questions. At the same time, the new method took away a lot of pressure and the children began to find examinations interesting and enjoyable instead of being stressful. A Comprehensive and Continuous Evaluation (CCE) system was introduced along with this, which took into consideration the overall personality of the student and reduced the dependence on a single final examination for deciding promotion to the next class. At present, the CBSE also has implemented CCE, but in a more flexible manner.

Kerala was also the first state in the country to introduce Information Technology as a subject of study at the High School level. It was started in class 8 with the textbook introducing Microsoft Windows and Microsoft Office. But within one year the government was forced to include Free Software also in the curriculum by protests from Free Software enthusiasts and a favorable stance taken by a school teachers association that had the majority of government teachers as its members. Eventually, from the year 2007, only GNU/Linux was taught in the schools, and all computers in schools had only GNU/Linux installed. At that time, perhaps even today, this was the largest installation of GNU/Linux in schools, and made headlines even in other countries. Every year, from 2007 onwards, about 500,000 children pass out of the schools learning the concepts behind Free Software and the GNU/Linux operating system and applications. The state is now moving towards IT Enabled Education. Eventually, IT will not be taught as a separate subject. Instead, all subjects will be taught with the help of IT so that the children will, on the one hand, learn IT skills and, on the other, make use of educational applications (such as those mentioned below) and resources in the Internet (such as textual material from sites like Wikipedia, images, animations and videos) to study their subjects and to do exercises. Teachers and students have already started using applications such as Dr. Geo, GeoGebra, and K tech Lab for studying geometry and electronics. Applications like Sun clock, Kalzium and Ghemical are also popular among teachers and students.

The initiative taken by Kerala is now influencing other states and even the policies of the Government of India. States like Karnataka and Gujarat are now planning to introduce Free Software in their schools, and some other states like Maharashtra are examining the option. The new education policy of the Government of India speaks about constructivism; IT enabled education, Free Software and sharing educational resources. Once a few of the larger states successfully migrate to Free Software, it is hoped that the entire country would follow suit in a relatively short time. When that happens, India could have the largest user base of GNU/Linux and Free Software in general.

References

1. http://www.columbia.edu/itc/mealac/pritchett/00generallinks/macaulay/txt_minute_education_1835.html
2. http://varnam.org/blog/2007/08/the_story_behind_macaulays_edu
3. http://en.wikipedia.org/wiki/Central_Board_of_Secondary_Education